# Interrupting History

# Studies in the Postmodern Theory of Education

Shirley R. Steinberg
*General Editor*

Vol. 404

---

The Counterpoints series is part of the Peter Lang Education list.
Every volume is peer reviewed and meets
the highest quality standards for content and production.

---

PETER LANG
New York • Washington, D.C./Baltimore • Bern
Frankfurt • Berlin • Brussels • Vienna • Oxford

Robert John Parkes

# Interrupting History

Rethinking History Curriculum after 'The End of History'

PETER LANG
New York • Washington, D.C./Baltimore • Bern
Frankfurt • Berlin • Brussels • Vienna • Oxford

Library of Congress Cataloging-in-Publication Data
Parkes, Robert John.
Interrupting history: rethinking history curriculum
after 'the end of history' / Robert John Parkes.
p. cm. — (Counterpoints: studies in the postmodern theory of education; v. 404)
Includes bibliographical references.
1. Historiography—Philosophy. 2. History—Philosophy.
3. History—Study and teaching. 4. Postmodernism and education. I. Title.
D16.9.P266    907.1—dc23    2011029204
ISBN 978-1-4331-1240-9 (hardcover)
ISBN 978-1-4331-1239-3 (paperback)
ISBN 978-1-4539-0218-9 (e-book)
ISSN 1058-1634

Bibliographic information published by **Die Deutsche Nationalbibliothek**.
**Die Deutsche Nationalbibliothek** lists this publication in the "Deutsche
Nationalbibliografie"; detailed bibliographic data is available
on the Internet at http://dnb.d-nb.de/.

© 2011 Peter Lang Publishing, Inc., New York
29 Broadway, 18th floor, New York, NY 10006
www.peterlang.com

All rights reserved.
Reprint or reproduction, even partially, in all forms such as microfilm,
xerography, microfiche, microcard, and offset strictly prohibited.

# Contents

Preface: Millennial Concerns ........................................................... vii
Acknowledgments ............................................................................ xiii
Note on Capitalization of the Word *History* ............................... xv

1 In the Wake of History ................................................................. 1
2 The New Curriculum History ..................................................... 21
3 At the End of the Grand Story .................................................... 43
4 The Struggle for Histories ............................................................ 71
5 Returning the Historiographer's Gaze ....................................... 99
6 Ghosts and Visions in the Curriculum ..................................... 127

References ........................................................................................ 135

# Preface: Millennial Concerns

As a way of situating my book, and performing a little *currere*, I would like to share a number of millennial concerns, framed in terms of an aspect of my own curriculum, or life "course." William F. Pinar, one of the most significant players in the reconceptualization of curriculum studies over the past four decades, uses *currere*, the infinitive form of *curriculum*, in order to privilege the autobiographical aspect of educational experience (Pinar, 1975). From this point of view, *curriculum* is read as the course of one's life rather than just a school syllabus document or the experience of school-based education. Thus, following Pinar, I begin with a concern that encouraged me to write this preface. Shortly after the millennium, a retiring president of the Australian Association for Research in Education, the dean of faculty at the university where I worked at the time, asked why we couldn't just return to "good old-fashioned forms of Marxist analysis." There was humor in his tone, but what was striking to me about his rhetorical question was the idea of a "return" to a particular pre-postmodernist form of analysis. The notion of "return" struck me as strange, given that I had never really been there in the first place. Of course, even a cursory glance at research texts produced in different times and places shows that they are marked by quite different peculiarities and regularities of style and concern. So here was my problem.

I was born the year that Michel Foucault's *The Order of Things* was published in France (1966); in the same year, the first English translation of Jacques Derrida's work appeared in the United States, and Roland Barthes was composing "The Discourse of History." Barthes's postmodern turn, marked by the production of *S/Z* (1970), was complete before I started school in 1971. When Derrida's *Of Grammatology* was translated into English by the postcolonial theorist Spivak in 1976, I was ten years old and facing the death of my grandfather, who had been my "da" in name and in spirit. When Foucault passed away in 1984, the same year Lyotard's report on the postmodern condition was translated into English, I was completing my final year of high school. Although I flirted briefly with an arts degree in 1985, it was another decade before I began studying for my Bachelor of Education degree. By the time I enrolled at the University of Sydney in 1996 the academy had been responding to postmodern and poststructuralist concerns for more than twenty-five years, and we had finally, and convincingly, entered into the postindustrial world of the Internet, in which Foucault's shift of concern from the "mode of production" to the "mode of information," as Poster (1984) describes it, seemed prophetic. Despite the existence of "old Marxists" in the faculty, poststructuralism had emerged as a distinct form of analysis that not only was agreeable to the postmodern sensibilities of those of us marked by the sign of erasure (Generation X), but also formed part of the intellectual space in which our postpunk academic subjectivities were being fashioned. Thus, although we might be haunted by Marx (as Derrida suggests, and my own critical pedagogy leanings betray), we can never *return* to Marx.

If the decline of Marxism can really be traced back to the fall of the Berlin Wall and the collapse of Soviet Communism, then there was little hope for me. It wasn't until 1996, well after Fukuyama (1989) had first announced the end of history, that I returned to study in the academy, which was already becoming a posthistorical institution (Peters, 1998) with the ghost of Marx lingering in those offices of a recalcitrant old guard who had yet to give up on the Revolution. However, even if both the Gen-Xers and the old guard were oblivious to Marx's passing, we knew that the end of the millennium was fast approaching. As primary school students, we Gen-Xers had calculated ourselves into that future many times, hardly believing that we would be adults, perhaps with children of our own, when the calendar finally had caught up with our imaginations. So millennial concerns had been part of our lives for a considerable period when Gorbachev and the Soviet Union finally went the way of Marx, and I do remember thinking in 1991 as I sat watching the (first) Gulf War unfold on CNN, oblivious to Fukuyama, that I finally might be experiencing the end of history. At the time, I didn't have Baudrillard's reassurance that this was just a televisual simulation of war (or as he described it in 1995, a high-tech form of one-sided electrocution), but I did have a baby son, which made the simulacra that much harder to resist.

Of course, we Gen-Xers were not the first generation to anticipate our coming-of-age at Armageddon, but for us, the end of history has *always* been shrouded in a radiation cloud (Anijar, 2004). This is probably why, when a friend at a dinner party asked what my writing was about, she was surprised at my answer that I was considering the implications of the end of history for History curriculum. It was self-evident to her that history had not ended, because events were still transpiring as we spoke. Her reaction demonstrated her investment in reading the end of history through the haze of a mushroom cloud, but it also revealed a great deal about a particular understanding of "history," and it indicated her lack of familiarity with "posthistorical discourse" in contemporary philosophy, politics, and history theory. What I took to be a topic of great importance from my location within the academy was regarded with incredulity at the dinner table. I make this point because despite being regarded by influential commentators as "a sign of the times," the end of history remains a somewhat esoteric concept with a number of diverse and conflicting associations (Jameson, 1998; Niethammer, 1992; Vattimo, 1991).

The idea that history is facing an inevitable end has been around for some time. Historians have noted, for example, that at the turn of the first millennium many European Christians expected the Messiah to return and engage in a "complete winding up of the created order and the imposition of a posthistorical age of divine rule" (Rayment-Pickard, 2000, p. 301). By the time of the Renaissance this view had been rejected by the European intelligentsia and replaced with a secularized Enlightenment view of the end of history as the self-perfection of humanity. However, the constant fear of imminent annihilation—which followed us through the Cold War and seems to be reignited by every new conflict, including the Bush Administration's War on Terror and recent tensions over rocket testing in the Korean peninsula—has constituted a social sphere in which the religious subtext of an impending apocalypse persists as a cultural undercurrent (Anijar, 2004; Giroux, 2001). Perhaps ironically, it is "technocratic rationality," a particular legacy of the Enlightenment functioning as the modus operandi of militarily invested governments around the globe, that has painted the apocalypse as more possibility than prophecy.

Over the last few decades of the twentieth century, end-of-history rhetoric emerged as a marker of intellectual debate over the status of history within neoliberal, poststructuralist, and neopositivist traditions. Although we really can only speculate about why end-of-history rhetoric erupted in a multiplicity of forms at this particular historical moment, the timing of its emergence suggests that it is part of, and a reaction to, a much broader secular millennialism, contingent upon the great social, cultural, and intellectual changes wrought during the late twentieth century. Manifestations of a secular "millennial sensationalism" appeared across a range of Western intellectual and media-driven discourses in the last two decades of the twentieth century (Feldstein, 2001). We would see the manifestation of a new world order as a result of the implosion of the Soviet Union; the anticipated failure of some critical computer systems as a result of the Y2K bug, which was itself intimately connected with the idea of time and a symbol of simmering anxieties about the information society (Fosket & Fishman, 1999); speculation the Earth would experience a cataclysmic collision with asteroid 1997XF11 in 2028, a prediction later challenged as inaccurate; fears that we would be wiped out by HIV/AIDS, a new indestructible plague; and in my own country, the urgency of Australia's push to become a republic, which was strangely ominous as we approached the centenary of federation, and invested with a millenarian romanticism (Wark, 1997). I do not mean to suggest that these millennial concerns were "false" because they were tied up in an apocalyptic fixation. HIV/AIDS still demands our attention, and has proven to be devastating in communities across the globe, particularly in Africa and parts of Asia; with September 11, we may well have moved closer to realizing a particular kind of new world order; and the inevitability of an Australian republic still seems a cautious bet, though its timing may no longer suggest an arcane destiny. The important point about this list of millennial declarations is that obsession with the end of history is not simply an academic phenomenon confined to the philosophical works that emerged on the French intellectual scene in the latter half of the twentieth century; instead, it has manifested in a variety of popular forms.

The focus of many films and television series and an important theme in an increasing number of books in the late 1990s, the millennium was clearly on our minds. A retrospective look may deem the millennium a twentieth-century obsession induced by an insatiable desire to create meaning—a motivation that drives the protagonist in the books by Umberto Eco and the readers of a Haruki Murakami novel. What Gould (1997) has called "millennium madness" may have given "to the more academic theories a greater resonance with the temper of their times than is customary," suggesting that there is "at least an 'elective affinity'" between the fall of communism, the end of modernity, and the end of the millennium, "even if we would be hard put to specify casual links" (Kumar, 1995, pp. 151-152). Likewise, Frederic Jameson's assertion in *Postmodernism, or, the Cultural Logic of Late Capitalism* (1991, based on an article originally published in the early 1980s) that "these last few years have been marked by an inverted millenarianism, in which premonitions of the future, catastrophic or redemptive, have been replaced by a sense of the end of this or that" (p. 1) is also pertinent. Reflective of the apocalyptic turn in philosophy stretching back to the post-World War II 1950s and the apocalypticism expressed in popular culture prior to the millennium, talk about the end of history was part of the millennial spirit of the times, a key discourse in the context of the fin de siècle (Berkhofer, 1995; Derrida, 1994).

While it may be that end-of-history discourse proliferated towards the turn of the millennium because of long-standing anxieties or the perennial search for meaning, it was reworked within poststructuralism into a decidedly anti-millennial form. Take for example Foucault's (1971/1994) resistance to ideas of continual development towards a shared finality; Derrida's (1994) rejection of teleological narrative as little more than a confidence trick; Lyotard's (1991) skepticism about the future offered by science, which he argues is motivated by an obsession with human survival beyond the supernova of our own sun; and

Baudrillard's (1992) loss of faith in both history and its end/ings as reality and its representations implode. Regardless of the reasons for the widespread emergence of end-of-history rhetoric, it remains, like its conceptual cousins "the demise of the author" and "the end of man," intuitively problematic. Certainly, the end of not just the century but also the millennium was bound to have an influence on the academic theories under consideration (Kumar, 1995) as well as the academic curriculum of the late twentieth century.

Although placing the proliferation of end-of-history rhetoric within its contemporary historical context has been an interesting and necessary intellectual exercise, the substance of this book is not actually concerned with the end of history as a millennial discourse per se. Instead, it explores representative positions on the end of history that emerged in contemporary political and philosophical debate, and the significance of those positions for school History. In particular, my concern is with contributions to end-of-history discourse that emerged in the second half of the twentieth century, after World War II, in the countdown to the year 2000. Had I adopted a different periodization, figures such as Hegel, Nietzsche, and Marx would have figured more prominently in my analyses, because at least one current stream of thought is indebted to their much earlier theorizing (see Fukuyama, 1992). I am aware that the periodization I have adopted here makes end-of-history discourse seem more a manifestation of, or reaction to, a form of secular millennialism than it might have otherwise. But what is important for this book is the meaning of the end of history and the problems it poses for History as a school subject, rather than its attachment to or its operation as an artifact of the (second) millennium itself.

I defend my decision to confine this work to discourses that became popular in the late twentieth century on the basis that postwar end-of-history discourse emerged from a context increasingly dominated by globalized capitalism, postmodern sensibilities, and fast-paced information technologies. Certainly the social and historical context in which the end of history was discussed by Hegel, Nietzsche, and Marx is quite different from the context in which Foucault, Derrida, Lyotard, Baudrillard, and Fukuyama produced (and sometimes exchanged) their views. I suggest that postwar end-of-history discourse is of a different genus than the nineteenth-century variety, and deserves to be considered in its own right. Legacies of earlier thinkers are discussed only where this assists understanding end-of-history rhetoric as it operates in contemporary discourse (thus, references to Hegel, Nietzsche, and Marx are not completely absent). My aim is not to develop a history of end-of-history rhetoric, an objective common in the area of philosophy, in which an idea is tracked to and from its apparent origin, or in which a series of analyses "move towards the present, demonstrating the gradual production of an adequate theory," an approach troubled by postmodern theory and rejected by R. J. C. Young as the production of white mythologies (1990, p. vi). Instead, I have elected to confine my study to the development of a curricular response to that end-of-history discourse that is closely associated with our times: the end of the Cold War after the collapse of Soviet Communism; the turn of a new millennium; the spread and obsession with information communication technologies; the rise of mass media; and most importantly, the epistemological crisis associated with the widespread ascendancy of postmodern skepticism within the humanities.

In confining my exploration to contemporary ways of thinking about the end of history, I aim to explore the challenges and possibilities arising from a postmodern conception of the school curriculum and the practice of a *posthumous* history pedagogy. In this preface I have explored concerns that end-of-history discourse is nothing but a passing fad thematized by—perhaps even contingent upon—a conjunction of calendar, theory, and autobiography; but that is not to trivialize its usefulness as a problematic. We have already passed the limiting horizon of the millennium, and the end of history continues to signify important debates in the academy, some of which problematize the possibility of history itself. Regardless of its own "historical ground," I assert the effectiveness of the end of history as a kind of heuristic or "diffractive lens" (Gough, 1998) through which to re-imagine History curriculum, particularly at this time when neoliberals and conservatives would have us give up the ghost in our struggles for critical and effective histories.

# Acknowledgments

This book developed out of an intellectual project that is now a decade long, which inevitably means there are many people to thank for their advice and support. Firstly, I owe a debt of gratitude to Bill Green, undoubtedly one of Australia's premiere curriculum scholars, for introducing me to the field of reconceptualist curriculum inquiry, and helping me find a home for my work. I owe special thanks to my close friend, colleague, and collaborator Eva Bendix Petersen for challenging me to articulate the political and ethical dimensions of my project; I hope I have met the challenge of her provocations. I am always in debt to the collegiality and limitless support of another good friend and colleague, Kalervo Gulson, who read and commented on several draft chapters and provided rich and thoughtful criticism. I must also thank Jenny Gore, who as my doctoral supervisor and now as Head of School has always shown the greatest confidence in me; and my first Head of School, Jo-Anne Reid, and Dean, Bob Meyenn, from whom I have taken great inspiration. Finally, I thank my family, whose love and support of "the professor" allow me to take pleasure in the work.

# Note on Capitalization of the Word *History*

In order to eliminate confusion that may arise over the referent of the term *history*, I follow the convention of recent History curriculum studies (see Clark, 2004) rather than the work of Jenkins (1999, 1997), who describes "uppercase History" as metanarrative, and "lowercase history" as the practice of historians. This convention, while useful, does not allow distinction between the practice of the discipline and the learning and teaching of the discipline, a distinction important to this study. Therefore, in this book *History* (with a capital *H*) refers to the subject taught in schools and universities (as with Economics, Mathematics, or Geography) and *history* (with a lowercase *h*) refers to the academic discipline or "the past" itself. Where I wish to make clear that "history" is being mobilized with metanarrative associations, it is placed "under erasure" through the use of quotation marks. The only exceptions to these rules occur (1) where the referent is left deliberately ambiguous (and therefore potentially multiple) when my discussion is focused upon the end of history; and (2) where normal punctuation conventions dictate the necessity of capitalization.

CHAPTER ONE

# In the Wake of History

Twenty years after the fall of the Berlin Wall, the end of history remains a motif of our times. Signifying both a crisis in historical ways of knowing and our location on the threshold of a new social order, the end of history is perhaps the only description of the "postmodern condition" upon which influential commentators agree (Vattimo, 1991). While neoliberal conservatives celebrated the end of history—perhaps prematurely, after the collapse of Soviet Communism—in the inevitable global acceptance of the ideologies of free-market liberalism and democratic capitalism (see Fukuyama, 1992), those whom we might call "methodological postmodernists" (e.g., Barthes, Baudrillard, Lyotard, Derrida, and Foucault) invoked the end of history throughout the latter half of the twentieth century as a symbol of a crisis of confidence in the discourse of modernity and its realist epistemologies.

This loss of faith in the adequacy of representation is a defining feature of fin-de-siècle postmodern thought, and has been perceived by many positivist and empiricist historians as a threat to the discipline of history, with its professed desire to recover and reconstruct "the truth" of the past. Postmodernism has been described by a number of historians and social critics as an attack on historical reason and the epistemological foundations of history as a discipline; they assert that postmodernism is willfully obscurantist and politically paralyzing, has little to do with the practice of actual historians, and has little to offer serious historiography (Evans, 1997; McCullagh, 2004; Zagorin, 1999). These defenders of the project of empiricist history, as well as some postmodernists, argue that if we accept postmodern social theory, historical research and writing become untenable. This concern with the status of historical truth parallels widespread anxieties about the postmodern social condition of contemporary life, in which we have to rethink our stories amidst complex social conditions that throw into question any grand narratives that attempt to transport us towards a millennial ending or cocoon us within a singular catholic metanarrative.

Since the early 1990s a growing body of work has considered the implications of postmodernism for education. Likewise, there has emerged a significant historiographical literature—produced slightly later, due to the slow adoption of postmodern thought within the discipline—that addresses the postmodern critique of historical representation. This literature includes survey and synoptic texts (see, for example, C. G. Brown, 2005 and Thompson, 2004) as well as sometimes polemic works produced by the most vocal advocates of postmodern history, including the highly influential *Re-thinking History* (Jenkins, 1991) which occupies an important place on many reading lists, possibly due to its seminal status and accessibility. There is also a small but significant reactive genre that seeks to protect the discipline against an "invasion" of postmodern social theory (Evans, 1997; McCullagh, 2004; Windschuttle, 1996). However, although many of these texts explore in detail the influence of postmodernism on history, their focus is almost unanimously on history as a discipline, not History as curriculum. It is fair to say that that while Berkhofer finishes his significant *Beyond the Great Story: History as Text and Discourse* (1995) with a call for the reflexive writing and teaching of history, the only notable examples from the opposite side of the debate are Jenkins's *Re-thinking History* (1991) and Windschuttle's *The Killing of History* (1996). Yet, both of these texts limit their concern to the teaching of History in the academy; neither addresses in any substantive way the problem of History in the school curriculum, thus almost entirely neglecting the concerns of the majority of curricularists.

Works that do address the implications of postmodern social theory for History and Social Studies education are quite limited in scope and number. While the discipline of history was slow to engage postmodern thought, the arena of History and Social Studies curriculum has been even less receptive than its "parent" discipline. The only text that devotes a substantial amount of space to the problem of postmodernism is *Social Studies—The Next Generation: Re-searching in the Postmodern* (Segall, Heilman, & Cherryholmes, 2006). This deliberately provocative collection partially thematizes postmodernism and its implications for social education, and it may be unique in devoting more than a single chapter to such concerns. Peter Seixas's chapter "Schweigen! die Kinder! Or Does Postmodern History Have a Place in the Schools?" in the edited collection *Knowing, Teaching and Learning History* (2000) is another rare engagement that seriously examines the implications of postmodernism for the teaching of school History. This is not to deny the significant and substantive recent work that explores the development of historical consciousness from perspectives marked by the "narrative turn" in psychology (Straub, 2005). However, this literature rarely, if ever, acknowledges a link to postmodern theorizing, claiming its scientificity and legitimacy through a less politically oriented sociocultural theory—Gergen's (2009, p. 13) acknowledgment of the influences of postmodernism on social constructionism is a significant exception. In addressing this dearth of direct engagement with postmodern thought by deliberating over the implications of postmodern social theory for History as curriculum—a disciplinary domain that has demonstrated resistance to theory in general, and skepticism towards poststructuralism in particular—it is hoped that this book will open new possibilities for rethinking History curriculum. But before we can engage seriously with end-of-history discourse and its implications for History as curriculum, it is necessary to understand what is meant by "history."

## History as Unreliable Signifier

An untutored reader could be excused for thinking that assertions of the end of history are the equivalent of proclamations of the end of the world; of course, occasionally they have been just that (see my preface). Confusion arises in part because of a linguistic condition in English in which the sign *history* has a number of competing referents. Those who have investigated the etymology of the word have argued that it is derived from either the Greek word *istor*, meaning "witness," or the Greek word *historia*, meaning "to investigate" (see Ashcroft, 2001; Le Goff, 1992). No English speaker who has thought about the issue can ignore the presence of the word *story* within *history*, leading to conclusions that *history* is properly the story of the past. In standard English, when we speak of history we are referring to knowledge about "the past" in the form of: (1) the academic discipline taught in universities and practiced by professional scholars; (2) the school subject, which typically has an ambivalent relationship to the academic discipline; or (3) the record of past events in particular human societies, the oeuvre of a particular author/historian, or the archives of a "civilization" that purport to retell the past as it was. Yet, we might also be referring to the past itself; the aggregate of everything that has ever happened; or just our own set of life experiences (i.e., when we talk of a "personal history"). The distinction between what actually happened in the past and our knowledge of what happened—or what Stanford (1994) calls "history-as-event" and "history-as-account," respectively—is generally accepted in the discipline. This distinction is evident in the work of positivists and postmodernists alike. The difference in their views usually comes down to what this distinction is taken to mean. For the positivist historian it means there is a past that can be recovered through careful research and analysis and subsequently re-presented, or retold, as histories, even if the history that is reconstructed is influenced by the concerns of the present or modified by the historian's interpretive choices (E. H. Carr, 1990). In contrast, in much postmodern and poststructuralist critique it is taken to mean that there is a pro-profound distinction between the sign (history text) and its referent (past event), such that one cannot say with any firm reliability that one is commensurate with the other. Indeed, postmodern and poststructuralist theory points to the complete unrecoverability of the referent. From this later position, history may be framed as a narrative that attempts to reconstruct, through a denial of its own historicity and the removal of all trace of its perspectivalism, a radically uncertain past (Ermarth, 1992; LaCapra, 2004).

Attempting to make the complicated concept of the end of history more comprehensible, Jenkins (1995) distinguishes between "uppercase History"—the belief that the procession of events we refer to as "history" has some inherent meaning or significance, or that human societies are evolving towards some optimal endpoint (a proposition shared by Hegel, Marx, Kojeve, and Fukuyama, among others)—and "lowercase history"—the actual practices of studying and writing historical narratives, the work of the professional historian. The origin of the professional approach is often attributed to the German historian Leopold von Ranke, but some have argued that Herodotus and Thucydides set the templates for the discipline (Curthoys & Docker, 2006). Jenkins's framework allows him to clearly distinguish which history he is arguing is coming to what end, and that framework is present when I examine the end of history in contemporary theory and its implications for History curriculum (though my use of upper- and lowercase conventions follows Anna Clark rather than Keith Jenkins; see my "Note on Capitalization"). However, even using Jenkins's distinction, the multiple meanings of *history* present a particular problem for any work that seeks to discuss the subject. Those multiple referents have been one of the stumbling blocks in the defense of the discipline, where all too often debate has deteriorated into polemics as authors slip between referents and at times stop making sense of what really is at stake.

This unreliability of the signifier *history* manifests itself in debates over the status of History/history by making the end of history itself a floating signifier whose meaning shifts depending on the discursive tradition drawn upon. The singularity of focus suggested by the idea of rethinking History curriculum after the end of history obscures the complexity and multiplicity at the heart of such a project, because there is not just one end of history but many. Navigating through the celebrations, lamentations, invocations, and proclamations that arise in and around end-of-history discourse, I argue that the empiricists' claims that History/history is being "murdered" by postmodern and poststructuralist approaches to studying the past are at best inaccurate. Claims that postmodernism is "killing history" arise out of a particular conception of history as a discipline, and are very likely the result of a "strong grammar" within the historiographic field that works to protect the borders of the discipline against the kind of "invasion"—from literary and cultural studies—lamented by the critics. It is this "strong grammar" that often leaves historians describing their practice as if historiography was an unchanging art. Thus, any challenge to this grammar is taken as an assault on the whole enterprise of history as a discipline.

Claims that history is under siege also emerge from a misunderstanding of the poststructural and postmodern position in contemporary theory, a position in which, far from being left without history, we are left with (almost) *nothing but history*, albeit in a "weak" form, stripped of its "metaphysical buttressing" (Roberts, 1995, p. 9). What this suggests is that postmodernism—at least in some of its poststructuralist forms—is a movement that extends the gaze of historians so that nothing escapes it, not even themselves. As such, history is hardly at an end under this kind of regime, *but it is transformed*, forced into reflexivity as it is pushed to its logical conclusion *where everything and everyone is historicized*. As a result of appropriating the gaze of the historiographer, histories—as interpretations of the past—come to be viewed as somewhat unreliable representations. Resultantly, a hermeneutic position emerges in which histories are understood as historical products themselves, to some degree "prejudiced" or conditioned by the period in which they were written, and constituted within the "horizon" or limits of the cultural paradigms of their authors. Understanding history as an "unreliable signifier" foregrounds the crisis of representation and legitimation that Lyotard (1979) associates with "the postmodern condition" of incredulity towards metanarratives—those "master narratives" that might be described as ahistorical representations masquerading as histories, which claim the status of universal truth while failing to acknowledge their own historical origins.

## Theorizing the Postmodern

Much of this book is devoted to exploring the various meanings of the end of history that are mobilized in contemporary theory. In the section that follows I provide a brief summary of the understanding of postmodernism and its central concerns. Of course, this definitional discussion is not neutral, and inevitably it moves in a reductive direction that is arguably at odds with postmodern thought itself. Nonetheless, presenting some of the main claims made about postmodernism is necessary before moving on to the details of the project that guides this book.

Postmodernism is notoriously difficult to define. Understood as an elusive and sometimes incoherent phenomenon, postmodernist thought emerged in the academy during the late twentieth century as an apocalyptic discourse intent on demolishing once carefully elaborated certainties via an extended and multifaceted polemic against foundationalism, essentialism, and universalism. Inheriting the terminal impulses of Nietzsche and Heidegger that claimed God and philosophy in turn, postmodernism has had a range of influences and antecedents. In some ways it seems to rehearse aspects of the philosophy of the ancient Greek school of skeptics, and from a different perspective, to push to their radical conclusions the philosophical arguments of the American pragmatists. Of course, it would be neither very postmodern nor historically accurate to suggest that the skeptics and the pragmatists are direct progenitors of postmodernism, despite Eco's amusing assertion that soon even Homer will be claimed as a postmodernist (Southgate, 2003). However, there are parallels in some of their philosophies, and in the work of the contemporary American philosopher Richard Rorty these ideas find a common home.

Used as an epithet for the "cultural condition" of late capitalism and the present "status of knowledge" in postindustrial societies, postmodernism appears as a cipher whose meaning must be indefinitely suspended (Lyotard, 1979). During the period of its more self-conscious impact on the humanities, an attempt was made to define postmodernism as both a mode of theorizing about societies and a period in social thought. This distinction developed into a common understanding that there are two main forms of postmodernism, the *methodological* and the *historical* (Cahoone, 1996; Denzin, 1994). Some scholars argue that methodological and historical postmodernism are intertwined, and thus postmodernism is best understood as constituted by "neoliberal forms of governmentality . . . the emerging postindustrial society in the West structured by the so-called new information economy . . . [and a] crisis of cultural authority" (de Alba, Gonzalez-Gaudiano, Lankshear, & Peters, 2000, p. 128). Because I am at least partially sympathetic to this argument, I will first attend to postmodernism as a historical epoch and style to set the context for my exploration of postmodernism as a methodological discourse.

## Historical Postmodernism

As a *historical* claim, postmodernism is typically mobilized to signify that the cultural organization of modernity has undergone fundamental change, and that a radical break with past social trends has taken place. Other scholars use the term to mark significant social and cultural transformations while still articulating a closer continuity with the modern, and even go so far as to suggest that the postmodernization of culture does not transcend modernity as a historical epoch, but instead constitutes a significant challenge to modernity as an intellectual enterprise. Understanding postmodernism as a historical claim thus involves exploring "the postmodern" (or "postmodernity") as both a particular cultural style and a unique social condition (Best & Kellner, 1997; Lyon, 1999).

A historical style in art and architecture that is dominated by anachronism, collage, allegory, and pastiche, postmodernism has been associated with "the end of art," a thesis that proposes that we have reached a condition in which the metanarrative of art history is over, so art no longer can be defined by its place in a historical or developmental progression. This leaves postmodern (or perhaps more accurately, posthistorical) artists free to produce art in any form they please. In its postmodern manifestation, this often means the artist rehearses and remixes older forms (indicating that the *telos* of art's history has been reached), or renders the everyday as art (problematizing any axiological foundations from which to view art). Posthistorical art is therefore characterized by the lack of stylistic unity (Connor, 1997; Danto, 1997).

Similarly, as a historical movement in literature, postmodernism has been associated with tendencies towards self-conscious irony and disruption in the form of fabulism, metafiction, and surfiction, forms of fiction that draw attention to themselves as fiction (Chabot, 1988). Postmodernism in literary studies has been associated with the idea of "the death of the author" (Barthes, 1968/1977), marking the impossibility of restricting meaning to the author's intentions, and the denial of univocal authorship as a result of the inevitability of textual repetition (intertextuality), an idea shared by earlier formalist theories. The "death of the author" also has been associated with the poststructural recognition that "author-ity" is always an artifact of a discursive regime rather than a simple fact of writing (Foucault, 1969/1994). Whether such trends in art and literature actually represent a new style that breaks with the modern, and whether they are in their current manifestation dependent upon or independent of postmodernism as a social condition, remain subjects of debate. However taken as expressions of "the postmodern," these artistic and literary movements suggest the overlapping of postmodernism as style and social condition.

Some scholars have argued that as a *historical social condition*, postmodernism is the result of a transformation from nineteenth-century industrial society to late twentieth-century information society in which the distortions of time and space resulting from new technologies for travel, telecommunications, and information transfer have come to shape the contemporary scene. Commentators have also described this particular reorganization of the social as a shift from the politics of production to an obsession with consumption, in which it

> is *the* factor, *the* principle, held to determine definitions of value, the construction of identities, and even shape the global ecumene. As such, tellingly, it is the invisible hand, or the Gucci-gloved fist, that animates the political impulses, the material imperatives, and the social forms of the Second Coming of Capitalism—of capitalism in its neoliberal, global manifestation. (Comaroff & Comaroff, 2000, p. 294, emphasis in the original)

Frederic Jameson (1991) agrees, depicting postmodernism as the historically specific logic of late (consumer-focused multinational) capitalism in which value is determined by the vagaries of the market, where consumption is the primary motivator. Within this milieu multinational capitalism has reworked the social and economic relationship between production and consumption in such a way as to make consumption the underlying principle of the information society and the driving force of the global knowledge economy. Stated another way, "postmodern culture replicates, reproduces, and reinforces the logic of consumer capitalism" (S. Shapiro, 1995, p. 192).

As a logic of consumption, the cultural style and social condition of postmodernism are brought together. This is perhaps clearest in the writings of the French social theorist Jean Baudrillard. Baudrillard has been described by Douglas Kellner as a postmodern McLuhan, and aspects of his work can be read as an update of Debord's theorization of contemporary society as spectacle (D. Kellner, 1989). Although marked by eclecticism, Baudrillard's analyses of contemporary culture are based most strongly on "classical exchange theory as a theory of social determination" (Gane, 2000, p. 35). He has argued that within postmodern society, the social value of "objects" is created by differentiating consumer items from each other (Baudrillard, 1988). This differentiation results in part from contemporary society's capacity to reproduce "the code" (i.e., create copies of an unrecoverable original) and "brand" the replicas (as "identifiable" and "identical"). Subsequently, consumer goods come to have both a value determined by the market (made up of their "use value" and "exchange value") and a "sign value" determined by the social status they confer upon, or the "identity" they make possible for, the consumer (McLaren & Leonardo, 1998).

Like the postmodern art of Andy Warhol, new technologies make possible the endless replication of the object/sign/style, and therefore the construction of "indiscernible counterparts" for everyone (who can afford them). The expression "indiscernible counterparts," which comes from art theory, suggests the impossibility of determining the difference between, for example, a shovel used to dig dirt, and a shovel created as a work of art. Here we take it further: The demarcation between copy and original has imploded. As a consequence of the mass production of consumer objects and social signs, "indiscernible counterparts" are produced that replicate an unrecoverable original, now lost amongst clones. Thus, theorists who argue for historical postmodernism as a description of the present moment in Western societies depict "the contemporary" as a society dominated by a capitalist logic of style and consumption in which "sentimentality and history become less pertinent because an almost perfect replica of the object can be (re)produced... [and] people become functions of consumer society as they are motivated to purchase more and more objects in order to feel part of the social milieu" (McLaren & Leonardo, 1998, p. 218).

Baudrillard believes they do this because consumer objects carry a "sign value" that is "consumed" in the act of exchange, conferring status on the consumer. This conflation of object/style/status reinforces the logic of capitalism via a marking of the individual by the list of what they consume, and therefore lends weight to the suggestion from some quarters that "postmodernist rhetoric has been profitably capitalized on by neoliberalism in order to update its longed-for project of cultural hegemony" (Hopenhayn, 1993, p. 98). Trapped within a matrix of market ideology, the argument advanced here is that the individual plays the consumption status game whether he/she wants to or not, and typically without any conscious awareness of his/her complicity in "the game."

Baudrillard (1983) couples his analysis of the dominance of the object with a vision of society in which the broadcast media have come to rule our lives and reality appears to have "imploded," with the result that it has become impossible for us to determine the difference between the real world and its "hyperreal" televisual simulation. This is perhaps best exemplified by the first Gulf War (1991), which Baudrillard argued "would not" and "did not" take place. According to Paul Patton in his introduction to Baudrillard's infamous text *The Gulf War Did Not Take Place* (1995), "the Gulf War was instant history in the sense that the selected images which were broadcast worldwide provoked immediate responses and then became frozen into the accepted story of the war: high-tech weapons, ecological disaster, the liberation of Kuwait" (Patton, 1995, p. 3). Baudrillard argues that the "war" in the Persian Gulf was both a media-driven "virtual war" (p. 30) and "an ultra-modern process of electrocution" (p. 61), but not an actual war because no Iraqi who took part had "a chance of fighting," and no American who took part "a chance of being beaten" (Baudrillard, 1995, p. 61). Thus, despite the claim that during this campaign "the amount of high explosives unleashed during the first month of the conflict exceeded that of the entire allied air offensive during WW II" (Patton, 1995, pp. 1-2), Baudrillard denies that a *real* war took place. For Baudrillard, what did happen was the analogue of the film *Capricorn One* (1978), "in which the flight of a manned rocket to Mars, which only took place in a desert studio, was relayed to all the television stations in the world" (p. 61).

It is not that Baudrillard is denying history when he asserts that the Gulf War did not happen. The theory of hyperreality is no dupe for alleged "Holocaust deniers" such as David Irving who are said to engage in "massive falsification of historical evidence, manipulation of facts, and denial of truth" (Evans, 2002, p. 10), and deliberate "misrepresentation, mistranslation, misleading phrasing, and imperfectly varnished deceit" (Guttenplan, 2001, p. 223). Baudrillard acknowledges that the United States and its military partners dropped bombs on Iraq and killed thousands of people, but he is not writing "history." Baudrillard's "high risk writing strategy, courting equally the dangers of contradiction by the facts and self-refutation," is designed to be "less a representation of reality than its transfiguration" (Patton, 1995, p. 6), less history than a challenge to the instantaneous history of the media report. Patton argues that Baudrillard's essays can be understood as a response to the media's first-draft version of history, as well as a challenge to the manner in which the events have been portrayed and an interrogation of the nature of war as a televisual simulation and media event. As Best and Kellner (2001) suggest, during the Gulf War "images and representations of the war, disseminated by government and media outlets, replaced the events of the war itself, providing a hyperreal experience of the war as a media spectacle" (p. 74). In the postmodern world of hyperreal simulation, Baudrillard (1992) argues that events have gone on strike, and all we are left with is their indiscernible media simulacra. It is this criticism of the process by which representation comes to be indiscernible from reality in media society, rather than a refutation that something actually took place, that is the intended meaning of Baudrillard's Gulf War denial.

Perhaps because so much of what is said to constitute the postmodern is either "recycled modernity" or renovation within the ruins of modernity, the notion of a postmodern style and a postmodern era is explicitly rejected by commentators who argue that the claims for a distinctive postmodern artistic aesthetic are contradictory and unconvincing, and that much of the scholarship supporting "the postmodern" as a break with industrial capitalism "grossly exaggerate[s] the extent of the changes involved, and fail[s] to theorize them properly" (Callinicos, 1989, p. 135). Yet, as a critic of postmodernism who has gone to great pains to argue against any suggestion that the latter half of the twentieth century saw a radical break with the past, Callinicos concedes that the term *postmodern* is usefully understood as a floating signifier utilized by "a socially mobile intelligentsia in a climate dominated by the retreat of the Western labour movement and the 'overconsumptionist' dynamic of capitalism in the Reagan-Thatcher era . . . to articulate its political disillusionment and its aspiration to a consumption-oriented lifestyle" (Callinicos, 1989, pp. 170-171). Callinicos's criticism of postmodernism as a historical social condition—and of those he believes to be advocating this thesis (such as Baudrillard and Lyotard)—hinges on a specific rejection of the idea that capitalism has mutated into a form that has left industrialization behind. He is evidently prepared to concede that postmodernism may be used as a sign to demarcate a particular sociohistorically located intellectual trend, but this trend still must be understood to be underpinned by industrial capital. Resultantly, he argues that postmodernism is more an intellectual orientation than a definable aesthetic. It should be acknowledged that Callinicos was writing several years before the advent of the public Internet, and almost two decades after his critique, postmodernism as signifier is still afloat and is being utilized by a generation of scholars who were still at school during the Reagan-Thatcher era. It may be that only time will tell whose stance on postmodernism as a historical phenomenon (or otherwise) proves correct, but at this moment, postmodernism no longer seems to be a passing fad, as some of its early critics predicted.

It is important to note that despite the fact that the emergence of postmodernism as an intellectual orientation appears to have coincided with the arrival of so-called postmodernity, it would be a mistake to conflate the two. Arguably, it is not synchronicities, dependencies, or overlaps in their development that connect postmodernity and postmodernism, but instead a set of resemblances. Certainly the pathways to postmodernism and postmodernity have been many and varied, and any genealogy of postmodern thought is inevitably partial. Thus, it is probably unproductive and only partly accurate, as well as ironically self-defeating, to define methodological postmodernism as the intellectual orientation of academics fashioned by postmodernity. Nothing is simple when it comes to defining any aspect of postmodernism.

## Methodological Postmodernism

As a methodological position, postmodernism is neither a systematic theory nor a singular or unified discourse. It may seem to the observer that postmodernism is used as a label for such a wide range of ideas that it is empty of any meaning (Rosenau, 1992). Perhaps best described as a continuum of critique that shares cynicism about claims to truth in the human and social sciences, postmodernism is often depicted as a minefield of conflicting concepts, marked by a pervasive nihilism that resists any tendency to totalize. A range of concepts have been proposed as postmodern philosophies, including:

> the death of the subject, the repudiation of depth models of reality, the rejection of grand narratives or universal explanations of history, the illusion of the transparency of language, the impossibility of any final meaning, the effects of power on the objects it represents, the failure of pure reason to understand the world, the de-centering of the Western logos and with it the de-throning of the "first world," the end of a belief in progress as a natural and neutral panacea, and a celebration of difference and multiplicity. (P. Slattery, 1997, p. 3)

This is some list. Certainly there has been some agreement that postmodernism typically "takes the form of self-conscious, self-contradictory, self-undermining statement"; invested in the trope of irony, it "manages to install and reinforce as much as undermine and subvert the conventions and presuppositions it appears to challenge" (Hutcheon, 1989, pp. 1-2). Connor asserts that "post-modernism as method is basically a revolt against the rationality of modernism, a deliberate attack on the foundation character of much modernist thought" (1997, p. 322). Working with a poststructural understanding of the rational, we might argue that postmodernism is simply a different form of rationality to "modernist reason," rather than the jettisoning or rejection of reason and rationality altogether (see Foucault, 1983/1994). To think otherwise is to accept that methodological postmodernism is simply a particular form of irrationality, either devoid of its own logic or constituted by the supplanting of logic by a valorization of aesthetics and experience. However, it is only subscription to the modernist binary of "logic" versus "rhetoric" that sustains the claim that postmodernism is a form of irrationality. In contrast, considering postmodernism as a form of reasoning reveals that methodologically its rhetorical logic challenges realism (arguing that there is no unmediated access to the world, and that what counts as "reality" is constructed in the process of attempting to know the world); rejects essentialism (claiming there is no universal human nature that is consistent across cultural landscapes and historical epochs); and disrupts foundationalism (asserting that there can be no statements of value or claims to truth that will be universally acceptable, because they are typically intelligible only within the sociohistorically specific disciplinary rules that have made them possible, or within the discursively established ethos that have given them credibility). These three signature postmodern philosophies are often defined by the motifs of the end of history, the death of the subject, and the death of the author, respectively (Parkes, Gore, & Elsworth, 2010).

In practice, methodological postmodernists—whom Breisach (2003) refers to controversially, but rather usefully, as poststructuralist postmodernists—typically refuse to accept that there are any transcultural, transhistorical, or transcendent grounds for interpretation. In exploring the postmodern challenge to history and the genealogy of various forms of postmodernism, Breisach actually differentiates between two types of postmodernism: structural postmodernism (which he associates with the period 1945 to 1965) and poststructural postmodernism (which came to prominence in the late 1960s). The defining feature of structural postmodernism—which is not to be confused with structuralism, per se—was the "retention of a knowable world of objectively given structures and forces" (Breisach, 2003, p. 22). Common to both forms of postmodernism, according to Breisach's analysis, is a belief that humanity will enter a period of history that is beyond modernity, called the *posthistoire*. According to Breisach's schema, poststructuralist postmodernists (such as Foucault, Lyotard, Derrida, Baudrillard, and Deleuze) are identified by their rejection of the privileged status of modernist theory, and thus enter into forms of postmodernism. In contrast, structural postmodernists (such as Cournot, Kojeve, and Fukuyama) can be identified by their belief that we are about to enter a period of quietude—the final stage of history—having realized a world based on a balance of "recognition" and "equality," and thus they profess visions of postmodernity (or more correctly, posthistory) as the stage beyond modernization.

Poststructuralism, which has come to be associated more closely with postmodern social theory than any other single philosophy, was widely used as a label for those critiques of modernity and Enlightenment philosophy that became the signature of continental philosophies prominent during the late 1960s. Originally a French form of methodological postmodernism, poststructuralism emerged partly as a result of the political disillusionment that followed the student and worker strikes of 1968, and partly as a reaction to the scientific pretensions of structuralist thought. Structuralism, which was the dominant social theory at the time, cast "human behaviour as rule-governed transformations of meaningless elements" (Dreyfus & Rabinow, 1982, p. xix). Among the poststructuralists, Barthes led the shift away from the search for deep structures that were believed to preconfigure meaning towards the concentration on the problem of representation. Foucault's work also demonstrates something of this shift.

As a thorough critique of "modern theories rooted in humanist assumptions and Enlightenment rationalist discourses" (Best & Kellner, 1991, p. 27), poststructuralism is often characterized by a respect for that which might be described as specific, local, different, and peculiar, and by a rejection of theories that propose universal, foundational, or essential norms of human social and cultural life. Where explanations are provided, they are given tentatively, cautiously, and reluctantly, as descriptions from the author's own praxis or position or as a set of self-proclaimed fictions, rather than as totalizing discourses that claim universal applicability or truth claims that articulate the discovery of some deep meaning concealed from consciousness. What is rejected by many poststructural postmodernists is the transcendental self, the disembodied, rational hero-norm of the Enlightenment who masquerades as ahistorical, asexual, acultural, and classless while simultaneously masking a (socially constructed) white masculine subjectivity. In place of the metaphysical or transcendental subject, methodological or poststructuralist postmodernists propose decentered, fragmented, material subjects, producers, and products of the discursive practices of their unique historical circumstances. Not only do these postmodern subjects lack an underlying ahistorical unity, they also are split or fragmented within themselves as a consequence of their participation in contradictory discourses and practices.

In attempting to encapsulate methodological postmodernism, some scholars draw upon an often quoted distinction between ludic, spectral, or skeptical postmodernism and resistance, critical, oppositional, or affirmative postmodernism. When this distinction is accepted, the scholarly work of poststructuralists and deconstructionists is categorized as either (1) a self-indulgent form of aesthetic free play that ignores politics, and might even lend support to the status quo, or (2) a material intervention that goes beyond a textual theory of difference, recognizing the shaping effect of the social and historical context (Ebert, 1996; Kincheloe & McLaren, 2003; Rosenau, 1992). However, the distinction between skeptical and affirmative postmodernism actually may be "conceptually misleading and historically false" (de Alba, et al., 2000, p. 129). If resistance postmodernism is characterized by the notion that texts are material practices that embody conflicting social relations—which could very well be an axiom of some poststructuralist works, particularly Foucault's—then I'm not sure that ludic and resistance postmodernism aren't just two different ways of reading postmodernism, or two different uses of postmodern theory, rather than discrete forms. Arguing that discourse is constitutive of social relations (after Foucault), or that there is no outside text (after Derrida), does not mean there is no world outside of language (and therefore no real political struggles). Rather, it means there is no unmediated access to reality, and that discourse is constitutive—as far as our perspective on things is concerned—rather than unproblematically descriptive, of "what is" (restating the challenge to realism highlighted earlier). Postmodernism is thus not an extreme form of idealism that denies the world, though it does reflect a degree of Kantian subjectivism. Nor is postmodernism the opposite of modernism, though it remains skeptical about the particular form of reasoning that underpins a great deal of modernist thought. Postmodernism doesn't have to mean denying a critical project, but it does mean remaining cautious of any claims to truth.

## Methodological Postmodernism and the Problem of Historical Representation

Postmodernism's challenge to the epistemological foundations of history as a discipline has been considerable, taking the form of academic publications that might be described as favorable, fair, and fearful. Much of the literature sounds either celebratory (by postmodernists) or mournful (by positivists). The main issues have centered on the role narrative construction plays in historical inquiry. For the contemporary historian, one of the central problems that postmodern social theory presents has been described as a crisis of representation. In principle, this means that poststructuralists as methodological postmodernists typically reject the idea that our representations unproblematically correspond with reality; instead, they take the position that reality is never known outside of our systems of representation, so our representations can be said to shape, write, constitute, or inscribe our "reality" rather than mirror it.

From the perspective of postmodernism, our representations of the world constitute reality as we know it. That is not to say that representations actually form the world itself, as some critics of methodological postmodernism have suggested, but they do predispose us to view and engage with the world in certain ways. Like the German philosopher Immanuel Kant, this leaves us not in the position of denying that a world exists outside our own mind, but in a state where although we can believe there is something we might call reality, we cannot know the true nature of that reality. This is where postmodernism meets pragmatism. Whereas pragmatism argues that the truth value of a map (of reality) hinges on its usefulness (to navigate that otherwise unknowable reality), the postmodern position is marked by a rejection of "naïve realism [which] holds that objects in the real world conform or correspond precisely to our representation and our understanding of them" (Munslow, 2003, p. 56), manifesting a "profound distrust of the idea that referential language works through mirroring or mapping reality" (Potter, 1996, p. 68). While postmodern social theory accepts the arbitrariness of the sign, it inverts our commonsense perspective that signs reflect things in the world and replaces it with the view that our understanding of things in the world is constituted by the sociohistorical sign systems we have inherited, appropriated, and evolved in the course of our sociolinguistic "development." In this view, the world—as we know it—is constituted by the sign, rather than the (existence of the) sign being dependent on the world.

It is highly unlikely that any historian other than a hagiographer would be inclined towards the sympathetic logic of romanticism, and it would be setting up the discipline of history as a straw man to suggest that most historians endorse anything like naïve realism. Yet, many historians do subscribe to other forms of realism. For example, there are historians who subscribe to an empirical-analytic philosophy that suggests it might be possible to "discover explanations that reflect the rational structure of nature through empirical research, the inference of its meaning and the representation of its findings as the truthful descriptive statement" (Munslow, 2003, pp. 40-41). There are also historians who seek to discover general laws operating behind the machinery of history. In both cases it is the will to know, expressed as a conceit that we can come to understand and accurately represent what happened in the past, which brings positivist and empiricist historians into conflict with poststructuralists. Methodological postmodernists of all persuasions typically deny the capacity of language to act as a transparent mode of representation; they argue that there is no unmediated access to the past, and that when attempting to write histories, all we are left with is partial traces of the past that are open to multiple, conflicting, situated interpretations and explanations.

As this brief overview indicates, although methodological postmodernism has challenged the foundations of much historical work, the implications of the problem of historical representation have been largely neglected in the field of curriculum, with only a few exceptions (see Brickley, 1994; Segall, Heilman, & Cherryholmes, 2006; Seixas, 2000). One of the ways I will attempt to address the problem of postmodernism for History as curriculum is through an examination of the "culture wars" and their impact on History curriculum.

## History and the Culture Wars

Taking seriously Ivor Goodson's argument that "social histories of school subject[s] need to be undertaken in national and local milieux" (1992, p. 25), this book reserves as the main context for its deliberations and ruminations the mandatory secondary school History curriculum in New South Wales (NSW), Australia. Specifically, it explores the central problematic of this book—History curriculum after the end of history—in relation to changes to the compulsory junior secondary History curriculum in NSW during the period defined by two important temporal markers, Australia's bicentennial (whose significance I discuss in chapter 4) and the millennium (whose significance for postmodern theory I discussed in the preface). Although in some sense it might be possible to discuss the central problematic in purely philosophic and theoretic terms, Goodson's work makes clear that attempts to study school subjects as abstract categories, or universal structures, divorces them from the wider social, political, and cultural assemblages and relations that provide them with form and meaning. Thus, while conceptual issues are given primacy in this study, the case studies I will examine do more than simply anchor the discussion; they function as a case through which deliberations in terms of the problematic are situated to render them meaningful, purposeful, and intelligible.

Mandating for the first time the study of Australian history, the 1992 NSW Years 7-10 History Syllabus (Board of Studies NSW, 1992) was a watershed curriculum document. Responding to the social conscience of the times, the syllabus did more than simply ensure coverage of Australian history; it incorporated "social histories" about, and from the perspective of, women and Australia's Indigenous peoples, and it framed them as legitimate alternatives to hegemonic, Eurocentric, patriarchal master narratives of the nation, challenging conceptions of history as a grand story. The social meliorist changes to the NSW History curriculum of the early 1990s set the syllabus on a collision course with politically conservative historians and socially conservative politicians, and it became an important site of struggle in a series of heated and highly public "history wars." At the core of these skirmishes over history was a concern that the historical consciousness of the nation's youth was being hijacked by left-wing radicals intent on installing a "black armband" (mournful, shameful, and somber) view of the nation's past, a view associated with political correctness, revisionist historiography, and postmodernism. The conservatives' position was championed by Prime Minister John Howard, who was keen to see schools dispense with the black armband history promoted during the term of his predecessor. Of particular concern was the representation of frontier life during the pre-federation period. A shift in the language that traditionally had described British colonization as "settlement" to an unprecedented acknowledgment of the Aboriginal perspective on colonization as "invasion" generated a great deal of angst among the conservative intelligentsia in NSW, Queensland, and Victoria, where similar curricular changes occurred (Davison, 2000; S. Macintyre & Clark, 2003). It was this angst that led to more recent reactionary proposals for a national "shared narrative" approach to History curriculum (Melleuish, 2006), driving the movement towards a national curriculum.

This Australian case is by no means unique; similar conflicts have occurred over History education in the United States, the United Kingdom, and Canada (see Nash, Crabtree, & Dunn, 1998; Phillips, 1998; G. H. Richardson, 2002). These parallel conflicts have been referred to as history and culture wars. At their heart is a concern over national culture, and the cultural literacy of the citizenry. The importance of school History as a battlefield in these history and culture wars should not be underestimated. History curriculum operates as an apparatus for the social re/production of national identities, but what is at stake in each of these history wars is not only national identity, but also our conceivable future. If this volume may be understood as foregrounding the exploration of History curriculum after "the end of history," then it is useful to understand one of its main subtexts as a concern with theorizing a postmodern curricular response to the history wars. Lundgren (1991) argues—from the standpoint of reproduction theory—that the problem of representation is the central problem of curriculum theory; if this is so, then the practical question arising for History curriculum amidst the history wars must be, how should History curriculum (re)present history after "the end of history"? There is no easy answer to this question. However, by exploring History curriculum as an important site of conflict in the culture wars particularly through the lens of poststructuralist and postcolonial theory, I will attempt to open new possibilities for History as curriculum that have been overlooked in the struggle for critical and effective histories.

## Reading This Book

In this chapter I have outlined the social and theoretical contexts for this study, defined the study's central problematic, and located my project within internationally resonant debates over History education.

Chapter 2 provides an orientation to the project. I begin by briefly mapping the curriculum field, paying particular attention to the critical-reconceptualist trajectory in curriculum theory and the significance for curriculum history of recasting curriculum as text and discourse. I locate my project within what has been called the "New Curriculum History," then set out the terms of the book's deliberation, analysis, and critique, casting poststructural discourse analysis as an important approach to curriculum inquiry within the New Curriculum History.

In chapter 3 I explore the way in which end-of-history discourse is mobilized in contemporary theory. My explorations begin with a close reading of the works of the economist and political scientist Francis Fukuyama. Representative of a contemporary neoliberal vision of history, it is probably impossible today to discuss the idea of the end of history without referring to his controversial and conservative thesis that triumphantly announces that modernity's goal of "the recognition of human freedom" is not a fantasy, but has been realized with the collapse of Soviet Communism, symbolic of the defeat of all viable alternatives to political and economic liberalism. Fukuyama's thesis is read with and against the writings of the French postmodern social theorists who assert that both history and its end are logographic illusions; and remain skeptical of a Eurocentric historicism that projects history as a grand story of human progress and universalizes the cultural mythologies of the West.

In chapter 4 I explore how the end of history as the rejection of history as a singular, universally shared, and all-encompassing "grand story" has manifested within school History curriculum. The focal point for my study is the social meliorist changes to the curriculum, and the cultural politics surrounding those changes, in NSW, Australia, from the bicentennial of the nation in 1988 to the millennium. I situate this case in relation to similar conflicts and culture wars over History education in Canada, the United States, and the United Kingdom. In these nations, History curriculum changes, with their emphasis on new and revisionist social histories, are read as promoting a "critical pedagogy of counter-memory." Following the political backlash against the socially critical curriculum changes in late twentieth-century History education, I conclude by exploring some of the limitations of counter-memory as critical history, arguing that the interjection of counter-narratives into the curriculum is a necessary but insufficient response to the problem of historical representation.

Chapter 5 provides an analysis of the missed opportunities for "critical practice" that are evident in the case studies of attempts at radical History curriculum reform. Synthesizing insights into the "nature of history" derived from the writings of contemporary philosophers of history, I argue that what remains uncontested in the struggle for critical histories are the representational practices of history itself. Integrating models of historiography and history pedagogy inside a frame provided by Ashcroft's (2001) analysis of the modes of action by which postcolonial subjects resist interpellation and inscription within dominant representations of the historic past, I argue that if

History curriculum is to be a critical/transformative enterprise, it must attend to the problem of historical representation. I conclude this chapter by proposing a way beyond "counter-memory" as critical history.

I bring the book to a close in chapter 6 by returning once again to the central problematic of the study. Drawing inspiration from the metaphor of curriculum ghosts and visions (see Doll & Gough, 2002), I explore History/history (after the end of history) as both ghost and vision—as stories of the past that haunt us, and narratives that we might use to conjure new futures for ourselves and others. Finally, I attempt to sketch some of the ethical and political implications of a History curriculum that places historical representation as its center, recognizing the productive power of the historical imagination to both haunt and inspire, to subjugate and set free.

CHAPTER TWO

# The New Curriculum History

In this chapter, the terms of the book's deliberation, analysis, and critique are set out. It begins by briefly mapping the curriculum field, focusing particularly upon what has been called the critical-reconceptualist trajectory in curriculum theory, and the significance for curriculum history of its recasting of curriculum as text and discourse. Combining approaches typically identified with history, philosophy, and literary studies on the one hand, and empirical analysis, and experimental science on the other, the field of curriculum theory has no single methodological foundation. While there are no commonly agreed "canons" to guide the process of curriculum theorizing, nor any widely accepted techniques of analysis that could be used as a standard to assure the reader of the fidelity of my approach, it is possible to situate this work within what has been called the New Curriculum History. Avoiding a truth-seeking hermeneutic, the New Curriculum History is representative of what has been described as a "textual turn" in the field of curriculum studies that draws upon poststructuralist (deconstructive) and hermeneutic (interpretive) approaches to curriculum conceptualization and critique (Baker, 2009; Pinar & Reynolds, 1992). Such approaches have been responsible for the reconceptualization of curriculum theory and curriculum history as forms of textual interpretation and pedagogic discourse analysis. As a form of textual interpretation and pedagogic discourse analysis, postmodern critical-reconceptualist curriculum theory (and the New Curriculum History) often adopts "reading and writing strategies" such as diffraction, as well as deconstruction, as ways of opening "lines of flight" for rethinking curriculum (Gough, 1994; Reynolds & Webber, 2004).

## Reconceptualizing Curriculum History

According to Pinar, "curriculum theory is a distinctive field of study, with a unique history, a complex present, an uncertain future" (2004, p. 2). He argues that in comparing curriculum theory with educational psychology, sociology, and philosophy, we should note that only curriculum theory can locate its origin within the field of education itself. Studying curriculum means understanding that "curricula are historically formed within systems of ideas that inscribe styles of reasoning, standards, and conceptual distinctions in school practices and its subjects," and therefore should be understood as "a practice of governing and an effect of power" that is implicated in the constitution of particular rationalities, identities, and subjectivities (Popkewitz, 1997, p. 151). In investigating curriculum as a site of subjectivity formation, it is important to note that curriculum theory is no unified practice, nor has it ever existed as anything like a monolithic discourse. The practice of curriculum theorizing remains multiple, fractured, and contested, and conceptions and cultures of curriculum vary, sometimes dramatically. Kemmis and Fitzclarence have argued that "the central problem of curriculum theory is to be understood as a double problem of the relationship between theory and practice, on the one hand, and of the relationship between education and society, on the other" (1986, p. 22). Attempts to understand and navigate trajectories in curriculum theory frequently focus on how scholars address either one or the other of these two central problems.

## Orientations Towards the Central Problems of Curriculum Theory

When the first problem—the relationship between educational theory and practice—is the focus of curriculum theory, heuristics tend to define the variety of roles adopted by the curricularist. For example, James B. Macdonald's (1975) somewhat dated but still efficacious map of the field identifies three distinct approaches to curriculum theory: (1) a form of evaluative curriculum philosophizing that uses theory as a guide for engaging in curriculum development and research; (2) a form of curriculum conceptualizing that uses theory to build curriculum constructs that can be tested empirically for the purpose of determining the most efficient and effective curriculum prescriptions and pedagogical practices; and (3) a form of intellectual "free play" that uses theory to articulate and critique conceptual schema, to reconceptualize contemporary curricular practices, or to generate new curriculum orientations and possibilities. In practical terms, this tripartite scheme can be rearticulated as a distinction between bipolar tendencies in curriculum scholarship: the curricularist as consultant or educational designer who works to design effective courses, pedagogical practices, and/or units of study; and the curricularist as generalist or theorist/critic who questions taken-for-granted assumptions about education (Cherryholmes, 1987; Petrina, 2004).

It is possible to depict the ways different curriculum scholars have engaged with the theory-practice problem as the result of their commitment to one of three orientations that produce different forms of knowledge. Thus, educational research may be conceived and conducted as a concern with: (1) the theoretic (propositional knowledge in the form of warranted conclusions, or "knowing that..."); (2) the practical (judgments in the form of defensible decisions, or "knowing I/we should..."); and (3) the technical (skills in the form of productive procedures, or "knowing how...") (Gough, 2003, pp. 4–6). While deliberative curriculum inquiry is essentially concerned with "the practical," much of radical curriculum theory has been concerned with "the theoretic" and has positioned itself against "the technical." Despite the importance of these various forms of knowledge, there is always an inbuilt danger that "a curriculum perspective that 'chooses' not to answer the commonsense questions appears to be naïve, obfuscating, needlessly difficult, or simply wrong, confused, or fuzzy" (Reynolds & Webber, 2004, p. 8).

If the second problem—the relationship between education and society—becomes the focus of curriculum theory, then we can identify a different set of orientations in the field of curriculum scholarship. Because of the way in which scholars deal with the problem of education and society, they can be identified as being system-oriented, system-supporting, system-indifferent, or system-opposing theorists. Others have suggested that curriculum scholars are inevitably: (1) social transmissionists who adopt an empirical-analytic orientation associated with the traditional model of curriculum design defined by the Tyler Rationale, which is concerned with the efficacy of curriculum as "knowledge transfer" from one generation to the next, and attempts to gain knowledge about effective pedagogy through methods of direct observation or carefully designed and controlled intervention; (2) interpretativists who adopt a reconceptualist orientation that encourages attempts to understand curriculum as lived experience and/or human meaning-making activity, and is concerned with understanding curriculum, its generation, evolution, operation, and effects; or (3) social reconstructionists who adopt a critical-theoretical orientation, associated with various forms of radical curriculum theory, that attempts to make explicit the implicit or hidden assumptions instantiated through curriculum as social practice, and who aim to use curriculum as a vehicle of liberation and emancipation, societal transformation, individual empowerment, and/or cultural critique (Aoki, 2005; Marsh & Willis, 2003). Such distinctions can be closely related to the technical, hermeneutic, and praxis-oriented knowledge interests articulated by the Frankfurt School critical theorist Jürgen Habermas. When constructed in this way, praxis-oriented curriculum inquiry often is positioned by its practitioners in opposition to what they perceive as the "instrumentality" or "technocratic rationality" of technically oriented curriculum theory (see Kincheloe & McLaren, 2003).

Sometimes scholars develop heuristics that do not distinguish between the two central problems of curriculum theory, because they believe in the importance of considering the theory-practice and education-society problematics together. This results in hybrid schema. For example, Huebner (1966/1999) has identified the deployment of five "value systems" in the practice of curriculum theory that result in discussions of curriculum from viewpoints that he describes as technical, political, scientific, aesthetic, and ethical. Each of these viewpoints results in different curriculum conceptions and prescriptions. Alternatively, Kliebard (1987) identifies curricularists as either mental disciplinarians, social efficiency experts, developmentalists, or social meliorists, depending on whether they were concerned with acculturating youth, testing a curriculum prescription, instantiating a psychologically informed course design, or correcting the "ills of society" through educational intervention. In another schema, Eisner and Vallance (1974) map constructions of curriculum as the development of cognitive processes concerned with the refinement and development of intellectual processes and operations; technology concerned with locating, testing, or developing the most efficient means to achieve desired curricular outcomes; self-actualization concerned with education as an enabling or self-empowerment process; social reconstruction concerned with the reform of society in the interests of producing a more just and democratic future for our children; and academic rationalism concerned with apprenticing the young into the knowledge, skills, and values of our cultural heritage to provide them with the tools required to participate in the Western cultural tradition. Despite the limitations of the various heuristics deployed by those attempting to map the curriculum field, it is typical practice to identify curriculum scholars with specific movements because of their utilization of common orientations to solving educational problems, and their particular conceptions of curriculum. Of all the contemporary approaches to curriculum inquiry, it is radical curriculum theory in its critical-reconceptualist form that has had the most influence on my approach in this volume.

## Radical Curriculum Theory

Although by no means a unified approach to the study of education, radical curriculum theory has two prominent and identifiable strands: reproductionist and reconceptualist curriculum theory. These strands in many ways overlap and borrow from each other, and they may be regarded as divergent trends within the reconceptualist movement itself, leading Cormack and Green (2009) to use the synthetic epithet "critical-reconceptualist" to refer to scholars working within this tradition. What has been called "reproductionist" curriculum theory is usually identified with the emergence of the "new sociology of education" movement that included the work of Michael Young and, a little later, Basil Bernstein in the United Kingdom, Samuel Bowles and Herbert Gintis in the United States, R. W. Connell in Australia, and Pierre Bourdieu and Jean-Claude Passeron in France. Radical curriculum theory also has roots in the American pragmatist and socialist movements of the early 1930s (Stanley, 1992). There are traces of this genealogy still discernable in the work of some contemporary radical curriculum theorists such as Henry Giroux. However, the writings of Giroux and other radical pedagogues have tended towards the adoption of a Gramscian and Althusserian form of neo-Marxist ideology critique, Marcusian emancipatory philosophy, and late in the development of "critical pedagogy," a turn towards the work of the Marxist-inspired pedagogical theory of the Vygotskian Cultural Historical School (see Kincheloe, 2004; Miedema & Wardekker, 1999).

In the 1980s radical curriculum theory was most readily associated with the work of Michael Apple, Henry Giroux, and Peter McLaren, who were in many ways foundational in the critical pedagogy movement (Kincheloe, 2004). In Australia, radical curriculum theorizing emerged most successfully in the form of the socially critical curriculum movement, which had particular impact in the area of English, and more broadly in educational action research. Much of the literature on feminist approaches to education may also be understood as a strand of radical theorizing, often favoring—like Giroux and McLaren—"pedagogy" over "curriculum," placing emphasis on education as a set of practices whilst remaining in many cases a "theoretical" discourse (Gore, 1991). Sharing vocabulary drawn from neo-Marxist writers such as Gramsci, Marcuse, and Althusser, and concerned with issues of ideology, hegemony, critical consciousness, cultural capital, and social reproduction, reproductionist curriculum theories both contrast with and complement the more "hermeneutically oriented" approaches within the reconceptualist strand of radical curriculum theorizing. Although neither approach has had the kind of impact in "mainstream" Australian curriculum theorizing that marks the emergence of a movement (Green, 2003), both these orientations have significance for this book, for it is as a work of critical-reconceptualist curriculum history that this study attempts to engage with its central problematic, History curriculum after "the end of history." Exploring the commitments, methods, and methodological issues of critical-reconceptualist curriculum theory and its relationship to the New Curriculum History forms the focus of the remainder of this chapter.

## Curriculum History and the "Textual Turn"

When Pinar published his influential collection *Curriculum Theorizing: The Reconceptualists* in the mid-1970s, he described it as "a report of a movement just under way" (1975, p. xi). Only a few years later, when discussing the emerging body of reconceptualist curriculum theory, he remarked that "while the writing published to date may be somewhat varied thematically, it is unitary in its significance for the field" (Pinar, 1979, p. 13). Despite its initial adoption and continuing use of conceptual tools from existentialism and phenomenology in order to understand the nature of educational experience, and somewhat later, its appropriation of poststructuralist methods, what links the reconceptualists is not a consistent methodology but the theme and function of their work. The three markers of critical-reconceptualist curriculum work—(1) an interest in going beyond the limits of the technicist Tyler Rationale; (2) the deployment of various forms of theory (usually with a continental European genealogy); and (3) an underlying neo-Marxist orientation or emancipatory intent—help to blur the distinction that some scholars make between reproductionist and reconceptualist curriculum theories. Yet, while downplaying differences in approach, these markers do define the space of radical curriculum theory, broadly conceived (W. M. Reynolds, 1989).

With a view of curriculum as a "complicated conversation," the dominant modes of inquiry for scholars working within the critical-reconceptualist movement are not "scientific" or "techno-rationalistic," but rather historical, philosophical, and literary (Pinar, 2004). Scholars working within this tradition frequently challenge notions that reconceptualist inquiry is a "retreat from practice" (see Wraga, 1999), with arguments that "curriculum discourse should be marked by richness, diversity, discordant voices, fecundity, multiple rationalities, and theories, and should be touched by humanity and practicality in a hundred thousand contexts" (Morrison, 2004, p. 487). In the early 1990s the North American curriculum scholar Edmund Short explored this diversity, fecundity, and multiplicity as it applied to curriculum inquiry in an important article in *Curriculum Perspectives*, the Australian education field's premiere curriculum studies journal.

According to Short (1991) in his thorough overview of inquiry methods in curriculum studies, historical inquiry aims to understand and explain human actions and associated events that occurred sometime in the past. The most striking features of historical inquiry are its application of "relatively standard" methodologies and its use of compelling storytelling as a means of providing explanation. In contrast, in Short's view, the fundamental purpose of philosophical inquiry is to grapple with life's central questions; its scope is broad, covering issues related to epistemological, metaphysic, aesthetic, ethical, logical, axiological, ontological, and cosmological problems. Its form of inquiry follows a process of intellectual and conceptual analysis through which questions are raised about contemporary problems or taken-for-granted constructions; answers are proposed; the implications of answers are explored; and the reasonableness of any answers are subjected to further interrogation. It is often identified by a form of dialectic inquiry that relies on a cyclic process of analysis, synthesis, and criticism. Finally, literary inquiry in Short's scheme embraces forms of both artistic and hermeneutic inquiry; whereas artistic inquiry attempts to help us understand the human experience as depicted through creative artworks, hermeneutic or "interpretive" inquiry seeks to develop an understanding of the meaning people attach to their experiences and actions. Typically, this involves a procedure of identifying the meanings in a text associated with the topic of inquiry and examining these meanings in relation to each other, the whole text, and the text's context. Depending upon whether this act occurs inside a conservative, critical, or poststructural frame of reference, there will be different expectations in terms of the "truth" that is realized through this process.

The adoption of historical, philosophical, and literary modes of inquiry within critical-reconceptualist curriculum studies recasts curriculum theory as the interdisciplinary study of educational experience in whatever forms it takes. This stands in contradistinction to narrow views of curriculum theory as limited to the study or design of a school district's planned scope and sequence guides or official published syllabi. The redefinition of curriculum as the "course" of our individual and collective educational experience can be seen clearly in the field. However, the "reconceptualization," as it is known, did not stop with the appropriation of a phenomenological hermeneutic. Implicated in the movement from modernism to postmodernism in the field of curriculum inquiry, the reconceptualization has its roots in the critical hermeneutic tradition, the impact of which has been "a shift from 'reproduction' to 'representation' as an organizing principle for curriculum research and critical pedagogy" (Green, 1993, p. 202). What the reconceptualization has meant for the field is a broadly realized "textual turn," the application of a wide range of insights, interpretive tools, methods, and heuristics from continental philosophy, literary theory, social history, and cultural studies to an understanding of curriculum as social text.

## Reading Curriculum as Text

Understanding curriculum as text requires an appreciation of contemporary literary, social, and hermeneutic theory. Despite the fact that critical-reconceptualist curriculum theory has increasingly drawn on an impressive array of theoretical traditions and, as a result, has no single conception of "text" that it consistently mobilizes, there are a number of intuitions about the nature of text that are widely shared by contemporary literary, social, and curriculum theorists. In the latter half of the twentieth century the term *text* was used in a range of disciplinary fields to describe any cultural object, including fashion, food, gestures, actions, and even the human body itself, not just that which is written down on a page. Using text as a paradigm, contemporary philosophical hermeneutics—as the theory of interpretation—underpins much of the critical work conducted in the social sciences, and has come to read the world, lived experience, and all human activity as a text. Adopted by hermeneutists, poststructuralists, postcolonial theorists, postmodernists, critical theorists, and curriculum reconceptualists as a flexible term that accommodates all human practices, products, and representations—including curriculum—, *text* becomes a synonym for "material culture." Accepting material culture as text, curriculum (as cultural practice and educational experience) is rendered capable of being "read" (Olsen, 1990; Silverman, 1990).

Once curriculum is understood as a text in this way, it can be "read" by teachers, students, and educational administrators. It problematizes research that assumes a stable relationship between planned and enacted curricula, or between educational experience and its documentation and interpretation. Rendered as text, curriculum becomes subject to negotiation as the agency of its "readers" is exercised through individual interpretation. Constituted independent of its readers, the text is never "a fully imagined and fully controlled product of its author's mind" because inevitably it carries a surplus of meaning, or at least it can be read in a variety of ways that go beyond the author's intended meanings (Fuery & Mansfield, 2000, p. 145). Curriculum as text is thus incapable of representing the world in an unproblematic way; rather, "the world it 'represents' is manifold and diverse, always subject to interpretation, construction and reconstruction" (Kemmis, 1993, p. 52). This particular kind of understanding of *text* has led some researchers to argue that "texts do not exist on bookshelves: they are processes of signification materialized only in the practice of reading . . . [ensuring that] the reader is quite as vital as the author" (Eagleton, 1983, p. 74). Because a text is always the product of a specific sociocultural situation, and its interpretation is inevitably tethered to events occurring around the time of reading, *text* has no final or determinate meaning—it remains an inexhaustible galaxy of signifiers and a seamless weave of codes and code fragments, such that their logic does not match their rhetoric (Eagleton, 1983; Silverman, 1990). Rather than being self-contained entities, texts constitute their boundaries via rhetorical means, and they are constituted by intertextuality, the transformation and repetition of structures across texts. In other words, texts are never isolated products of an author's mind, but instead reproduce and rework structures and ideas that can be located in other texts. The intertextual relationships that are activated, including not only references to ideas drawn from other texts but also repetition of textual structures in composition, make texts less stable entities than they appear. Resultantly, *text* must be understood as "a totality of composition that bears within itself possibilities of meaning that overflow grammatical and syntactic arrangement" (Gallagher, 1993, p. 6).

The suggestion that meaning is not solely an artifact of grammatical and syntactic arrangement does not mean that "anything goes" in textual interpretation. Rather, it should support recognition that meaning is constructed or interpreted alongside and in response to the text as a result of the reader's sociohistorically constituted subjectivity and culturally contingent register and genre-based reading expectations, rather than derived or extracted from something that is found within it. Meaning in this sense is always multiple and, more importantly, relational—never solely or inherently a property of text. Thus, we should work on the assumption that "all readers are writers, [and] that the text is constantly being reinvented by readers" (L. Richardson, 2001, p. 36). Understanding the process of reading as an act of (re)writing, R. J. C. Young argues that "text functions as a transgressive activity which disperses the author as centre, limit, and guarantor of truth, voice and pre-given meaning" (1981, p. 31). The text, by inviting the birth of the reader, is the death of the author (Barthes, 1968/1977).

We must be mindful, however, of Gallagher's assertion that "built into the very act of reading, and conditions implicated in the situation of the reader and in the structure of the text . . . [are the] conditioning factors [that] constitute the limits within which the reader constructs an interpretation of the text" (1993, p. 5). While the text precludes any possibility of a singular theory or method of reading, the author's linguistic and tropic choices haunt the text, making some readings more or less likely. Stated another way:

> The text mediates: it is neither a direct expression of reality, nor is it totally divorced from it. So meaning in the text is dual. It is both to be found in the text's organization and syntax and in the relation of the text to the world. (Tilley, 1990, p. 332)

We might add that, in addition to emerging from the relationship of text to world, and reader to (authored) text, meaning is determined by the "cultural tools" or "sociocultural templates" that mediate these relationships, whether in the guise of text-forms or reading strategies. Conceptualizing curriculum as text draws attention to the "semiotically mediated" nature of the educational encounter. Practically, this means that as individuals engage with and appropriate the physical and symbolic tools made available in the curriculum, they both reproduce culture and simultaneously transform it via mutations they introduce into the social through unexpected interpretations and novel tool-use, a consequence of the demands of unique and situated performance. In sociocultural terms, curriculum functions as a culturally framed and socially mediated educational experience that constrains possible outcomes and experiences through its representational strategies and structures, and simultaneously provides possibilities for the agency of individual learners as they navigate and negotiate unique situations, and in the process, it redefines the educational experience (Engestrom, 1999; Wertsch & Penuel, 1998).

The meaning of curriculum as text for curriculum inquiry can also be understood, in part, from a useful comparison with educational policy research methodology. Jenny Ozga, exploring educational policy as text, has argued that "we should not restrict our understanding of texts to those that come with 'policy text' stamped all over them" (2000, p. 95). She makes the case that beyond

> White and Green papers, Bills and Acts of Parliament, regulations governing decision-making at all levels of provision . . . [we should] extend the category of policy text to include documentary or other materials that can be read as significant within the discursive parameters of an investigation, provided that detailed justification is given for their inclusion. (Ozga, 2000, p. 95)

I think it is clear from the critical-reconceptualists that the same case can be made for "curriculum text" in the kinds of historical, philosophical, or literary inquiry undertaken by the contemporary curriculum historian. In practice, this means broadening the base of the curriculum text from syllabus documents to textbooks, teaching resources, academic articles (that posit educational ideals or analyze the pedagogic effects of discourse), educational policy documents (where they describe the intended experience of students and educators), newspaper articles and editorials (that critique existing school practices and outcomes, or express opinions about ideal educational realities), statements made by education ministers during radio interviews, diagrammatic representations of a course or program in a university handbook, films that construct particular visions of the teaching profession, and so on. Even pedagogic "ideas" that can be located within and/or across texts, domains, and practices become a potential object of study. Sometimes curriculum inquiry has involved the production and interpretation of new texts for analysis, such as those that emerge from autobiographical inquiry as narratives of educational experience; we see the production of such curriculum texts in the work of the early reconceptualists (Pinar & Grumet, 1981). However, it also means, after the hermeneutic turn, using "text" as metaphor, reading "educational experience" as if it were a text, whether or not a textual object that records such experience (in written or oral form) was ever produced.

According to Mann, "to regard a curriculum as a literary object . . . means first of all to think of it as a set of selections from a universe of possibilities" (1975, p. 135). Because of the curriculum's inevitable selections and elisions, possibilities are opened for "reading" curriculum as an autobiographical, political, racial, gendered, aesthetic, queer, utopian, eschatological, institutional, theological, or historical text (Pinar, Reynolds, Slattery, & Taubman, 1995). The possibilities are almost limitless, but always involve some form of "disarticulation" of the text—the disruption of that which the author presents as common-sense, obvious, transparent, natural, given, or unquestionable, that opens the text up to critical questioning (MacLure, 2003). Accepting the "crisis of representation" that is implicated in curriculum theory's textual turn, the act of writing a text that interrogates curriculum becomes a method of inquiry that takes seriously Alison Lee's (2000) description of research as "(re)writing," in which the production of a new "intertextual text" is the method. Given that curricularists must be selective both in what they interrogate and in what they compose, no single critique is or will ever be exhaustive (Mann, 1975). However, a critique's success is perhaps best judged by the extent to which it encourages the reader to think differently about the problems that haunt the curriculum field.

## Discourse Analysis as a Mode of Curriculum History

The reconceptualization of curriculum theory did not stop with the recasting of curriculum as text. After its initial hermeneutic turn, the field of curriculum studies continued to show signs that its practitioners were experimenting with new ways of engaging in reconceptualization. In the early 1990s a second wave of reconceptualist theorizing—or if one prefers, a third wave of curriculum theorizing—appeared. Some of the theorists involved in the first forms of reconceptualist inquiry began to adopt approaches to curriculum theory that were noticeably influenced by poststructural deconstruction and various forms of postmodern social theory. The 1990s also saw an increasing attention in curriculum scholarship to issues of language, representation, and knowledge, drawing particularly upon poststructuralist theory as an important intellectual resource. In *Expanding Curriculum Theory: Dis/positions and Lines of Flight* (2004), Reynolds and Webber proclaimed the emergence of a new generation of postmodern curricularists who work as "Deleuzian nomads... preferring to 'do curriculum' on an alternate playing field" (2004, p. 11). Appropriating methods from various forms of poststructural theory, the intellectual "nomad" typically challenges "an idea, concept, trend, movement, or act, and then immediately puts it under erasure, challenging his or her own presumptions to knowledge, power, and will in curriculum theorizing" (2004, p. 203). Certainly, there has been a turn to

> cultural studies and the virtually ubiquitous post discourses . . . which draws on the work of the original reconceptualists . . . but which takes erstwhile supposedly radically untraditional characteristics (such as theorizing about non-school pedagogical spaces, theorizing social justice) for granted and concentrates on pushing the theoretical limits of curriculum theorizing. (Wright, 2000, pp. 9-10)

This particular kind of approach to curriculum theorizing is enabled by the possibilities that arise through a conceptualization of curriculum as "pedagogic discourse"—discourses about pedagogy, and discourses that have a pedagogical effect (by inscribing a particular set of meanings and possibilities). It relies on a critical insight of poststructural discourse theory: the impossibility of making statements outside of discourse. Thus, any statement made by the researcher or scholar is subject to the same "suspicion" as any statement analyzed by a discourse theorist. To place a Foucauldian spin on Derrida's controversial statement "il n'y a pas de hors-texte" (1976), there is no "truth" outside of discourse/text, because it is discourse that provides the truth-value of any claim made.

## Conceptions of Discourse in Educational Research

Let me begin my exploration of "discourse" in curriculum theory by repeating Stephen Ball's claim, made inside a somewhat different frame, that text and discourse are related but distinct cultural artifacts (Ball, 1993). The exact nature of this relationship depends upon the definitions of text and discourse to which one subscribes. The phenomenologist Ricoeur, for example, has asserted that "text is any discourse fixed by writing" (1991, p. 106). Whatever his intention, this limits the definition of *text* to a written artifact, and for the reader of Ricoeur, it renders discourse simply speech. Foucault (1978/1994) cautioned against the tendency to reduce discourse to text, but he was speaking of text as a "material object" rather than a "material practice." As a way of reworking or rewording Ricoeur's proposition, we might say that text—as both material object and material practice—is constituted *by* discourse, and that discourse bleeds beyond the boundaries of a single text, working within and across texts, forming a network of intertextual relations. Before we can fully appreciate these statements and their significance for the New Curriculum History, we need to understand what is meant by the term *discourse*.

There are multiple conceptions and definitions of *discourse* circulating in contemporary theory, and a wide variety of ways in which "discourse analysis" is taken up as a practice in educational theory specifically (MacLure, 2003; Mills, 1997). It would seem that almost the full range of possible conceptions has been mobilized within the field of curriculum studies. Any historically oriented study of the concept of discourse reveals a complex genealogy emerging from the interaction of ideas across the domains of structuralism, poststructuralism, linguistics, post-Freudian psychoanalysis, neo-Marxism, and the field of cultural studies. It is important to note that although a great deal of contemporary research credits Foucault with originating the widespread adoption of the term *discourse*, it has been argued rather convincingly by Sawyer (2002) that it is not the strict Foucauldian definition that is typically mobilized in contemporary scholarship. Sawyer claims that the more likely origin of the "broad usage" of the term, particularly if we look at how it is used, is two other French theorists, the Marxist Michel Pêcheux and psychoanalyst Jacques Lacan, and many of the theorists who worked in the emerging field of British cultural studies during the 1960s and 1970s. Foucault added to the confusion himself, stating in *The Archaeology of Knowledge* that despite his own formal definition, he has used *discourse* in a range of ways, "treating it sometimes as the general domain of all statements, sometimes as an individualizable group of statements, and sometimes as a regulated practice that accounts for a number of statements" (Foucault, 1969/1972, p. 80). While the common or broad usage of the term often fluctuates between these various senses, with different disciplines placing more or less emphasis on one definition or another, two particular conceptions seem to dominate educational literature: We might describe them as the literary (or cultural) and linguistic definitions.

Within Literary and Cultural Studies, *discourse* operates as a synonym for sets of "authoritative statements" that are said to stand in "intertextual relationship" with one another. Texts thus instantiate and are constituted by and as "discourse," or sets of "authoritative statements." These "authoritative statements" or "master narratives" not only inscribe particular relations of power, but also are so seductive that often it is impossible, difficult, or dangerous to think otherwise. Understood in this way, we might suggest that "discourse" functions as a kind of scaffolding within which particular forms of reasoning are constructed. Such "authoritative statements" not only constitute the "flesh" of the text, but also discursively construct its boundaries and its "intelligibility" to different audiences as fact or fiction (Cherryholmes, 1987; Popkewitz, 2001). Mobilized as a term for "authoritative statements," "discourse" has been heavily influenced by Foucault, whether or not he can be claimed as its origin. Foucault's insight that "it is in discourse that power and knowledge are joined together" (1980, p. 100) pervades the mobilization of discourse theory in education.

For Foucault (1991), "discourse" was understood as a series of statements that form the objects of which they speak, consisting of words actually spoken or written that are or can be grouped according to certain rules that make their existence as authoritative statements possible. Foucault does not conceptualize the "rules" that form the "conditions of existence" of a discourse as the constraints and affordances of a linguistic grammar; instead, they are rules of formation for objects, operations, concepts and theoretical options, or the conditions that broker the limits and forms of expressibility, conservation, memory, reactivation, and appropriation. These rules determine not only what can and cannot be said but also what may be considered true or false within a given discipline, community, or institution at a specific historical moment; or as Foucault expresses it, "discourse can be both an instrument and an effect of power" (1980, p. 101). Importantly, Foucault's concern with discourse centers on what he describes as "the archive," the sum total of authoritative statements that have been made in a given field, discipline, or institution. Foucault's conceptualization of discourse presents the possibility of understanding curriculum as archive, or a series of statements that either instantiate a pedagogical intent or that have engendered, or are likely to result in, an educative effect. In a Foucauldian sense, "discourse analysis" is, therefore, the study of "knowledge systems" (Popkewitz, Franklin, & Pereyra, 2001), constituted by "*serious* speech acts: what experts say when they are speaking as experts" (Dreyfus & Rabinow, 1982, p. xx, emphasis in the original), or what is articulated and accepted within a discipline, community, or society.

Practically, Foucault's discourse analytics attempts to "define the play" between intradiscursive, interdiscursive, and extradiscursive dependencies: "between the objects, operations and concepts of a single formation," "between different discursive formations" or disciplines, and "between discursive transformations and transformations outside of discourse . . . discourse and a whole play of economic, political and social changes" (1991, p. 58). According to Baker and Heyning (2004), within educational research, the adoption of Foucault-inspired approaches to "discourse analysis" has resulted in a tendency towards historicization and philosophizing projects that provide insight into the "conditions of possibility" for certain curricular or pedagogic discourses; denaturalization projects that challenge the universality and normativity of particular educational practices; and critical reconstruction projects that marshal towards reconceptualizing the curriculum imagination, or a particular policy or pedagogic practice. While this book is readily identified as a work of critical reconstruction, it is clear that such a project overlaps in significant ways with historicization/philosophizing and denaturalization approaches, and may not be possible without them.

Although versions of Foucault's definition of discourse, and approaches to discourse analysis purportedly influenced by Foucault, are widely mobilized in educational research and have had some play in the field of curriculum studies, an alternative definition that has arisen within the discipline of linguistics enjoys currency in education studies more broadly. In linguistics, *discourse* is typically defined as language in use. This conception of discourse has led some linguists to focus almost exclusively on the grammatical (syntactic, graphophonemic, phonological, semantic, pragmatic, and morphological) rules used by a speaker to construct meaning in different communicative situations and cultural contexts, resulting in emergent subdisciplines such as "conversation analysis." In other words, linguists studying "discourse" are concerned with how the mobilization of linguistic resources to construct meaning varies as a function of communicative purpose, cultural and situational context, and relationship between interlocutors. They typically study language as social semiosis, a set of signifying resources to be deployed for social purposes. Within such a sociolinguistic perspective, "discourse," or more correctly, a "discursive formation," appears as the regularly repeated written or spoken text-forms (registers and genres) that are the conventions for making meaning under specific sets of conditions constituted by purpose, context, and audience. Discourse therefore operates as a culturally constituted limit condition, and also manifests via a set of socially shared presentational, orientational, and organizational resources that shape linguistic and nonlinguistic behavior (Halliday, 1985; Lemke, 1995).

Given the context-bound regularities that are apparent in the reproduction of specific forms of discourse, the sociolinguist James Paul Gee has proposed that human beings navigate between alternate "discourse communities" (Gee, 1990). Gee's suggestion, redolent of Vygotsky's distinction between everyday and scientific thinking, is that we each acquire a "primary discourse" from our home/family environment, and learn a number of "secondary discourses" within scholastic and ultimately work-related institutions. Here, understanding and controlling one's own language use in different situations becomes the key to successfully negotiating social life, and the capacity to do so is frequently depicted as a kind of social capital that curriculum plays an important part in distributing. Thus, a key feature of the analytical approach adopted by linguists studying "discourse" as "language in use" is the close, systematic attention to linguistic and semiotic variation across differing situations and contexts. This approach to discourse analysis differs from literary and cultural studies approaches in its attention to the grammatical choices that are made to construct meaning, and in its functional "linguistic" method—based upon the work of Halliday (1985) and his systemic functional linguistics school—rather than an intertextual "literary" methodology.

Oftentimes, linguistic and cultural definitions of discourse are married, as is the case in the various forms of Critical Discourse Analysis (CDA). Practitioners of CDA can be identified by their attempts to understand how textual and discursive practices mirror the sociopolitical structures that dominate individual lives, constructing their "practice" as a form of "ideological critique" that relocates discourse and text within the context of their production and consumption. Drawing upon the close systematic analysis of the language choices deployed within texts, the CDA analyst attempts to provide concrete examples of how a text constructs an unequal social world. An important contribution to CDA has been Gee's conceptualization of *discourse* with a lower-case *d* as "language-in-use" and *Discourse* with a capital *D* as (1) "sayings-doings-thinkings-feelings-valuings" (Gee, 1990, p. xv); or (2) "words, acts, values, beliefs, attitudes, social identities, as well as gestures, glances, body positions, and clothes" (Gee, 1992, p. 107); and (3) a particular social group's form of life or their way of being in the world. Despite the focus on "discourse," approaches that purport to be forms of CDA vary, but typically they all adopt a strategy that involves exposing, through the use of linguistic and semiotic tools, the ways in which text (including social practice as text) operates as an ideological instrument, a tool of an often invisible cultural politics. CDA not only works across, and often blurs, the distinction between the various definitions of discourse articulated in the preceding pages, it also adopts an approach to discourse that is informed more by critical theory than poststructuralism, despite its claims, because discourse (as ideology) is seen to conceal realities as much as it constructs them (Fairclough, 1995).

While the space created by the blurring of definitions is also the operative domain of curriculum studies, the approach to discourse analysis adopted by the critical-reconceptualist is typically literary rather than strictly linguistic. This has particular consequences for curriculum history. One realization it has produced is that there is no escaping discourse (given that "discourse" is considered to be embodied in, and to shape, both statement and social practice). Subjectivity is understood as an artifact of discourse, socially and historically contingent. Unsurprisingly then, the New Curriculum History promises no trans-subjective truths from research. There is no "essence" to be recovered by the act of interpretation, nor any ultimate "foundation" that can authorize the method of inquiry.

The recognition that the researcher is as much subject to the effects of discourse as that which is studied, and that this phenomenon affects interpretation, marks a moment of self-reflexivity in curriculum studies. Reynolds and Webber argue that:

> the purpose of discourse analysis [in curriculum theory] is not to determine what the discourse means, but to investigate how it works, what conditions make it possible (its exteriority), how it interacts with nondiscursive practices, and how it is connected to power and knowledge. (Reynolds & Webber, 2004, p. 7)

Further, within a poststructuralist approach to curriculum inquiry, attention is likely to be given to the effects of statements, such as the "subject positions" they permit and create, rather than to their grammatical forms (B. Davies, 1993). Pedagogic or curriculum discourse analysis for the New Curriculum historian thus is not a way of constituting the object of analysis as an everyday classroom speech act or vocal exchange; instead, "discourse" is deployed as a way of highlighting how "serious statements" made within or about education constitute and coordinate particular forms of knowledge that form our ways of reasoning about the self and the world at particular historical moments and social circumstances (Popkewitz, 2001). This insight has implications for the objects of curriculum history.

# Reading Curriculum as Discourse: Methods of the New Curriculum History

James B. Macdonald (1975) has asserted that the objects of analysis for curriculum theorizing are inevitably statements about (1) forms of knowledge and ways of knowing—the "nature" of what is to be taught and how it is learned (epistemology); (2) pedagogical decision-making processes and educational realities—what can be taught and learned within the limits of the educational situation (ontology); and (3) valued skills, concepts, and experiences—what is currently being, or should be taught (axiology). Statements arising about curriculum from within the field defy any single mode, ranging across the "descriptive, explanatory, controlling, legitimating, prescriptive, and affiliative" (Huebner, 1975, p. 256). Pronouncements inescapably tend towards normative or idealistic statements about what curriculum should be, or descriptive statements about what curriculum actually is or how it has been enacted and experienced (Smith & Lovat, 1995). A discursive formation—"curriculum" from the perspective of the New Curriculum History—is both educational experience and an "archive" of statements that govern our way of thinking about education (and the particular disciplinary knowledges it has generated or appropriated). Understood in this way, curriculum is "an ensemble of methods and strategies that inscribe principles for action" or set the parameters for particular styles of reasoning (Popkewitz, 1997, p. 163).

In order to understand how curriculum constructs particular "styles of reasoning" or constitutes sociohistorically specific "rationalities," it is useful to draw on Eisner's tripartite model of curriculum. In *The Educational Imagination* (1979) Eisner argues that the explicit curriculum—that knowledge (and "system of reasoning") that is advocated in the official documents of a state or district education authority—is only a small component of what schools teach and students learn. He argues that in understanding the total curriculum of a school (and for our purposes, the "rationalities" it constructs), it is just as important to consider what he terms the "implicit curriculum"—what a school teaches because of the ideas and values it instantiates through its physical organization, timetabling methods, organizational structure, and so on. The implicit curriculum, which is not formally stated or even "consciously" intended, is defined by the messages that students actually receive or the meanings they construct. In many ways, it is similar to the "hidden curriculum," with some important differences in how it is operationalized as a concept in curriculum theory.

A central concept in radical curriculum theory, the hidden curriculum has been understood as those outcomes from schooling that are not explicitly intended by educators yet still arise as a result of the tacit teaching of norms, values, and dispositions that are learned in the process of coping with the routines and expectations of the educational institution (Apple, 2004a; Seddon, 1983). Thus, it is best understood as a "covert curriculum" that is deeply implicated in social reproduction. Whereas the hidden curriculum is almost always cast negatively as a mechanism for the maintenance of the hegemony of the classes who can exercise the most power in a society, the implicit curriculum seems to be constructed as a more generous notion. Closer to Dewey's idea of "collateral learning" that understands the "latent outcomes" of this covert curriculum as potentially positive as well as negative (Hlebowitsh, 1993, p. 9), the implicit curriculum does not immediately imply (as hidden curriculum frequently does) a pedagogical device responsible for the production of an ideologically laden "false consciousness." In conception, the implicit curriculum "fits" more readily with a Vygotskian notion of education in which the social and tool-mediated activity of schooling simultaneously reproduces and transforms culture. For Vygotskians, education operates as a "construction zone" in which knowledge is co-constructed by participants, and curriculum (as educational experience) becomes the crucible in which culture and cognition create each other (Cole, 1985; Engestrom, 1999). From this perspective, it is unnecessarily reductionist to understand the covert curriculum as solely an instrument of social control. Inevitably, like all aspects of the curriculum, it both constrains and enables particular ways of thinking, acting, being. Such effects are independent of whether a given curriculum or pedagogy is visible or invisible (Bernstein, 1990).

For Eisner, the curriculum is not constituted only by what is taught explicitly or visibly according to official syllabi, and implicitly or invisibly through its social practices; it is constituted also by that which is not taught, or what he terms the "null curriculum." The null curriculum makes clear how the curriculum functions to construct a system of reasoning. Eisner argues that the null curriculum is formed as a result of those intellectual processes that are emphasized or neglected by schools, and the content or subject areas that school curricula addresses or ignores. It is worth quoting at length Eisner's conception of the null curriculum. According to Eisner:

> There is something of a paradox involved in writing about a curriculum that does not exist. Yet, if we are concerned with the consequences of school programs and the role of curriculum in shaping those consequences, then it seems to me that we are well advised to consider not only the explicit and implicit curricula of schools but also what schools do not teach. It is my thesis that what schools do not teach may be as important as what they do teach. I argue this position because ignorance is not simply a neutral void; it has important effects on the kinds of options one is able to consider, the alternatives that one can examine, and the perspectives from which one can view a situation or problem. The absence of a set of considerations or perspectives or the inability to use certain processes for appraising a context biases the evidence one is able to take into account. A parochial perspective or simplistic analysis is the inevitable progeny of ignorance. (Eisner, 1979, p. 83)

What this means for curriculum theorizing, and curriculum history, is that it is important to attend to not only the curriculum that is advocated, and the curriculum that is enacted or experienced, but also the knowledge that is neglected. The curriculum therefore embodies a particular system of reasoning validated in part by its neglect of alternate forms. Eisner argues that real consequences emerge from a null curriculum, because any voids in an educational program withhold from students ideas and skills that they might have used. However, Eisner is not arguing for the impossible—a curriculum that teaches everything. In his own words, he provides the following caveat:

> I am not suggesting that any of us can be without bias or that we can eventually gain a comprehensive view of all problems or issues. I do not believe that is possible . . . Such a perspective requires omnipotence. Yet if one mission of the school is to foster wisdom, weaken prejudice, and develop the ability to use a wide range of modes of thought, then it seems to me we ought to examine school programs to locate those areas of thought and those perspectives that are now absent. (Eisner, 1979, p. 83)

Therefore, Eisner's notion of the null curriculum opens possibilities for curriculum critique not only in terms of what is planned or enacted, but also on the basis of what is missing or absent. The null curriculum is, therefore, singularly important as a methodological tool, because as Eisner notes, the concept "allows one to raise questions about what children are learning that would never be identified if one were to focus only on the intended goals of the explicit curriculum . . . [and places us] in a position to evaluate the consequences of each" (Eisner, 1979, p. 85). In naming the null curriculum, Eisner, though not a poststructuralist himself, provides a useful resource for conducting poststructuralist curriculum inquiry.

When used as part of a poststructural or deconstructive curriculum inquiry, the null curriculum moves from being simply a description of what is not taught as part of the official and unofficial curriculum to become an important methodological tool. One of the important tasks of poststructural studies of curriculum "is to figure out why and how opportunities are provided and why other opportunities are bypassed. Curriculum, in part, is a study of what is valued and given priority and what is devalued and excluded" (Cherryholmes, 1987, p. 297). By identifying the specific forms of reasoning that are valued in a curriculum and examining those forms in relation to the styles of reasoning that are neglected, a picture develops of the curriculum as a system of governance that is constitutive of subjectivity via its selection of particular ways for individuals to construct and organize their views of who they are. Stated another way, curriculum and pedagogy are social practices of self-formation (Palermo, 2002; Popkewitz, 2001).

As a methodological construct, the null curriculum enables the researcher, given the application of different frames or lenses, to determine how curriculum is implicated in the production of specific rationalities. For example, if I wanted to understand what forms of hermeneutic theory had been taken up in curriculum work and what forms were neglected or ignored, then a text such as Shaun Gallagher's *Hermeneutics and Education* (1993) would be useful because it provides a typology of various forms of hermeneutic inquiry. In his own inquiries, Eisner uses an aesthetic lens to demonstrate that the creative arts remain in many ways a null curriculum in U.S. schools. Following Donna Haraway's approach to the history and philosophy of science, Gough (1998) adopts a diffractive approach to curriculum inquiry that highlights how fiction—speculative or science fiction particularly—may be utilized as an effective means of posing new options and alternatives through "narrative experiments" with figures such as "the cyborg" that expose the limits inscribed within curriculum constructions of our collective past, present, and future. Such "diffractive lenses" open possibilities for the poststructural reclamation of earlier hermeneutic work in the curriculum field by functioning as tools in deconstructive inquiry that invite interpretation and the seeking of understanding as a goal, but resist the attraction of naming any particular reading as an ultimate truth.

The notion of the null curriculum complements deconstructive curriculum inquiry. The null curriculum functions in many ways like the "absent presence" in deconstruction, defining a curriculum's system of reasoning by what it neglects or deliberately rejects. As Hall notes, deconstruction "seek[s] out the unspoken and unwrittens—silenced truths that haunt the texts marked by their absence" (1999, p. 9). In its initial appropriation by academics in U.S. universities, deconstruction was associated specifically with a strategy that challenged conceptual oppositions within a text through overturning the text's implicit hierarchies. Concerned over the problems generated by such reductive definitions, Derrida has declared deconstruction to be neither a theory, a philosophy, a school, a method, a discourse, an act, nor a practice (Derrida, 1990). Resisting definition, Derrida has asserted that "deconstruction is inventive or it is nothing at all" (1989, p. 42). Of course, the precise meaning of Derrida's refusal that deconstruction is a method hinges on what we mean by the term *method*. If the concept of method suggests something that is highly systematized and closed, then deconstruction is definitely not a "method" (Royle, 2000). However, deconstruction is not devoid of all definition:

> Deconstruction not only teaches us to read literature more thoroughly by attending to it as language . . . it also enables us to interrogate the covert philosophical and political presuppositions of institutionalized critical methods which generally govern our reading of a text . . . It is not a question of calling for the destruction of such institutions, but rather of making us aware of what we are in fact doing when we are subscribing to this or that institutional way of reading. (Derrida, 1984, p. 125)

Therefore, it would be safe to say that deconstruction is an analytical strategy that systematically exposes the multiple ways that any text can be interpreted, problematizing any attempt to close on a singular meaning (of text or method). In this sense, deconstruction may be understood as a "radical hermeneutic" tool of the New Curriculum History that understands meaning as a product of the play of signs, which it aims to keep in play through engagement in acts of reading and interpretation that resist the desire for closure on a final meaning (Caputo, 1987).

Despite the problems of defining actual deconstructionist methods, Boje has attempted with "apologies to Derrida" to outline moves that he believes can be identified as signature deconstructionist strategies (2001, p. 22). Boje's list includes practices of making visible unstable binaries; recovering absent voices; subverting definitions by listing variations; reversing dualities; articulating dissensus; finding exceptions to stated rules; tracing the unsaid; and renarrating and resituating text. This list of strategies provides a good description of the methodological scope of those forms of the New Curriculum History that can rightly be called poststructural curriculum theory or deconstructive hermeneutics. The New Curriculum historian may well recognize their work as deconstructive or genealogical, investigating how systems of curricular or pedagogic ideas change over time and how power is always implicated in any change, but they must also acknowledge their lack of innocence, as they inevitably engage in "authorial practices such as restatement, paraphrasing, quotation and elision, all in the name of creating historical narratives with explanatory power" (Cormack & Green, 2009, p. 233). Recognizing that historical work is a textual practice that involves not only examining and interpreting textual data but also the production of new texts brings a reflexive turn to the work of the New Curriculum historian, and any attempt at defining the methods of the New Curriculum historian should be tempered by Cormack and Green's suggestion that curriculum discourse analysis "is at once symptom and technology, and hence as much a mode of transgression as it is a matter of discipline and method" (2009, p. 223). With this warning in mind, I take up the challenges of the New Curriculum History in the chapters that follow, exploring—through deconstructive readings and genealogical inquiry—the emergence of "end of history" discourse in contemporary theory and its influence within History education.

CHAPTER THREE

# At the End of the Grand Story

As an economist who once worked for the political science department of the RAND Corporation, and a member of the policy planning staff of the U.S. Department of State during the Reagan era, Francis Fukuyama unsurprisingly has a conservative outlook. It is probably impossible to discuss the idea of "the end of history" today without referring to his controversial and conservative thesis built upon themes he draws from Kojeve, Hegel, Nietzsche, and Marx. Fukuyama's thesis is the most widely known contemporary academic manifestation of the resurrected utopian dream, assuring us of our arrival at history's terminus. Fukuyama's end of history spin does not involve the rejection of modernity's master narratives; instead, Fukuyama announces triumphantly that modernity's goal of "the recognition of human freedom" is not a fantasy—it has been realized in the history of the present. The manifestation of a Hegelian end of history metanarrative, Fukuyama's work announcing the arrival of the West at the telos of history ("the end" of the grand story) stands in opposition to the writings of the French postmodern social theorists (such as Barthes, Baudrillard, Derrida, and Foucault) who assert that both history and its end are linguistically generated illusions. In this chapter I read Fukuyama with and against the methodological postmodernists as a strategy to illuminate the multiple meanings of the end of history in contemporary theory.

I turn to the work of Fukuyama as the contemporary theorist most responsible for popularizing the idea of the end of history, and arguably the most articulate representative of a neoliberal vision of history. I begin by attempting to articulate the main aspects of his utopian end-of-history thesis. I follow this by exploring some of his more recent work, which seems to indicate a concern that without careful intervention, we may find ourselves "back in history" as society falls into various states of dystopia. Fukuyama's dystopic concerns demonstrate the conservative line that underscores all his writings, (and the neoliberal agenda more generally), and they make for a useful comparison with similar concerns in the work of the postmodern philosopher Jean-François Lyotard. I then problematize both their readings of the posthistorical subject by discussing them in relation to the image of the posthuman/posthumanist "cyborg" as it emerges in the work of Donna Haraway and others. Following lines of criticism developed in *Specters of Marx* (1994), I document Derrida's deconstruction of Fukuyama's thesis, which reveals its idealistic closures. I then proceed to examine an alternative conceptualization of the end of history mobilized in contemporary theory by Jean Baudrillard. His conception of the end of history reads the present as marked by a "loss of history," the result of history's displacement by media spectacle. Baudrillard's rejection of the grand story of history as a seductive illusion is then contrasted with recent developments in the area of postcolonial theory, which argues that history is a "white mythology" that serves to constrain humanity within the metanarrative of Western (neo)colonialism, partly by constructing whiteness as the invisible norm against which all others are compared. This analysis of end-of-history discourse in contemporary theory invites speculation about the political uses and abuses of history and the impossibility of history as a "grand story" after historical and methodological postmodernism.

## The Neoliberal as Last Man of History

Fukuyama's original essay on the subject of the end of history was published in *The National Interest* shortly after the fall of the Berlin Wall. The coincidence in the timing was more than serendipitous. For Fukuyama (1989), the fall of the Berlin Wall, the collapse of the Soviet Union, and the resultant end of the Cold War, were all events that marked the triumph of liberal democracy over its rival socialist modes of political and economic organization. Taken together, and read through his enthusiastic commitment to political and economic liberalism, these events appeared to signal, for Fukuyama, arrival at the end of history; that is, arrival at the terminus of history, where history is "understood as a single, coherent, evolutionary process" (Fukuyama, 1992, p. xii), or "a coherent, directional evolution of human societies taken as a whole" (Fukuyama, 1995). Fukuyama's thesis not only celebrates the triumph of free-market capitalism over the Soviet socialist system, but also reinstates a metanarrative of progress. Interestingly, Fukuyama appears to be unconcerned by the epistemological crisis that occurred across the humanities, casting doubt on notions of universal progress, and he remains optimistic, despite the rise of global Islamist terrorism and the continuing communist regime in Korea, that he was correct in his original end-of-history thesis that "the process of modernization was . . . a universal one that would sooner or later drag all societies in its train" (Fukuyama, 2002a, p. 8). His vision is a legacy of the historical and cultural epoch we usually refer to as the Enlightenment. It is, as Jenkins (1999) would note, a vision of "history" in the upper case, in which making history is synonymous with making progress (in Fukuyama's sense, movement towards the realization of a liberal capitalist utopia). It is a view of the post-Cold War period as a posthistorical era that is effectively beyond ideological conflict. It is built around a belief that we have arrived at the end of the grand story of humanity.

Fukuyama's widely read essay engendered a range of reactions, some positive, many highly critical, and there are even alternative readings of the same historical events that suggest it was utopian thinking itself that could be found in the rubble of the Berlin Wall (see Rusen, 2005). In any case, supported by a storm of publicity, Fukuyama's essay caused such a stir among academics and political commentators that he expanded it into what became a best-selling book, *The End of History and the Last Man*, which in its post-Cold War triumphalism was very much a product of its times (Furedi, 1994). The book was followed by a number of essays published during the 1990s, many of which manifested Fukuyama's attempts to clarify and restate in ways more acceptable to a hostile audience his speculative end-of-history thesis (see, for example, Fukuyama, 1995). As recently as 2002 he returned to the topic in a response to the events of September 11, 2001, which appeared to critics of Fukuyama's work to suggest a serious problem for his thesis. For many, the events of September 11 demonstrated that international ideological conflict was not dead, and that although liberal democracy's old adversary, socialism, might now be relegated to the pages of history, liberalism had a new foe in reactionary Islamist fundamentalism (Zakaria, 2001). Could this mean that Fukuyama's proclamation of the end of history may have been premature?

Fukuyama's response to this question was that September 11 was simply "a serious detour" on the way to the global acceptance of political and economic liberalism (2002a, p. 8). In his view, there is no escaping history, no escaping the current of "modernization and globalization," which he sees as "the central structuring principles of world politics" (2002a, p. 8). In fact, it is clear that Fukuyama sees September 11 as "a desperate rearguard action" that seeks to challenge globalization and modernization, but which ultimately will be "overwhelmed by the broader tide of modernization" (2002b, p. 11). The events of September 11 therefore do little more than assure Fukuyama of the steady advance of modernization throughout the world, which he associates with the acceptance of the ideology of political and economic liberalism (which we might characterize in its contemporary form as neoliberalism). Yet, despite his confidence about the global march towards liberal states, Fukuyama often is ambivalent about which countries are currently living at, inside, or after the end of history. While some would argue that in *The End of History and the Last Man* Fukuyama's end-state of history was implied to exist in contemporary America (Roth, 1995b), Fukuyama's more recent comments are a little more cautious. Take for example his post–September 11 declaration that "the Europeans are certainly right that they are living at the end of history; the question is, where is the rest of the world?" (Fukuyama, 2002a, p. 24). For those who accept Fukuyama's thesis, this is an important question. However, his neoliberal supporters need not despair, for Fukuyama provides at least a partial answer to this problem.

Although we have yet to arrive at the full realization of a global liberal utopia, according to Fukuyama's reading of the political events of the last two decades of the twentieth century the world has entered a period where all alternatives to liberal democratic capitalism have been revealed as inadequate. His thesis—in his own words, part empirical, part normative—is speculative, based on a quasi-Hegelian view of history, a view that follows Hegel in conceptualizing the history of the world as nothing other than progress towards the consciousness of human freedom (Williams, Sullivan, & Mathews, 1997). Such a view is what Karl Popper (1957/1986) referred to as *historicist*, in the sense that it looks for universal laws or trends that sit behind or underlie social developments and historical change. For Popper, the philosophy of Marxism was one of the clearest examples of historicist thinking. From a postmodern perspective, the fundamental flaw in Fukuyama's historicist thesis is his equating of "human freedom" exclusively with a particular historically locatable form of politico-economic liberalism. By reading a unique set of historical events as universal exemplars, Fukuyama reinstates a metanarrative of progress while presenting his thesis as a simple (even self-evident) historical description. Because metanarratives gloss the situated, historically and culturally embedded nature of events, usually presupposing some grand underlying theme or principle, they are really historicist (or perhaps more accurately, ahistorical) narratives that masquerade as histories.

Fukuyama defends against attempts to dismiss his thesis as simple historicist speculation by asserting that it is possible to argue on empirical grounds that human societies will increasingly adopt free-market capitalism, or as he prefers to call it, "economic liberalism," as their mode of economic production; socialist modes, after the collapse of the Soviet Union, have been demonstrated to be inadequate. This argument forms what he considers to be the strongest argument of his thesis. He also argues that societies increasingly will be inclined to adopt liberal democracy ("political liberalism") as the preferred mode of government because of an innate human need for recognition—to be seen and valued—that only democracy has been shown by history to meet. His evidence for such a statement is that

> the fall of the regimes in Poland, Hungary, East Germany, and Czechoslovakia was the direct result of the death of Marxism-Leninism in the original homeland of the world proletariat, the Soviet Union [resulting in a] remarkable consensus . . . over the viability and desirability of economic and political liberalism. (Fukuyama, 1990, p. 75)

This, he suggested five years later, is the weak aspect of his argument (Fukuyama, 1995). For Fukuyama, the global movement towards economic and political liberalism indicates that we are living at the end of history, that is, at a time when history has moved beyond ideological conflict to leave liberalism as "the last man standing."

In an attempt to clarify his original thesis, in 2002 Fukuyama argued that:

> [T]he "end of history" hypothesis was about the process of modernization. Progressive intellectuals around the world spent much of the last century and a half believing that historical progress would result in an evolution of modern societies toward socialism. In more recent years, they have held that societies could modernize and yet remain fundamentally different culturally. My hypothesis was that there was such a thing as a single, coherent modernization process, but that it led not to socialism or to a variety of culturally-determined locations, but rather to liberal democracy and market-oriented economics as the only viable choices. The process of modernization was, moreover, a universal one that would sooner or later drag all societies in its train. (Fukuyama, 2002a, p. 8)

It is debatable whether Fukuyama is correct about both the direction and universality of history. Certainly, his argument makes visible a particular modernist metanarrative of the ultimate movement of history towards a specific *telos*, or optimal endpoint. However, Fukuyama's end of history utopia is not a vision shared by his fellow historicists Marx, Hegel and Kojeve. In the preceding passage Fukuyama differentiates his end-of-history thesis from that of Marx, who depicted the end of history as the arrival at a socialist utopia. Likewise, Fukuyama differentiates his view from Kojeve (1969), who despite being cited as support for Fukuyama's Hegelian doctrine of Universal Recognition, agreed with Marx that the end of history is to be realized in a universal socialist state. In the process of distancing his ideal utopia from the Marxist/Kojevean desire for a socialist state, Fukuyama constructs a utopia that is in some sense closer to Hegel and his idealist proposition of the universal acceptance of "freedom" as the goal of history (albeit "freedom" of a particular sort). For Fukuyama this manifests itself as the realization that economic and political liberalism is the only viable option for human beings in modern societies. He is able to argue this because in his view, it is only liberalism that satisfies the human desire for "recognition"—a form of recognition that, under neoliberal managerialist philosophy, can operate as a force for both freedom and subjugation (McCarney, 1994; Phelan, 2010).

According to Fukuyama, Kojeve was visibly wrong about the *telos* of history, as the collapse of European communism has demonstrated, because he ignored the role of mediators such as business corporations that increase the possibilities of "recognition" in a civil society; Fukuyama clearly believes that these mediators are absent in a communist state. Thus, while drawing on the insights of Marx and Kojeve, Fukuyama anticipates a very different *telos*, one that rejects the ideology of socialism in favor of the promise of a free-market liberal utopia, which Fukuyama believes is the politico-economic embodiment of Hegel's goal of a society built on "universal recognition" of freedom. Fukuyama does not conceptualize his utopia as "radically egalitarian," but as a society in which human freedom and social equality are offered to the maximum extent possible (Bertram, 1994; McCarney, 1994).

According to Fukuyama's speculations, based on his observation of the development of modern societies,

> [T]he logic of a liberal and democratic political order becomes more pressing as societies develop economically, since reconciliation of all diverse interests that make them up requires both participation and equality. The unfolding of modern natural science drives economic development, and economic development drives—with lags, setbacks, and wrong turns—a process of political development in the direction of liberal democracy. We can therefore expect a long-term progressive evolution of human political institutions in the direction of liberal democracy. (Fukuyama, 1999, p. 280)

Fukuyama's assertion is plain. If a society has not yet "modernized," it will be forced to at some point in the future as a result of the increased pressure of the global marketplace for absolute participation. Because modernization involves the appropriation and development of sophisticated technologies, it requires the mobilization of labor and vast resources in a particular direction. Societies undergoing modernization are therefore forced to move towards various forms of consensual politics. For Fukuyama, the result of moving in this direction is that, perhaps after experiments with alternative philosophies such as socialism (or even religious fundamentalism), liberalism will be recognized as the only viable political and economic theory, the only political and economic philosophy that works in harmony with a unified, globalized market economy. As he argued in his first major book, liberalism is also the only political philosophy that (at least in principle) allows all voices to be heard, and thus provides the recognition of individuals that he believes our "human nature" demands (Fukuyama, 1992).

The vision of history offered by Fukuyama is a relatively linear, teleological one. Deviations from the *telos* are to be interpreted not as a failure of the thesis, but as temporary deviations and setbacks that ultimately will be supplanted by the adoption of political and economic liberalism (the arrival at Fukuyama's utopia). In *The Great Disruption* (1999) Fukuyama provides an account of the massive social change that occurred from the 1960s to the 1990s as industrial nations began the transformation into information societies. In this work, Fukuyama again restates his conservative vision of history as a linear, progressive, directional development, albeit with a minor modification to account for the unpredictable rise and fall of "social and moral values." Beginning by restating his end-of-history thesis, Fukuyama asserts that:

> [I]n the political and economic sphere, history appears to be progressive and directional, and at the end of the twentieth century has culminated in liberal democracy as the only viable alternative for technologically advanced societies. In the social and moral sphere, however, history appears to be cyclical, with social order ebbing and flowing over the space of multiple generations. (Fukuyama, 1999, p. 282)

While Fukuyama remains satisfied that his global, liberal, democratic, free-market utopia ultimately will be achieved, his premillennial tome appears to show signs of concern that his end of history utopia could move further from our reach than originally conceived, or at least fall under threat from a variety of sources. This concern is thematized in Fukuyama's later works, demonstrating that despite his confidence in the ultimate manifestation of his liberal utopia, he remains uneasy about the potential of "technologically advanced societies" to slip into states of social, economic, moral, and political dystopia. Such a concern was subtly present as early as Fukuyama's *The End of History and the Last Man* (1992), the title of which contained an implicit warning that we had better not be like Nietzsche's "Last Man" lest our complacency and experience of "physical security and material plenty"—the effect of living after the end of history, after all ideological battles were over—leads to the reigniting of history, with all the conflict that this suggests (Sim, 1999). There is, therefore, an important justification for the examination of Fukuyama's dystopic concerns, as they remain the flip side of his end-of-history thesis. It is the examination of Fukuyama's dystopias that I now turn.

## Fukuyama's Dystopia: The Return to History

If we were to charge Fukuyama with naïvete because his teleological, liberalist end-of-history thesis leaves no space for radically new forms of political and economic life to emerge as a consequence of the impact of unforeseen technologies in the future, then we should not be surprised that in his later work he appears to recant, at least partly, in response to exactly this notion. In response to critics, Fukuyama's subtly revised argument is that because technology shapes the forms social life often takes, we will not experience the absolute end of history until we reach the end of science (Fukuyama, 2002b). That is, we will not be living at the end of history until we reach the end of technoscientific progress. Thus, Fukuyama's latest work simply adds a second problematic trajectory to its already contested teleology.

For Fukuyama, the problem with suggesting that the end of history hinges on an "end of science" is that we have no way of determining if and when we have reached the final form of technoscientific development. If, as Popper has argued, "the course of human history is strongly influenced by the growth of human knowledge" and "we cannot predict, by rational or scientific methods, the future of our scientific knowledge," then he is right in asserting that "we cannot, therefore, predict the future course of history" (Popper, 1957/1986, pp. vi–vii). Fukuyama's suggestion that the end of history will be reached after "the end of science" is self-defeating, because science cannot logically have an end, at least not one that we know is the end (despite the "popular idea" that we are coming close to knowing all that we can know, as argued in Horgan, 1996). Unmistakably, Fukuyama's thesis relies on a commitment to a historicist vision of history (and science), a commitment to formulating hypotheses about invisible trends underlying social change, and, therefore, predictions about the direction of history. I must make clear here, however, that I am not advocating, in challenge to Fukuyama, that technoscience has the potential for unlimited progress. Rather, I simply suggest that the future forms technoscience takes are never perfectly predictable, and may well be radically different from its present forms. This has been forcefully argued in the work of Thomas Kuhn (1970), who sought to demonstrate that scientific progress is frequently the jettisoning of a previously held paradigm in favor of a new one that is not necessarily contingent on its predecessor. Likewise, much of Foucault's oeuvre could be interpreted as a challenge to the idea of progress in the human sciences. Interestingly, these critiques do not concern Fukuyama, who once again demonstrates a capacity for ignoring the epistemological challenges to his thesis, asserting instead a commitment to his own brand of historicist empiricism and allegiance to "the grand story" of modernization and its myth of perpetual progress.

As noted earlier, in his final premillennial work, *The Great Disruption* (1999), Fukuyama examines the shift that has been occurring in the "developed" world, from an industrial to an information society. He asserts that during this period of transition, or as he calls it, the "Great Disruption," the countries involved experienced an epoch characterized by "moral decay." As evidence for the "moral decay" associated with the Great Disruption of the 1960s to the 1990s he cites high crime rates, illegitimacy statistics, and indices of low levels of trust in major institutions. He ignores issues relating to improvements in the working conditions of the socially disadvantaged and the increasing status of women in Western societies—these would disturb the dark picture he paints. Furthermore, many scholars would challenge Fukuyama's assumption that the measures he has selected indicate anything about levels of morality in the general population. Instead, they tell us a great deal about Fukuyama's values.

Exploring the moral dimensions of the end of history further, Fukuyama suggests in this later work that

> there is a strong logic behind the evolution of political institutions in the direction of modern liberal democracy, one that is based on the correlation between economic development and stable democracy. . . . This same progressive tendency is not necessarily evident in moral and social development. (Fukuyama, 1999, p. 10)

Fukuyama's first dystopia thus is a descent from the end of history into social disorder and chaos. According to his logic, if we leave unchecked the "excessive individualism" that the Great Disruption encouraged, then we may be unable to enjoy the fruits of the end of history. We will be like Nietzsche's lazy, hedonistic Last Man who forgets what it is like to live in history, with its conflicts and dangers. Fukuyama's problem, Roth argues, is "how will we keep ourselves hard after getting what we wanted" (Roth, 1995b, p. 171)? He notes "the ambivalent liberal in *The End of History* looks around and sees satisfaction, then worries, American-style, about the dangers of too much satisfaction" (Roth, 1995b, p. 171). Of course, the parallels between the Last Man of history and the politically apathetic, distrustful youth of the 1990s is striking, and cannot go unnoticed by Fukuyama, who is eager to place developed nations at the end of history, and intensely worried by the prospect of what we might term "a return to history."

Fukuyama's historicism comes to his aid in providing hope that this dystopia will not circumvent the end of history. He argues that "there is a bright side . . . social order, once disrupted, tends to get remade once again, and there are many indications that this is happening today" (Fukuyama, 1999, p. 6). Accordingly:

> [W]e can expect this to happen for a simple reason: human beings are by nature social creatures, whose most basic drives and instincts lead them to create moral rules that bind themselves together into communities. They are also by nature rational, and their rationality allows them to create ways of cooperating with one another spontaneously. (Fukuyama, 1999, p. 6)

Thus, while Fukuyama is unsure of a way to maintain moral order over time, again he is sustained by a vision that the social disorder of the Great Disruption is starting to recede, and will retreat due to certain "essential features" of human behavior evident in cyclic trends observable over "the course of human history." Such a view relies on a view of humanity that is shared by more mainstream historians such as Pirenne, who once asserted that a relatively stable human nature is a core assumption of all attempts at historical construction, because "one cannot comprehend men's actions at all unless one assumes in the beginning that their physical and moral beings have been at all periods what they are today" (Pirenne, 1970, p. 30). Interestingly, at its extreme, such a position suggests the impossibility of writing a history of "the Other," and locates moral behavior as a universal trait rather than an emergent sociocultural phenomenon subject to variation from place to place, and over time. It would appear that the commitment to a relatively stable and universal human nature, or at least assumptions about relative consistencies in human behavior, invites metahistorical speculation about meanings concealed in the grand sweep of a cyclical or teleological history (Bullock, 1970). According to Bhabha:

> [T]he idea that history repeats itself, commonly taken as a statement about historical determinism, emerges frequently within liberal discourses when consensus fails, and when the consequences of cultural incommensurability make the world a difficult place. At such moments, the past is seen returning, with uncanny punctuality, to render the "event" timeless, and the narrative of its emergence transparent. (Bhabha, 1996, p. 59)

Although Bhabha was not talking about Fukuyama here, he might as well have been, so closely does his description of a general liberal strategy accord with Fukuyama's rhetoric. Once again, Fukuyama's thesis emerges in striking opposition to postmodern conceptions of the end of history, which are built on an opposing assumption: that humanity has no universal, essential, enduring subjectivity; no inevitable trajectory; nothing like a universal "human nature"; nothing to hang a universal morality on.

The concern about a moral dystopia stopping us at the gates to the end of history is only one of Fukuyama's apprehensions. He is also concerned that recent developments in science will lead to a nightmare world where the end of history may be permanently eluded or deferred as humanity is altered beyond recognition. Fukuyama's second dystopia is unambiguously the emergence of a posthuman world driven by an unrestrained technoscientific establishment. In *Our Posthuman Future: Consequences of the Biotechnology Revolution* (2002) Fukuyama proposes three scenarios—two of which are borrowed from Aldous Huxley's *Brave New World* (1931/1989), a text he addresses in his introduction—that are likely to occur if technoscientific progress remains unaccountable to "moral" values. In the first dystopic scenario, human beings use designer drugs to alter moods and personalities to the point that there is no longer any excuse for not being in a state of perpetual happiness. The consequence of such a scenario, Fukuyama wants us to recognize, is the social stigma and potential ostracism that might occur as a result of "having a bad day," which will no longer be acceptable. The film *Equilibrium* (DeBont, Foster, & Wimmer, 2002) exaggerates such a scenario, where people who fail to take their "mood" drugs—to keep them in "equilibrium"—are executed as traitors to the state. In Fukuyama's second scenario, advances in medicine make possible life spans of well over 100 years, causing a range of unforeseen problems such as increased mental rigidity as people age and a decreasing interest in sexual reproduction resulting from an inability to make oneself attractive to the opposite sex—welcome to universal test-tube reproduction.

In his final dystopic scenario, Fukuyama worries about the likelihood of science transforming our world into the kind of place depicted by H. G. Wells in *The Island of Dr. Moreau* (1896/1996), in which genetic manipulation results in chimeras and interspecies hybrids—humans whose capabilities have been enhanced by animal DNA, with unforeseen terrifying effects. Likewise, Fukuyama shows concerns about the eugenic possibility of "designer babies," whose genes are manipulated to produce specific characteristics in future generations, a scenario prophesized by Frank Herbert in his Hugo and Nebula award-winning book *Dune* (1965/1981), where the religious order of the Bene Gesserit attempts to manipulate bloodlines in order to produce the Kwisatz Haderach, an all-powerful messiah. A similar theme is evident in Herbert's lesser known *The Eyes of Heisenberg* (1966/1976), in which genetic science has become bureaucratized to the point where all embryos have their genes "cut" in order to produce a race of near-immortal "optimen." Fukuyama warns of potential social effects of the gene manipulation scenario, such as children blaming their genes, or their parents who "selected" their genes, for all their own failures. He also suggests the possibility of the development of a new underclass whose failures are blamed on the contamination of their human genes with animal material. We might also ask what happens to those who can't afford modification: Will they produce a new underclass of the less than biologically perfect, who are excluded from particular kinds of jobs due to identified defects in their DNA? One can see such a dystopia in the film *Gattaca* (DeVito, Shamberg, & Nicols, 1997), in which an ordinary guy with a heart defect must assume someone else's identity in order to attain the career he's dreamed of. In a moment that reveals the liberal-humanist emancipatory undertones of his thesis, Fukuyama asks, "What will happen to political rights once we can breed some people with saddles on their backs, and others with boots and spurs?" (2002b, p. 23).

Fukuyama's concerns for the advent of a technoscientific dystopia appear to be based on his enduring commitment to notions of an essential human nature. In Fukuyama's first postmillennium book he argued that "whatever the academic philosophers and social scientists may think of the concept of human nature, the fact that there has been a stable human nature throughout history has had very great political consequences" (Fukuyama, 2002b, p. 28). For Fukuyama, the growing scientific interest in biotechnologies may reopen the possibility of systematic social engineering such that in a generation or two, we may find ourselves in a posthuman future in which technology has provided us with the capacity to gradually, and dramatically, alter our human nature. Such comments make Fukuyama seem completely oblivious to the telling critiques of essentialism and humanism that have emerged within the academy since the late 1960s and early 1970s (see, for example, Henriques, Holloway, Urwin, Venn, & Walkerdine, 1984). I think he is right to recognize the potential of science to alter the human subject, or to produce new types of subjects, but wrong about the idea of a "human essence" that is being reshaped by bioscience. We may recognize in retrospect that what is being reshaped is the ahistorical, universal subject of history: Not "an essence," but the concept of a unified, transhistorical self. At least, that's an alternative perspective from the point of view of the methodological postmodernists.

Given his commitment to essentialism and humanism, Fukuyama shows concerns that

> the posthuman world could be one that is far more hierarchical and competitive than the one that currently exists, and full of social conflict as a result. It could be one in which any notion of "shared humanity" is lost, because we have mixed human genes with those of so many other species that we no longer have a clear idea of what a human being is. It could be one in which the median person is living well into his or her second century, sitting in a nursing home hoping for an unattainable death. (Fukuyama, 2002b, p. 302)

However, his concerns are not only for the social costs of a posthuman future, but also for what such a future might mean for liberal democracy. If we suspend the arguments concerning essentialism and humanism for a moment, and accept Fukuyama's belief in a stable human nature, then we would have to agree that if "human nature shapes and constrains the possible kinds of political regimes," then "a technology powerful enough to reshape what we are will have possibly malign consequences for liberal democracy and the nature of politics itself" (Fukuyama, 2002b, p. 20). Fukuyama's answer to the problem of a "return to history" ushered in by the radical alteration of "human nature" is to encourage the development of legal and institutional restraints on scientific innovation and experimentation. Interestingly, Popper in his critique of historicism predicted that such a strategy was the one most likely to be adopted by the historicist/utopianist, arguing that "the uncertainty of the human factor must force the Utopianist, whether he [sic] likes it or not, to try to control the human factor by institutional means" (Popper, 1957/1986, p. 21). Although Fukuyama's *Our Posthuman Future* wasn't written until twenty years after Popper's polemic against historicism, the main thrust of its argument—indeed, its reason for being—is predicted in Popper's critique. Ironically, the goal of Fukuyama's historicism, "liberal democracy," shares a remarkable affinity with Popper's "open society" (Roth, 1995b). Popper, however, never suggested that his utopia was inevitable.

## Fukuyama Unborn or the Posthistorical Cyborg

It is interesting to note that Fukuyama's posthuman dystopia shares a remarkable affinity with aspects of the apparently anti-technoscience end-of-history discourse that emerged in the work of the postmodern philosopher Jean-François Lyotard. Famous for his assertion that the postmodern condition can be characterized by incredulity towards metanarratives, a consequence of the agonistic struggle between incommensurable language games, Lyotard is no supporter of historicism. Plainly, when he asks "Can we continue to organize events on the basis of the Idea of a universal history of humanity?" he is positioning himself in opposition to totalizing narratives that purport to affirm a universal history (Lyotard, 1989, p. 317). Likewise, his mantra against the credibility of metanarratives places him in direct opposition to the kind of end-of-history thesis argued by Fukuyama. It is not surprising then to find that Lyotard does not share Fukuyama's faith in political and economic liberalism, which is evident when he argues that "'May 1968' refutes the doctrine of parliamentary liberalism . . . the 'crises of 1911 and 1929' refute the doctrine of economic liberalism. And the '1974-9 crisis' refutes the post-Keynesian adjustments that have been made to that doctrine" (Lyotard, 1989, p. 318).

Yet, despite his rejection of metanarrativist history and his refutation of liberalism's credibility, Lyotard's vision of a posthuman apocalypse brings him closer to Fukuyama than one might expect. As Sim argues, Lyotard's depiction of the end of history is "a singularly bleak one at that, of both the end of history and the end of the world" (Sim, 1999, p. 25). It is a vision of a posthuman nightmare world produced by an unrestrained technoscientific establishment intent on replacing flesh with some form of hardware that will act as a platform for "thought" so that consciousness can continue without a body. Lyotard, in ironic mode, argues the logic of such a commitment, since "while we talk, the sun is getting older," and eventually, he assures us, the sun is going to expand to engulf our planet, and life on Earth will be over (Lyotard, 1991, p. 8). In typically provocative fashion, Lyotard rehearses the argument that humanity must escape the impending solar apocalypse (4.5 billion years from now) or be faced with extinction, or what he calls "the death of death" (1991, p. 10). According to Lyotard, this is "the sole serious question to face humanity today" (1991, p. 9).

Whether we are as concerned as Lyotard about "the death of death" or not, there is a great deal of evidence to suggest that "with the ever deeper incursion of science and technology into the natural world, society, everyday life, and our very bodies (e.g., with wearable computers, bionic implants, and modified genes), human beings and technology are imploding" (Best & Kellner, 2001, p. 151). Some are concerned that this implosion is likely to result in a situation where technology will become capable of creating a new generation without any human intervention. Although some people are generally favorable to such a blurring of the boundaries between technology and biology, others remain understandably cautious, recognizing the postmodern as an era of intense technological development in which humanity and its environments have the potential to codevelop into new, dramatic, and dangerous configurations (Best & Kellner, 2001; Kurzweil, 1999; Paul & Cox, 1996). Lyotard's essay seems to be a warning against this "co-evolution," but its matter-of-fact tone disguises its sardonic intent.

Concerns about technology and its potential to interrupt "the human" first emerged as a theme in Mary Shelley's *Frankenstein* (1818/1993), a tale that

> synthesizes the vision of scientific materialism—that modern science can produce wonders, including new life forms—with the stance of Gothic romanticism, which fears the ugly, the monstrous, the irrational, and the violent erupting and destroying of human hopes and life. (Best & Kellner, 2001, p. 159)

It seems certain that Fukuyama and Lyotard share Shelley's concerns, particularly as Lyotard (1991) uses the term *inhuman* rather than *posthuman* to describe the trajectory of "human development" in a world dominated by techno- and bioscience. Yet the problem shared by Fukuyama and Lyotard is a commitment to a "natural-technological" binary that fears technology will effectively terminate humanity. This particular fear is not unique to the theorists under discussion here; it can be identified as a genre in contemporary film and speculative literature. Anakin Skywalker's transformation into the evil cyborg Darth Vader and the rise of the "clone army" in *Star Wars: Attack of the Clones* (Lucas, 2002), the domination of humanity by machines in *The*

*Matrix* (Silver, Wachowski, & Wachowski, 1999), and the dismembering of robots at a carnival in *A. I. Artificial Intelligence* (Speilberg, Curtis, & Kennedy, 2003) are all moments in contemporary cinema that highlight the enduring fear of man being replaced by machines.

Not all theorists who predict a shift towards the posthuman are as disturbed as Fukuyama and Lyotard by the prospects of an "enhanced" or "modified" humanity. Donna Haraway's "cyborg manifesto" (1985) represents an important chapter in the area of cyborg politics, working against the natural/biological and artificial/technological binaries that prefigure and fuel much of Fukuyama and Lyotard's pessimism. Invoking the mythological figure of the cyborg to collapse distinctions between the natural and artificial, Haraway's manifesto has been described as "a complex interpretation of the cultural, social, and economic milieu at the end of the millennium" (Cutler, 2001, p. 190). On a mission to tear down "the Berlin Wall between the world of objects and the world of subjects, and the world of the political and the technical" (Haraway, 1997, p. 270), Haraway is at the forefront of a queering of technoscience, for which "the pedagogic task is to learn the rules of the game" (1997, p. 131), so that we might avoid "the end of the millennium . . . brands that mark us all in the too persuasive stories of the New World Order" (1997, p. 271).

Haraway, who identifies as a historian of science, argues that far from "destroying 'man' by the 'machine' or 'meaningful political action' by the 'text,'" postmodern criticism—with the figure of the cyborg as its subject—opens possibilities for moving beyond our dualist ontologies and oppositional politics (1985, p. 70). Further, the idea of the hybrid creature of the cyborg allows us to elude "seductions to organic wholeness" that prevent us from seeing the liberating possibilities of a politics that emerges from the merger of flesh and machine (1985, p. 67). It is a vision that agrees with Fukuyama's insight that the alteration of the human could lead to new political forms, but rather than see this as a catastrophe, Haraway proposes that this is a rare opportunity to rethink our politics. Celebrating—in a way that must be offensive to Fukuyama's liberalist idealism—the potential of the posthuman condition to provide us with new forms of political radicalism, Haraway affirms that "the cyborg is our ontology; it gives us our politics" (1985, p. 66). Such a politics, by virtue of its emergence from the hybrid cyborg form, is likely to invite "progressive people" to engage in the "transgression of boundaries," "potent fusions," and "dangerous possibilities" (1985, p. 71). Unlike Fukuyama's utopia, in which everyone is a political liberal, Haraway projects "heteroglossia" as the likely form of a cyborg's "radical cultural politics" (1985, p. 70).

Haraway's generally positive vision has spawned a scholarship on the political possibilities of the posthuman condition (see, for example, the contributions in Bell & Kennedy, 2000) that stands in contrast to Fukuyama's historicist, essentializing, and humanist commitments. While it is sensible to remain mindful of the potential dominating effects of new technologies and fusions of flesh and machine—powerfully depicted in *Star Trek*'s vision of "the borg," a species of imperialist cyborgs who wish to integrate whole species and cultures into their mind-numbing collective—being "cyborged" doesn't have to mean making "the Holocaust and the Gulag look like rehearsals" (Gray, 2001, p. 201). In *Cyborg Citizen: Politics in the Posthuman Age* (2001) Gray creates something of an inventory of the many ways in which we have been cyborged already, and will be cyborged in the future, from the colonization of our bodies by nanotechnologies, increasingly powerful biomedical agents, cosmetic simulacra, and interspecies organ transplants, to our use of information communication technologies that form humanity into a single "cyborg system" (2001, p. 194). The optimism of Gray's work stands in contrast to Fukuyama's pessimism, and while Gray concedes that "horror is possible, perhaps inevitable," he also reminds us that "resistance, even joy, should be just as possible," and that "cyborg epistemology shows that there is no inevitable dialectical lockstep; prosthetic additions are always possible—on the body and on culture, and therefore the future" (2001, p. 195). Gray renders history plastic. There can be no terminal interface that cannot be modified, enhanced, hacked, or supplemented in some way. Therefore, there can be no end to history, no final destination.

Avoiding the binary of the real and the virtual by drawing on Virilio's (1989) distinction that divides reality into virtual and actual events, we might underscore that the merger of flesh and machine, though "real," does not have to be "actual." The posthuman condition may manifest as a "virtuality" rather than an "actuality." According to Kroker and Weinstein we are living "at the edge of a fantastic intensification of a history that is yet to be written: the telematic history of the virtual body" (2001, p. 132). Rejecting Fukuyama's thesis "as an explanation of the fading role of ideology in the twilight days of the Cold War," they affirm that only "when history means the archiving of the human function and its recombination in the form of monstrous hybrids ... can we finally speak of non-history" (2001, p. 132). In concert with Fukuyama, Kroker and Weinstein resurrect Nietzsche's Last Man, reinscribing him as "the recliner" whose "flesh has crashed" right at the moment the media-net emerges, fusing commodity and desire (2001, pp. 143–144). In their vision of a telematic history on a "transition to nowhere," they see "history" as an irrelevancy "because its subject 'man' is no longer the protagonist of anything but cynical dramas on the media-net" (2001, p. 143). Telematic history is for Kroker and Weinstein the real (virtual if not actual) end of history. Fukuyama's fear of a return to history triggered by the boredom of the Last Man is challenged by Kroker and Weinstein's thesis. For them, the Last Man, the recliner, is sitting back with the remote control or Playstation controller, reentering an unexpected kind of history, in which a different kind of freedom is sought: a virtual freedom to archive, delete, copy, and recombine identities in forms that might outrage the sensibilities of more conservative liberals.

It would seem that what Fukuyama fears most from a return to history was announced by Foucault at the end of *The Order of Things* (1966/1994) and celebrated and given form by Haraway: fear for the demise of the human subject of history. If the historical positions itself against the natural, or in Fukuyama's case, is naturalized by the historian, then Haraway's cyborg is a disruptive figure, a terminator who ends Fukuyama's naturalistic history in favor of a being in which culture is not just context, nor simply inscribed on the surface of the body, but penetrates, indeed, constitutes the "flesh," wet and virtual. While the prophets of the virtual may want to signal the posthistorical nature of the telematic, there is also a different kind of history in the prosthesis, one in which the tool itself is an artifact of the cultural-historical milieu that marks the body as historical from the inside out. Therefore, Fukuyama's dystopia signals not a return to history, necessarily, but alternative posthistorical possibilities. If indeed we continue down the path of self-modification, it will be interesting to observe whether the Last Man of history remains Fukuyama's complacent Nietzschean clone or emerges as Haraway's radical cyborg who experiences history as part of the integrated circuit.

If the virtual will be the ground of a new history, then one wonders what Fukuyama would make of the claim that

> in this age of information overload, what is significant is no longer freedom of ideas but rather freedom of form—freedom to modify and mutate the body. The question is not whether society will allow people freedom of expression but whether the human species will allow individuals to construct alternate genetic coding. (Stelarc, 1997, p. 1)

Certainly the Fukuyama of *Our Posthuman Future* would have great difficulty in coming to terms with Stelarc's radical view of human freedom. But then, what is the ideal of freedom that Fukuyama's liberalism seeks? At least one critic, the deconstructionist Jacques Derrida, is highly skeptical of a form of freedom that seeks in its arrival at the *telos* to silence all other voices.

## Haunting Fukuyama: Specters of Derrida

Derrida's critique of Fukuyama goes beyond concerns that Fukuyama is engaged in an attempt to silence ideological opposition to liberalism in the wake of the collapse of the Soviet Union (which symbolizes for Fukuyama not only "the end of history" but also "the end of Marxism"). It also goes beyond Derrida's assertion that Fukuyama deals with only an idealized version of liberalist ideology and not its instantiated forms, which Derrida argues have "never been so much in the minority and isolated in the world," and which today operate in "a state of dysfunction," as they are always "distorted, as was always the case, by a great number of socio-economic mechanisms" (Derrida, 1994, p.79). Wendy Brown would undoubtedly agree, and notes that "the 'triumph of liberalism' heralded by Western pundits in 1989 was short-lived; within eighteen months, intense civil and constitutional conflicts revealed that neither *liberalism* nor *triumph* appropriately named what was unfolding" (Brown, 2001, pp. 7, emphasis in the original).

Derrida also points out the irony of Fukuyama's end of history claim, which relies on references to actual historical events (such as the fall of the Berlin Wall) to pronounce its "end," and yet disavows this strategy when critics identify events (such as September 11) that seem to discredit Fukuyama's hypothesis. In the latter case, Fukuyama quickly shifts to trans-historic and natural claims for his ideology, a move Derrida refers to as "the sleight-of-hand trick between history and nature, between historical empiricity and teleological transcendentality, between the supposed empirical reality of the event and the absolute ideality of the liberal *telos*" (Derrida, 1994, pp. 69, emphasis in the original). Thus, Derrida identifies for us a technique of metanarrative historians: emphasizing the events of their time where they support the vision of the *telos*, and emphasizing the *telos* itself where the events seem to discredit the metanarrative being proclaimed.

Perhaps Derrida's most enduring contribution to end of history debate will be his insistent claim that to write Marx or socialist ideology out of history will not be as easy as proclaiming the arrival of the liberalist utopia. According to Derrida, Marx will remain a specter, a ghost that haunts our thinking and philosophizing (a point I concede in my preface). Derrida's view is that we are all heirs of Marx in some sense, whether we construct our ideas around his theses or against them. In a sense, this is the explicit theme of *Specters of Marx*, the work in which Derrida seeks to demolish Fukuyama's thesis. According to Sim's reading of Derrida, "Marx is too deeply ingrained in our cultural heritage to be dismissed, as some of the more radical post-Marxist thinkers would have us believe" (Sim, 1999, p. 45). Further, Sim argues that "there can be no sudden break of the 'Marxism is dead' variety: to believe otherwise is to be philosophically naïve" (1999, p. 47). It appears, then, that despite his own references to Marx, Fukuyama remains naïve, engulfed in the "good news" of his own triumphalism (Derrida, 1994, p. 64).

## September 11: History's Return, or the Final Nail?

There have been many criticisms of Fukuyama's thesis, not the least of which argues that the specter of communism that liberalism apparently has defeated was no more than a rival brand of capitalism, and that Fukuyama's triumphalism is an instantiated form of "idealized liberalism" (Derrida, 1994). Fukuyama (1992) has defended his liberalist idealism by arguing that his thesis is based on empirical observations of the changes occurring throughout the world at the current time. Enlisting the support of recorded events, Fukuyama attempts to give credibility to a sensational suggestion. The seductive power of a selective empiricism is evident in Fukuyama's post–September 11 comments when he argues that "it is hard to see that Islamism offers much of a realistic alternative as a governing ideology for real world societies. Not only does it have limited appeal to non-Muslims; it does not meet the aspirations of the vast majority of Muslims themselves" (Fukuyama, 2002a, p. 8). To support this observation, Fukuyama uses the same strategy that he uses to support his end-of-history thesis: He selects specific favorable empirical examples. Citing only the Islamic regimes in Iran and Afghanistan, highlighting the apparent dissatisfaction of the Muslim populations living under these strict theocracies while ignoring the stable, successful, and relatively prosperous Islamic democracies in Malaysia and Indonesia, Fukuyama bolsters his thesis about the inevitable connections between liberalism, democracy, and free-market capitalism.

Considering Fukuyama's implicit dismissal of Islam as an ideological alternative to liberal democracy, Zakaria states that while Fukuyama may be correct that "radical Islam as an ideology . . . posed no threat to the West . . . we pose a threat to it, one its followers feel with blinding intensity. It turns out it takes only one side to restart history" (Zakaria, 2001, p. 70). According to Zakaria, the consequence of the recent internationalization of terrorism will be governments becoming "more powerful, more intrusive and more important . . . for the oldest Hobbesian reason in the book—the provision of security" (2001, p. 70). Zakaria's critique is a rejection of the notion that we are anywhere near seeing the widespread permanent adoption of political and economic liberalism. Instead, what we may see are governments that are more authoritarian, despite their professed allegiances to particular democratic philosophies. Using Fukuyama's own strategy to support Zakaria, we might cite the swing towards right-wing political parties in developed nations around the globe and the strengthened border protection and anti-civil liberty laws passed by governments concerned by the threat of terrorism (post-September 11 sedition and detainment without charge laws in Australia being a case in point).

Despite the fact that Fukuyama's work is often recognized as derivative of a broad Hegelian-Marxist tradition, Fukuyama's is a weak version of the Hegelian view of history. While Hegel was perhaps the first "modern" scholar to herald an end to history, he saw this end as arising out of a dialectical process in which thesis (an idea) and antithesis (an opposing, contradictory idea) would see a final resolution in synthesis (some new form that reworks the original idea after taking into consideration its contradictions and oppositions). Hegel conceptualized the resolution of his dialectic as the universal and reciprocal recognition of one's humanity, which, following the French and American revolutions, amounted to the universal acceptance of "freedom" as the ideal of humanity. Horrocks has argued that "Hegel never imagined the struggle to preserve this freedom would end. Wars would continue after the end of history" (1999, p. 15), but the ideal of freedom would not be supplanted as the goal of human society. There is good reason to believe that Hegel thought the Prussian state existed at the end of history, and that the Napoleonic wars already had moved Europe to acceptance of history's *telos* (Sim, 1999). Marx, revising Hegel's view of history with his own formulation of the historical materialist dialectic, disagreed.

According to Marx, the fulfillment of history would be achieved when the underclasses, alienated by the machinery of capitalism, inevitably rose up against the owners of capital, displacing them in the establishment of a communist state. Here Marx's materialism is at odds with Hegel's idealism. The "dictatorship of the proletariat" was not just an idea that had to be recognized or accepted, but also a reality that must be actualized. Fukuyama has been accused of collapsing distinctions between philosophers in order to enlist their support (Sim, 1999). Considered by some to be an heir to Hegel and Marx, Fukuyama reads their philosophies of history through Kojeve (from whom he gains his specific reading of the idea of Universal Recognition) and through Nietzsche (from whom he appropriates the idea of the Last Man). Although the empirical existence of opposing politico-economic systems is acknowledged in Fukuyama's thesis, there is no real dialectic through which the opposites are synthesized into a greater whole. For Fukuyama, one competitor is simply superior to the other, and the lesser must inevitably give way to the greater. Fukuyama's is not only the Hegelian-Marxist reading of historical development as progress in a particular political direction (although he does seem to hold this view), it is also predicated on a kind of intellectual Darwinism in which only the strongest or fittest ideology ultimately survives the struggle of social, economic, and political life. The flaw here is not the lack of a "true" dialectic in Fukuyama's view of history, but his unproblematized assertion that we have apprehended the ultimate form of human social life in economic and political liberalism. Despite differences in the works of Hegel, Marx, Kojeve, and Fukuyama, what they share is a teleological view of history, a view of history as a "grand story" in which events are inexorably moving our human societies towards a final utopian ideal or form. They differ only on the nature of the utopia and, perhaps, the process of arriving at this final form of human society.

The Marxist scholar and theorist of the postmodern Frederic Jameson seems to support Fukuyama's thesis when he argues that Fukuyama's end of history doesn't really mean "the end of time" but rather "the end of space," a consequence of the cultural fallout of a homogenizing globalism (Jameson, 1998). However, Jameson's observation about the effects of globalism also supports a concern that Fukuyama's thesis amounts to little more than an attack on cultural pluralism in its suggestion that in the long haul, we shall see "a continuing convergence in types of institutions governing the most advanced societies" (Fukuyama, 1992, p. 338). One might ask Fukuyama, can we have liberalism without McDonalds? Although he is never explicit on this point, the answer seems to be no, because it is impossible for Fukuyama to envisage a direction for history that does not result in the adoption of both economic and political liberalism (at some ultimate point). Furthermore, Fukuyama's end-of-history thesis may actually be, as LaCapra argues, "an ideological attempt to remain fixated at an existing historical condition, such as a market economy and limited political democracy" (LaCapra, 2004, p. 1). Consequently, we might say that Fukuyama's thesis equates history with ideology and conflates economic and political liberalism, and although it is evangelical in character, it does little to promote hope for the critics of late capitalism, because his representation of the future is one in which all opposition to liberal capitalist ideology is silenced.

## The Illusion of History

Depictions of the end of history in contemporary theory do not stop with Fukuyama and his dystopias. While Fukuyama's thesis may be read as an argument for the metanarrative of modernity, a great deal of contemporary postmodern and poststructuralist theory opposes metanarrative history generally, and the discourse of modernity specifically. In fact, when the end of history is discussed in postmodern social theory, it is the rejection of "the grand story" of modernization that is intended, not the celebration of modernity's final realization in the triumph of liberal democracy (Vattimo, 1988). One writer who has been at the forefront of discussions of the end of history as the rejection of the "grand story" has been the French social theorist Jean Baudrillard. Often considered to be at the fringe of postmodern scholarship, Baudrillard is usually either loved or detested. His controversial work as cultural critic and ironic philosopher has provoked accusations of intellectual shenanigans and earned him epithets ranging from "the Walt Disney of contemporary Metaphysics" (Norris, 1990) to the "New Manichean" (Bayard & Knight, 1995). However, there is much to take seriously in Baudrillard's work, even if his ironic and flamboyant style gives some readers the false impression that he himself doesn't take his subject matter seriously. While his work deals with a range of topics, his themes are drawn from his own "pataphysical" reading of contemporary life.

Baudrillard's unique contribution to end-of-history discourse spans several works, and it is arguably one of the enduring themes in his oeuvre, particularly during the 1990s—in the lead up to the millennium. In 1992's *The Illusion of the End* (cryptically subtitled *The Event Strike* in its French publication), the end of history appears as a subplot in his pivotal symbolic exchange and death; and informs the argument of what is perhaps his most controversial work, *The Gulf War Did Not Take Place* (Baudrillard, 1995). Far from providing a single thesis with regard to the end of history, Baudrillard develops throughout his writings a range of theories, from the idea that history no longer moves forward, but in reverse, to the notion that "news" has displaced history. For Baudrillard, one of the striking symbols of the late 1990s was the digital clock displayed on the Beaubourg Centre in Paris. Unlike most clocks that keep track of the forward march of time, the Beaubourg clock was set to countdown the seconds to the year 2000. Baudrillard (1998) theorizes this as history going in reverse. Proposed in the count down to the millennium, Baudrillard's views challenge both the teleological metanarrative history of Fukuyama and the unreflexive history of blind empiricists (Jenkins, 1999). Drawing on a rich intellectual tradition that embraces scholars from Marx to McLuhan, Baudrillard's work on the end of history offers surprising insight into the history of our times and the nature of historical consciousness in postmodernity. Given that I have discussed a number of aspects of Baudrillard's critique in the introduction to this volume, I will confine my comments here to those most relevant to the problem of history.

In contrast to Fukuyama's assertion that we have arrived at the terminus of history, Baudrillard (1992) argues that the whole concept of an end to history is an illusion, because for history to be at an end would imply that "history" (as the procession of events) had a teleology in the first place. Baudrillard rejects any pretensions to a history with some deep underlying significance. However, although his argument is that any "end to history" is simply an illusion, the idea of an end to history can only be sustained if we accept that there is no grand story of human society—no "history"—in the first place, because grand stories typically imply grand endings. So, for Baudrillard, providing an argument that demonstrates that any end to history is an illusion simultaneously terminates history as well. According to Baudrillard, there is no coherent unfolding of a grand plan, inescapable destiny, order in events, or concealed set of meanings to be revealed through life's twists and turns; and when events continue but have no significance, we are living beyond history (Lainsbury, 1996). In one stroke, Baudrillard's anti-Hegelian, anti-teleological, and anti-utopian thesis attempts to establish that both history and its end are illusions, and must be considered to be already over.

While Baudrillard's arguments may be aimed at bringing an end to metanarrative history, they are not the end to his thesis. Baudrillard's attack goes much further than suggesting that both history as a "grand story" and its end are illusions. He also argues that it has become impossible to practice history in any conventional sense, or even to write or tell histories in their conventional "lowercase" form. Baudrillard's argument is that late capitalist society has become increasingly fragmented, accelerated, and saturated with information, a consequence of its absolute dependence on technological innovations. He lucidly argues, on his own empirical grounds, that the pace of society, and particularly the central role of the high-tech media, have made history impossible, and so its reporting and recording functions have come to be replaced by "news."

According to Baudrillard (1995), there is no longer any time to reflect upon the past. Instead, we are left simply to consume the ongoing stream of news that floods into our living rooms and workplaces. Rather than living in history, or with history, it is Baudrillard's thesis that we are seduced by media-driven simulacra and simulations in which nothing "really" happens, because it is happening for us only on the television set or in the newspapers. For Baudrillard, "the event which is measured [neither] by its causes nor its consequences but creates its own stage and its own dramatic effect, no longer exists" (1992, p. 21). Now events only exist, according to Baudrillard, because of their "newsworthiness." That is to say, "events" are brought into and exist in the social world only when journalists have judged them to be newsworthy, not because they simply "happened." As I discussed in the introduction, Baudrillard's argument is captured by the idea that events are "on strike," and this allows him to assert controversially that the Gulf War did not take place (Baudrillard, 1995). With reference to what has become known as the First Gulf War, he can assert this because the Gulf War we know about is not the events that occurred in some Middle Eastern desert, but the "news story" we experienced watching the television news broadcasts and reading the daily newspapers. The history of the Gulf War we experienced in our living rooms, according to the new media, was one in which the only causalities were from surgical strikes to strategic targets; for Baudrillard, history as an inherently meaningful event was among those targets. The example of the Gulf War is used by Baudrillard to support his assertion that meaning can never be an essential characteristic of an event; rather, it is something constituted in its production as a news story or public narrative (Horrocks, 1999). For Baudrillard, reality and its representation have imploded in the news story, because televisual simulation has come to be indistinguishable from the event. Coupled with the filtering effects of the media that determine what is significant (newsworthy) and what is not—a function of taste and fashion as much as anything else—the result is not only the loss of history as a grand story, but also the loss of history as a quiet reflection on the past.

## History as a White Mythology

Baudrillard is not the only theorist to suggest that history as a "grand story" is simply an illusion. Internationally, a number of scholars have made the case that history functions as a set of "white mythologies" that provide narrative support for various forms of cultural and economic imperialism. The most significant of these scholars are Edward Said, Homi Bhabha, Gayatri Chakravorty Spivak, and the academics that make up the Subaltern Studies Group, including Dipesh Chakrabarty and Ranajit Guha. Considered together, these scholars belong to the field of critique known as postcolonial studies. According to R. J .C. Young, "post-colonial critique focuses on forces of oppression and coercive domination that operate in the contemporary world" and defines its terrain by "the politics of anti-colonialism and neocolonialism, race, gender, nationalisms, class and ethnicities" (2001, p. 11). Extending this position, Gyan Prakash has argued that one of the aims of postcolonial criticism is to critique the "historicism that projected the West as History" (1994, p. 175).

For Prakash, the conflation of history with the triumphant narratives of the West was a masterstroke of imperialism. In practice it meant that history, as a discourse that emerges from Europe, has tended to have a culturally specific teleology and to write about the peoples outside of Europe in ways that assume—in a manner surprisingly reminiscent of Fukuyama—that they will "come on board" in the journey towards the ultimate end or be left behind as "people without history." This embedded, often invisible, historicist agenda has resulted in histories that construct cultures ethnically different from the historian's as inferior. The power of this kind of history was not just its strategy of constructing the colonized subject as "different and other within the categories of knowledge of the West," but also, more profoundly, its ability to make the colonized see themselves as "the Other" (S. Hall, 1997, p. 112). According to R. J. C. Young, "the Third World was itself created as a representation, or as a set of representations, not only for the West but also for the culture whose representation was constructed" (1990, p. 159). He asserts that this was absolutely essential for the success of the European colonization of Asia, Africa, the Americas, and the Pacific Islands (including Australia) because nineteenth and early twentieth-century imperialism was both a territorial and economic power and a subject-constituting force. Following Spivak, Young argues that this means that "history is not simply the disinterested production of facts, but is rather a process of 'epistemic violence'" (1990, p. 158). Lands may be colonized by subduing the population through force or oppressive trade relations, but minds are colonized by inscribing the subdued population in the historical record as inferior, sometimes even subhuman. We see this, for example, in the construction of "exotic Orientals" in the case of Asia and the Middle East (Said, 1978), and a single unified "dying race" of Aborigines in the case of Australia's Indigenous peoples (Biskup, 1982; Russell, 2001).

In practice, the construction of the Other in the discourse of the colonizer meant that the only option for subaltern (colonized) Others was to attempt to clone themselves in the cultural image of the colonizer (Ashcroft, 2001). However, paradoxically, "if the colonizer does not always openly discourage these candidates to develop that resemblance, he never permits them to attain it either. Thus, they [the subalterns] live in constant and painful ambiguity" (Memmi, 1967, p. 15). This is particularly true of those who succumb, either by force or choice, to assimilation. Assimilation was a state-sponsored policy in pre-bicentennial Australia, and it has been making something of a comeback in public discourse since the emergence of Pauline Hanson's ultraconservative One Nation Party in the mid-1990s, and again since the events of September 11. When forced to assimilate, subalterns often find themselves liminal beings, removed from their own primary culture yet not completely accepted in the new culture—hybrid nomadic subjects, without place or path.

Derrida's analysis of the way in which binary logic is used to privilege one particular side of the colonizer-colonized dyad is useful here. Derrida's deconstructionist strategy, which may have been born of his own experience as a French Algerian alien in both France (the location of his tertiary education and emergence as a philosopher of international acclaim) and Algeria (the place of his birth and schooling), predicts the paradoxical effects of colonial discourse. Given the seduction of becoming part of "the institution," yet simultaneously experiencing the rejection of one's claim of status, one can aspire only to being a "well-behaving black," typically at the cost of one's indigenous heritage; this is an experience Australia's "stolen generation" know only too well. The binary logic of colonizer-colonized that privileges the culture of the colonizer as the norm against which all others will be judged ignores the complexity and multiplicity that is the lived experience of the Other. Take, for example, the tendency within the historical discourse of Europe to project Asia or the Middle East as "unified racial, geographical, political and cultural zone[s] of the world" (Bhabha, 1983/1997, p. 41), and to represent Australia's Indigenous peoples as a single racial group described by the epithet *Aborigines*, obscuring the fact that there is evidence that there may have been as many as 500 indigenous tribal groups speaking about 250 different languages prior to European contact (Russell, 2001). This construction of the Other as a unified group has particular effects. As Stuart Hall notes:

> Far from being grounded in a mere "recovery" of the past, which is waiting to be found, and which, when found, will secure our sense of ourselves into eternity, identities are the names we give to the different ways we are positioned by, and position ourselves within, the narratives of the past. (S. Hall, 1997, p. 112)

Events such as the hijackings on September 11, which resulted in the homogenization of ethically and religiously diverse Muslims in the consciousness of the West, repeat the same tired pattern in which power is affirmed by rendering the Other as a single manageable group. Although the age of European imperialism is over, history lingers (as both metanarrative and the narrative technology that positions us as peoples in relation to one another). The so-called rupture of "decolonization" has not resulted in the freedom we might have expected, and the historical discourse often "boringly repeats the rhythms of colonization with the consolidation of recognizable styles" (Spivak, 1997, p. 202). From Spivak's viewpoint, independence from the colonial power might free us of our foreign oppressors' armies, but it does not automatically free us of the discourses in which our subjectivities and identities have been inscribed. This is, quite obviously, a serious problem for the postcolonial historian.

It is of course difficult—if not impossible—to free ourselves from the inscriptive effects of the cultural discourse of history. Spivak (1997), reflecting upon a lecture delivered in London, problematizes the naming of the subject in everyday discourse (with its historical legacies). Spivak at home in the United States is "Indian" (as she would be in Australia), but in Britain she is definitely "Asian." In India, she would be "Bengali." She also might be thought of by some as representative of "woman," "feminist," "postcolonial theorist," or "poststructuralist." Therefore, she wonders, in delivering her lecture, who it is that speaks? Recognizing history as a cultural discourse is part of the answer to her question. According to Chakrabarty, we may well "attempt the impossible . . . by tracing that which resists and escapes the best human effort at translation across cultural and other semiotic systems, so that the world may once again be imagined as radically heterogeneous" (Chakrabarty, 1997, p. 244). But it must be attempted. While there may exist some potential for imperialist and indigenous systems to be "interruptive" of each other, with due caution, Chakrabarty points to an interesting dilemma he experiences as a postcolonial historian when he asserts that

> insofar as the academic discourse of history—that is, "history" as a discourse produced at the institutional site of the university—is concerned, "Europe" remains the sovereign, theoretical subject of all histories, including the ones we call "Indian," "Chinese," "Kenyan," and so on. There is also a peculiar way in which all these histories tend to become variations on a master narrative that could be called "the history of Europe." In this sense, "Indian" history itself is in a position of subalternity; one can only articulate subaltern subject positions in the name of this history. (Chakrabarty, 1997, p. 233)

Here Chakrabarty has captured the perpetual dilemma for the revisionist or insurgent historian—the impossibility of writing an alternative view of the past in a way that does not automatically, either through the structure of its form, or by virtue of its being alternative to the dominant discourse, position itself inside the ongoing subjugating narrative of a European historicism. As Ashcroft (2001) explains,

> the most profound hindrance to colonial history is not the absorption of colonial reality into Europe in this way. It is the dominance of the assumptions and methodologies of the master narrative of History itself, as a way of conceiving colonial reality. (2001, p. 98)

It is not surprising, given this dilemma, that R. J. C. Young draws attention to the fact that "oppositional historians can often unknowingly, or even knowingly, perpetuate the structures and presuppositions of the very systems they oppose" (1990, pp. 161-162). There are no easy answers, and no easy freedom from history.

What is clear from the perspective of postcolonial theory is that Fukuyama's end-of-history thesis inscribing humanity's trajectory within a neoliberal discourse of modernity deploys the same kind of metanarrative strategy as colonial history, albeit as a display of neocolonial discourse rather than "official" history. Subscribing to a relatively stable human nature throughout history, Fukuyama recapitulates the colonial strategy of universalizing the experience of Europe (and the United States), projecting the West as "history." Fukuyama's dismissal of the threat of politicized Islamic fundamentalism and his willful neglect of Islamic democracies in Southeast Asia in his end-of-history discourse seem to confirm a tendency towards a Eurocentric historicism, as does his attempt to reassert the discourse of history at a time when "we are witnessing the dissolution of 'the West'" as the master-category of history (R. J. C. Young, 1990, p. 20). If R. J. C. Young is correct that "postmodernism can best be defined as European culture's awareness that it is no longer the unquestioned and dominant centre of the world" (p. 19)—a realization that is itself an artifact of the cultural contact resulting from the colonial period—then history is indeed under siege by postmodernism, and Fukuyama's teleological thesis is no more than the death throes of the modernist metanarrative. Perhaps, then, the rise of the New Right (across "both sides" of politics) during the 1990s in nation-states such as Australia is part of a reactionary politics, troubled by the loss of (metanarrative) history, seeking unity under the invisible sign of "whiteness" and its cultural philosophies (i.e., liberalism, democratic capitalism, etc.). Fukuyama's end of history pronouncements thus can be understood as a call for history to stop where it is (or was), at the triumph of liberal democracy. Yet, given "[t]he conviction that history has reason, purpose, and direction is fundamental to modernity" (Brown, 2001, p. 5), it may be the project of modernity that actually has ended, as the innocence of history (and the discourses that rehearse its trajectories and teleologies) is called into question (Vattimo, 1988).

CHAPTER FOUR

# The Struggle for Histories

Over the last decade of the twentieth century the idea of history as a single grand story was called into question not only in the academy, but also in school curricula across much of the English-speaking world. The struggle to replace grand narratives of the nation with multiple and conflicting histories that often challenged and "revised" received wisdom set curriculum reforms on a collision course with conservative politicians and their media sympathizers. Such conflicts were referred to variously as "culture wars" or "history wars," and their boundaries typically were the nation-state with its imagined cultural, spatial, and temporal borders. The timelines and specifics of these conflicts vary somewhat from nation to nation, which is why curriculum histories must be tied closely to national milieu (Goodson & Marsh, 1996). This chapter focuses on the story of one particular "history war" and the curriculum that became one of its chief battlefields in the settler society of New South Wales (the largest state in the postcolonial nation of Australia) during the period from the nation's bicentennial to the millennium. As I explore this particular history curriculum war in detail I will make due reference to parallel conflicts in the United Kingdom, the United States, and Canada.

I chose to focus on the Australian case partly because it is in many ways emblematic of the struggles for histories that have occurred in History education across the English-speaking world. According to some observers, what was at stake in these "history wars" was the future of the nation, because as Tony Bennett has argued, "the shape of the thinkable future depends on how the past is portrayed and on how its relations to the present are depicted" (Bennett, 1995, p. 162). Wendy Brown agrees, asserting that "[the] struggle over what the past could mean in the present is at the same time a struggle for the future" (Brown, 2005, pp. 13–14). In other words, history as narrative constrains and enables particular ways of thinking about where we have been and where we are going. Thus Peter Seixas is in good company when he argues that these struggles over the national narrative arise because of "the power of the story of the past to define who we are in the present, our relations with others, relations in civil society—nation and state, right and wrong, good and bad—and broad parameters for action in the future" (Seixas, 2000, p. 21).

Accepting the underlying assumptions of such a position, Chris Healy interprets History curriculum as a political device that has historically "installed particular visions of history and trained people in ways of acquiring and interpreting social memory" (Healy, 1997, p. 73). Thus, although historical narratives often can be learned through all sorts of social interaction outside the classroom, and through consumption of history in a range of popular culture forms (M. L. Davies, 2006; Groot, 2009), the school curriculum serves as a specific site of sanctioned storytelling, and although it may be a site of disciplinary development or critical engagement, it also can be a crucible for the installation of "collective memory" (Seixas, 2000). Having explored the curriculum reforms of the 1990s and examined the ensuing political backlash, I will conclude this chapter with an examination of the complex and problematic relationship between history and memory, the significance of this relationship in terms of the struggles over curricular representations of the national past, and the pedagogical interventions that have been attempted in the name of a critical History curriculum.

## History's Last Stand

There are a number of factors that make the NSW History curriculum an interesting context within which to explore the emergence of "end of history" discourse in schools. An important site of scrutiny in the premillennial NSW state-based and federal inquiries into History education, NSW had become significant in Australian education, particularly during the late 1980s and early 1990s, as the place of History's "last stand" as a school subject (Halse, et al., 1997; Taylor, 2000). In the Commonwealth of Australia education has been a state rather than federal government responsibility since federation in 1901. It should be noted, though, that the national government has frequently achieved its education agendas through the use of incentive (read "compliance") funding regimes, arguably ignoring the political division of labor that followed the formal establishment of Australia as a relatively autonomous nation. Among the federated states of Australia, NSW remained unique in maintaining a discrete junior high school History subject despite decades of political pressure for a shared national Social Studies curriculum. In the mid-1990s History as a discrete subject (along with Geography and Commerce and a newly developed "Environmental Studies" strand) was subsumed into an integrated Social Studies curriculum titled "Studies of Society and the Environment" (SOSE) in all states but NSW. The move to integrate History with the social science subjects was one of the consequences of the Declaration of National Educational Goals (MCEETYA, 1989), otherwise known as the Hobart Declaration, which was rapidly translated into a series of national statements and profiles for the various "key learning areas" (KLAs) that had been formed as a way of standardizing curriculum across Australia (C. Harris, 1996). Arguably, the main thrust of the Hobart Declaration was the endorsement of an outcome-based national curriculum, the wholesale adoption of which would see History forgo its place as a discrete subject in every state except NSW. Although moves towards an integrated Social Studies curriculum and a unified "core" national curriculum had been gaining momentum for some time before the Hobart Declaration, all previous attempts at developing a core integrated social studies curriculum for Australian secondary schools had been unsuccessful. Hobart was successful largely because of the unique and historic consensus it achieved (and represented) among federal, state, and territory ministers for education, all of whom were signatories to the declaration. The Hobart Declaration was superseded by two later national statements, the Adelaide Declaration on National Goals for Schooling in the Twenty-First Century (MCEETYA, 1999), and the Melbourne Declaration of Educational Goals for Young Australians (MCEETYA, 2008). Partly as a result of the history wars I explore, the more recent debates and discussions that resulted in the Melbourne Declaration turned back the clock and led to the formation of the federally funded Australian Curriculum and Reporting Authority (ACARA), which has a historic mandate to develop a national curriculum with History as one of its four foundation subjects (the others being Mathematics, English, and Science). I will come back to this reversal of history a little later.

NSW's dissent from the Hobart Declaration took the form of establishing a Human Society and Its Environment (HSIE) KLA for primary (elementary) schools that included a history-inspired "change and continuity" strand consistent with the other states and territories, and the maintenance of a discrete History subject in the junior years of secondary school. This was largely due to the effective intervention of the NSW History Teachers' Association (HTA) and a local tradition in which History, in the living memory of many teachers, always had been taught as a discrete subject (Simpson, 2000). An introductory Social Studies curriculum in Form I (Year 7), followed by the possibility of an elective study of History in Forms II, III, and IV (Years 8-10), had been the pattern in NSW schools since the adoption in 1962 of the Wyndham Scheme, a discipline-based academic curriculum model. Throughout this period, instruction was guided by a prescriptive and chronological syllabus that was programmed in fortnightly slabs of content that remained relatively unchanged from 1957 until 1972 (Clark, 2003). Within this structure, Australian history may have been relegated to the elective streams, but the place of History as a school subject remained secure.

The success of History as a school subject in attracting elective enrollments during the 1970s and 1980s, particularly over rivals such as Geography, helped to secure the place of a discrete History curriculum during the early 1990s amidst anxieties over the role and function of History as curriculum within the new KLA structure (Duncan, 1992). Continued support for History as a defined area of study also came from the "History premier" Bob Carr, who served as the NSW premier on the cusp of the millennium from 1995 to 2005, and whose undergraduate degree in American history had instilled a passion for and commitment to the subject; Carr even authored a short patriotic tome on the topic, *What Australia Means to Me* (B. Carr, 2003). Carr's support went beyond advocacy for a discrete History subject to backing for the institution of a state-based history project award scheme and scholarships for the study of American history (his personal passion). This disputation over the continued status of History as a discrete subject in NSW had global significance, particularly in light of parallel conflicts over the social education curriculum in countries such as Canada and the United States (Seixas, 1993), leading Peter Seixas (1994) to argue that History is a "discipline adrift" in a sea of Social Studies, to its detriment as an area of study. But the notion that the NSW mandatory History curriculum represented History's last stand is not the main reason that it provides an interesting context for the exploration of the central problematic of this book.

The most important reason for using the NSW case to explore "end of history" discourse is that during the fight to maintain its borders in the early 1990s, History curriculum in NSW was rewritten as a "radical text" that made subsequent pre-millennium curriculum developments appear "reactionary." The "radicality" of the 1992 curriculum changes took a number of forms. The first involved the adoption of a firm position on what content knowledge should be "fundamental" to the History education of young Australians. There was an attempt to address the perennial problem of the lack of national content in the curriculum, which had been exacerbated by the structure of the History curriculum in the 1960s, 1970s, and 1980s that relegated Australian history to the elective years. Mandating 100 hours of Australian history content, the 1992 syllabus was described at the time by the HTA president Carmel Young as "a radical departure" from the syllabus it supplanted (C. Young, 1993, p. 3), going further than establishing a set of new basics and moving significantly away from previous curriculum constructions. It was surprisingly "radical" in another, more political way, for the 1992 syllabus "guard[ed] against the sway of a master narrative in history" by underscoring "the importance of selecting and promoting a full range of voices in the telling of Australian history" (1993, pp. 4-6), "voices frequently absent from the national narrative" (Clark, 2003, p. 173).

Endorsing a trend that had begun in the 1970s that moved History away from the rote recall of facts and dates, the 1992 syllabus was a watershed document in its "social meliorist" orientation. Strongly influenced by that "study of the social dimensions of past societies" that has come to be called "social history"—which had been struggling for over a decade to gain ground in U.S. schools (Stearns, 1982)—the NSW syllabus encouraged "real questioning from a multitude of viewpoints" (1982, p. 4). Organized around five focus questions that attended to issues of Australian identity, heritage, Australia's international relationships, women's experience, and Indigenous perspectives, the 1992 syllabus effectively changed school History in terms of both its orientation as an area of study and the definition of "the subject" that was studied. The incorporation of social histories from the perspectives of women and Australia's Indigenous peoples—perspectives that had been historically sidelined, or for a long time academically nonexistent—and the framing of these histories as legitimate alternatives to the master-narratives of "famous men" and "pioneering settlement" proved to be the most controversial aspect of the changes to the NSW History curriculum in the early 1990s (Parkes, 2007).

## The Climate of Reform: History as a Gendered Text

As critical approaches to Australian history began to emerge from within the academy during the 1960s and 1970s they inevitably had an impact on the history that was taught in schools. This impact initially took the form of an increasing focus on the construction of a nonprescriptive, student-enquiry-focused syllabus in 1972 that maximized the opportunities for teachers and pupils to choose content and approaches to suit their interests, the ability levels of students, and specific school circumstances (Johnston, 1982). Although the syllabus released in 1980 intensified the focus on the development of students' historical understanding, it was not until the early 1990s that the impact of the new History on the school curriculum took a decidedly more political turn, involving the incorporation of the perspectives of women and Australia's Indigenous peoples into the teaching of Australian history.

The 1992 History Years 7-10 Syllabus in NSW was made possible by the political climate that existed in the wake of the civil rights and social reform movements of the 1960s and the equity policy context of the late 1970s and early 1980s that had given rise to the publication of documents such as "Girls, School, and society" in 1975; "Towards Non-sexist Education" in 1979; the multicultural education policy statement and guidelines in 1979; and the Aboriginal education policy in 1982. Certainly we can say that these policies were influenced by a growing social conscience constituted in part by the discourses of feminism, neo-Marxism, and multiculturalism. It is also likely that the "new histories" that came to the fore in the late 1970s and early 1980s—social histories that emphasized the lives of ordinary people over the study of elites—legitimized the place in the NSW History curriculum of feminist and Indigenous perspectives on Australia's past (Osborne & Mandle, 1982). The growing influence of postmodern social theory that had made "history from below" an increasingly appealing option over more totalizing approaches to history in the academy probably also contributed to the climate of reform that encouraged curriculum developers to design a syllabus that could be described as socially meliorist (Allport, 1987; C. Young, 1987). Without doubt, one of the most important movements and philosophies to foster this climate of curriculum reform was feminism.

It is beyond the scope of this project to examine the impact of feminism upon education in any general sense. Instead, I will confine my comments to an exploration of history from a feminist perspective as a way into understanding the climate of History curriculum reform. From the standpoint of feminist theory, history is a gendered text. In *Feminism and Deconstruction* (1997) Diane Elam suggests that Western history has been dominated for centuries by narratives of "great men." Elam acknowledges recent feminist attempts to re-evaluate what counts as historical knowledge, and to make women appear in the historical record where previously they had been invisible. Natalie Zemon Davis's attempts to recover the voices of ordinary men and women in sixteenth-century France (Davis, 1987) is case in point, as is the work of June Sochen, who uses the neologism *her-story* to highlight a focus on women as the subject of the narrative that is told. Writing about women in the early days of American history, Sochen argues that "as any reader of history books knows, the overwhelming majority of evidence, of persons, and of events described in history narratives is about male exploits, male accomplishments, and male failures" (Sochen, 1982, p. 1). Armed with a commitment to write women's history, Sochen is one of an increasing number of feminist historians who have taken up the challenge to write histories from a woman's perspective, focusing on the private life of women, rather than the public life of men, as the object of the historian's gaze. Circulating within and beyond the academic history community, these feminist perspectives on the past were on the way to becoming commonplace at the time of the production of the 1992 syllabus.

While Elam believes in the importance of telling her-story, rather than just his-story, she underscores that "her-story is not one story," that there is no single story shared by every woman, and that "an injustice is committed when any one history purports to speak for all women everywhere, when it does not underline the incompleteness of its own narrative" (Elam, 1997, p. 69). Elam's comments grapple with a central problem of historical scholarship and curriculum development. Whenever events are historicized they are also, in a sense, "hypostatized." That is, there is a tendency for historical narratives to fix a reader's conceptions of "the past." The effect of this "fixation" is to leave history standing motionless, a snapshot of a much richer and more varied context than the form of narrative can capture, regardless of how pluralist or dialogic the style of the historian. When a story becomes history, it renders static a conception of "the past," and by virtue of its attempt to "get the story straight," allows some voices to be heard while silencing others. This fixing of history often produces "an account of the past that is fundamentally ahistorical" (A.-L. Shapiro, 1997, p. 12). That is to say, where the historian writes in such a way as to universalize the viewpoint of his or her narrative, the alternative possibilities that would normally remain in any rendering of "the past" become "flattened," and discontinuities are suppressed, implying that the present is the predestined result of some remote past rather than the result of unpredictable action, constant contestation, and contextual contingencies. Thus, even feminist histories may suffer from the problem of presenting the voice of their narrator as recording the universal viewpoint of all women. This is problematic, and it may be one of the factors that have given rise to the range of feminisms we see today, given that no one feminism speaks for all women (St. Pierre & Pillow, 2000).

Thinking in terms of school life, what the feminist critique of history reveals so sharply is the fact that "the traditional curriculum teaches all of us to see the world through the eyes of privileged, white, European males and to adopt their interests and perspectives as our own" (Rothenberg quoted in Berkhoffer, 1995, p. 170). This kind of criticism seeks to demonstrate, in line with poststructural and postcolonial theory, how historical narratives typically position the white, European male as the uncontested norm, or standard against which all others should be measured. Because it is unlikely that the viewpoints of other groups (such as gender, ethnic, indigenous, and class minority views) will be the same as the dominant phallocentric view, difference is registered as deficit. Histories that revise or question "the great story" of men are often declared to be ideologically motivated, whereas "the great story" is positioned as an objective reality. We see this particular strategy in the writings of Keith Windschuttle, who denies historical accounts of the massacres of Indigenous people in Tasmania as ideologically motivated while portraying his own counter-revisionist argument as "objective" history. It must be said, though, that Windschuttle's approach to historical scholarship is far from orthodox, and may share more in common with historical deniers such as David Irving (Taylor, 2008).

Certainly, any historian who takes seriously the feminist critique is forced to reread history as a gendered text. Historians of the 1960s and 1970s were alert to this issue, engineering a critical approach to Australian history that demonstrated a commitment to social histories from feminist, migrant, and Aboriginal perspectives and questioned established interpretations (Clark, 2003). This shift is often described as an interest in history from below; history from the viewpoint of those in the margins. While feminism was an important influence on the climate of reform that was a crucible within which the 1992 syllabus was produced, the context for curriculum reform in NSW was undoubtedly dominated by the bicentennial of the nation and the attention it brought to Aboriginal history. Feminist history left its mark on the 1992 syllabus, but it was the lingering effects of the bicentennial that brought an end to history as it had been known, serving as the blue touch paper for igniting the history wars in the lead up to the millennium.

## Bicentennial Australia and History as Social Memory

As the interjection of the perspectives of women followed the gender equity and women's liberation movements of the 1970s, it is no coincidence that Indigenous perspectives finally found a place in the NSW History curriculum when they did. Awareness that Australia's Indigenous peoples held a legitimate alternative perspective on the nation's history was thrust into public consciousness during the late 1980s through a growing body of works dedicated to the revelation of an Aboriginal history. Reynolds's groundbreaking *The Other Side of the Frontier: Aboriginal Resistance to the European Invasion of Australia* (1982) provided one of the first accounts of early European-Indigenous contact from the Aboriginal viewpoint. Advocated as a useful resource for gaining an Aboriginal perspective that could be incorporated into the curriculum, Reynolds's work challenged the traditional narrative of a nonviolent frontier and encouraged its readers to look at the past through Indigenous eyes (Prentis, 1993; C. Young, 1987).

Some of the shifts in Aboriginal history, including Reynolds's work, had been canvassed quite early in *Teaching History*, the journal of the History Teachers' Association (Farrell, 1980). More recent work by Veracini (2003b) documents "four waves" of Aboriginal historiography. According to Veracini, the first wave took place during the 1960s and 1970s, establishing an opposition between Aboriginal presence and absence in "Australian history." The second wave, during the late 1970s and early 1980s, explored issues of Aboriginal passivity and resistance in relation to colonization (it was during this second wave that Reynolds's early work had become a touchstone). The third wave, which emerged in the late 1980s and continued through the early 1990s, examined the tension between Indigenous strategies of confrontation and collaboration with the British invaders, and ultimately affirmed Aboriginal agency. The fourth phase commenced in the late 1990s and continues into the present. It involves debates over tension between unsurrendered Indigenous sovereignty and the extinguishment of Indigenous land rights (otherwise known as "native title"). Thus, though the "new Aboriginal historiography" in general refers to the tendency of historians in the latter half of the twentieth century to pay attention to Indigenous perspectives on the past, the central debates in the field have undergone a number of transformations. By the time the 1992 syllabus was produced, history educators who were keeping up with the academic debates were aware of literature that fitted into the first three phases of the debate. The development of a new syllabus in 1998 coincided with the beginning of the fourth phase of Aboriginal historiography, although polemic work that is central to many recent debates arguably continues the battles of the third phase (see Windschuttle, 2002, 2009).

Public awareness of a distinct Aboriginal perspective on Australian history came partly as a result of a series of grassroots protests that culminated in a day of mourning during the bicentennial celebrations of 1988. For many Australians, the call for a day of mourning by Indigenous elders at the time of the bicentennial was an important catalyst for reflection on the nation's past, bringing into sharp relief the disjuncture between the official story of 200 years of successful European settlement and Indigenous stories that described two centuries of displacement, occupation, and oppression. Placing an increasing emphasis on Aboriginal experience and perspective, the new historiography of the 1980s had moved towards detailed local and regional studies of Indigenous life that broke the "Great Australian Silence" around Indigenous history. This "great silence" had been sustained by an Anglo-Australian myth that the destruction of Aboriginal society in the face of colonizing forces was inevitable and complete; a belief in an uneventful frontier free of the founding violence of other nations; ignorance of (and disbelief when confronted with the revelation of) state-sanctioned Indigenous child-removal policies designed to foster "assimilation" throughout most of the postfederation/prebicentennial period; and the willful "drawing of a veil" over events by nineteenth-century historians already concerned about what it could mean for the national spirit and reputation if stories of frontier atrocities were widely circulated in Australia and abroad (J. Harris, 2003; Russell, 2001; Veracini, 2003a).

It must be stated that the 1992 syllabus stood in striking contrast to the 1957 syllabus, which still looked at Australia's Aboriginal people as a study of "stone age man" who remained at the "threshold of history" (Clark, 2003). This shift in perceptions of Aboriginal people, their culture, and their ownership of a legitimate history had taken generations to emerge. But once that shift occurred, the new perceptions rapidly impacted upon what was taught about Indigenous Australians in the curriculum. Interestingly, the History curriculum in NSW also seemed to be in tune with the legal climate of its day. In the same year the 1992 syllabus was published, the struggle for Indigenous land rights moved forward with the High Court's announcement of the Mabo decision, which in practical terms meant that Indigenous people had a right to dominion over their traditional lands, and that this situation demanded recognition within Australia's political and legal institutions (Ritter & Flanagan, 2003). The Mabo decision (and the Wik decision that followed in 1996) had important consequences for Australian history in particular, and for Australian society more generally. As Attwood has argued:

> Mabo and the new Australian history ends the historical silence about the Aboriginal pre-colonial and colonial past upon which the conservative invention of Australia and Australianness was founded, and since their Australia was realised through and rests upon that conventional historical narrative, the end of this history constitutes for them the end of Australia. (Attwood, 1996, p. 116)

It was this end of history that emerged in the 1992 syllabus. In a certain sense, the 1992 syllabus anticipated the Mabo decision and was already affecting possibilities for this kind of recognition within the school History curriculum. However, though popular with teachers, the apparent radicalism of the 1992 syllabus made it unpopular with conservative politicians, as well as at least one prominent Australian historian.

## "Hijacking" History and Whitewashing Public Memory

In *The History Wars* (2003) Stuart Macintyre and Anna Clark documented and in many ways challenged the growing concerns of a powerful New Right that sought to return Australia to a naïve, idealistic, "1950s view" of the nation's past. In their analysis, the nation's past had become the focus of a political battle tethered to issues of national identity, immigration, and the treatment of Australia's Indigenous population (past and present). That the incorporation of a revisionist Aboriginal perspective on Australian history triggered a series of political conflicts over the curriculum should not be surprising, because as Ashcroft has argued, "narratios are not neutral alternatives, but are themselves a feature of the power struggle continually waged in post-colonial societies. Contesting narratios struggle for authority over the explanation of the past" (Ashcroft, 2001, p. 89). Disputes over the content of the curriculum that followed the incorporation of Indigenous histories of Australia's colonial past were "simply the latest manifestation of a perennial concern about historical knowledge and national identity" (Clark, 2003, p. 172).

Only a couple of years before Macintyre and Clark's analysis of the "history wars," Graeme Davison published his own work in the popular press, *The Use and Abuse of Australian History* (2000). Davison's exploration of the contemporary uses and abuses of history in Australian society included a discussion of what he called the "Howard-Keating conflict." According to Davison, the newly elected prime minister John Howard accused the outgoing left-wing government led by Paul Keating of "hijacking" history, of officially sanctioning a "politically filtered . . . and distorted" view of our national past; Howard wanted to return to Australia's "real" history. For Howard, the leader of the main federal conservative party, the real history was one that Australians could be proud of—a history that documented what Australia had *achieved* over the past 200 years, rather than any perceived failings of the nation and its citizenry. Importantly, without ever stating it explicitly, the prime minister wanted a history that played down any injustices committed against Indigenous populations in the colonial past. Howard's resistance to the new Aboriginal history seemed to be motivated by a concern that acknowledging past injustices could require present or future governments to treat Indigenous peoples as a "special case" requiring compensation, at odds with his radical ambition to dismantle the "welfare state" and return Australia to an egalitarian paradise where everyone would be "treated the same." More importantly, Howard's resistance appeared to arise from a neoliberal individualism that is intuitively appealing to many Australians, which suggests that those of us living in Australia today should not be held accountable for what our forbearers did during our collective past. Keating, in contrast, was concerned that before Australia could go forward as a nation, "white Australia" must reconcile with its unwritten past: a past that lingers and has consequences for Indigenous communities today; a past in which Aboriginal communities were treated with a kind of disrespect that is out of step with contemporary social values.

The positions of Howard and Keating in the "history wars" were supported by their particular readings of the past (Nile, 2002). On the one hand, Keating's speechwriter, the historian Don Watson, drew on the work of Manning Clark and Henry Reynolds, both of whom had written "revisionist" histories of Australia that called into question what had been the dominant narrative until the late 1960s—a "white colonial" narrative. On the other hand, Howard's history—which seemed to be bound up in a desire to turn back the historical clock to the Australia of his youth—was forged through readings of the conservative historian Geoffrey Blainey. According to Blainey, Australia's collective memory is under siege from the "black armband" view of history. The notion of a "black armband" view of the past was first raised by Blainey (1993b) in his John Latham Memorial Lecture in April 1993, then followed by an article with the same theme in the conservative journal *Quadrant* (see Blainey, 1993a). However, it wasn't until the new Prime Minister, John Howard, used the phrase three years later as a political mantra against left-wing "revisionist" historians and political opponents sympathetic to revisionist histories that the term *black armband history* entered the national lexicon (Warhaft, 1993).

Blainey coined the phrase to describe the "mournful view" of the nation's past that was being promoted by the Hawke-Keating Labor government, who were drawing on the constructions of revisionist historians to challenge what they perceived to be a "public amnesia" in relation to the displacement of Indigenous peoples and the destruction of their societies by European colonization. Blainey contrasted the "black armband" view with what he described as the traditional "three cheers" view of Australian history. It was Blainey's view that the "balance sheet" of the past was firmly in favor of the achievements of "white society" since "settlement," and that any history that has an excessive focus on past wrongs promotes a "mournful" relationship with the nation's past that harms the nation and is ultimately inaccurate. Blainey's concern was that Australia's history was being rewritten by "radicals" intent on claiming the historical consciousness of "ordinary" Australians in the service of partisan politics.

Following Blainey's lead, the educationalist Kevin Donnelly (1997) has argued that there is a political bias present in what is currently taught in schools about the Australian nation's history. Donnelly has expressed particular concern about the teaching of "revisionist" or "black armband" accounts of the colonization of Australia that depict white "settlement" as an "invasion," a position that had been argued some years earlier by a host of journalists and commentators (see, for example, Koch, 1994; McGuinness, 1994; Partington, 1987; Wilkins, 1994). According to these journalists, the draft version of the 1992 syllabus represented the work of a "new establishment" that was hijacking our national past and infecting students' minds through the use of "politically correct buzzwords" that included terms such as *invasion, genocide, dispossession, Aboriginality,* and *terra nullius* (Clark, 2002, p. 20). Although critique during the early 1990s remained at the level of rhetoric and hyperbole, it was not long before a series of counter-revisionist texts on Australian history emerged. At the forefront of the new counter-revisionist history was Keith Windschuttle and his controversial tome *The Fabrication of Aboriginal History, Volume 1: Van Diemen's Land, 1803–1847* (2002).

Windschuttle's work, which attacked the new Aboriginal historiography and particularly its representation of frontier conflict, gained wide public and media attention. Windschuttle levels a number of criticisms at the new Aboriginal historiography. For example, he disputes the application of the term *genocide* to the treatment of Aboriginal populations in Tasmania. In that respect he is not alone, as the field remains divided on the contemporary use of the term *genocide*, with some scholars considering it inappropriate for the Australian context (Curthoys & Docker, 2001; Markus, 2001). His more controversial claim is that there was no organized resistance to European encroachment in Tasmania, and that accounts of a guerrilla war are fabrications based on exaggerations of the evidence for the numbers involved. Windschuttle's views have stimulated a series of rebuttals from scholars working in the field, and even provoked a critical response from the professional history teaching journals (Attwood, 2005; Clement, 2003; Poad, 2003). However, not all of the attention has been negative. *Washout: On the Academic Response to the Fabrication of Aboriginal History* (Dawson, 2004) is something of a counter-offensive aimed at Windschuttle's critics and those left-wing academics who generally support what has been called the "new Aboriginal historiography." Windschuttle's published polemics have ushered in the latest phase of the struggle over representation of the nation's past, which continues with the publication in 2009 of Windschuttle's latest sortie, *The Fabrication of Aboriginal History, Volume 3: The Stolen Generations, 1881–2008*. This latest offensive attacks the idea that Aboriginal children were forcibly removed from their parents as part of systematically racist government policies. By effectively writing history as a guilt-free narrative, Windschuttle, an apologist for Australia's past, seems to be committed to challenging every aspect of established Aboriginal historiography.

The comments from Blainey, Donnelly, Howard, Windschuttle, and a host of conservative journalists reflect what might be described as a "white backlash" against the "radical histories" of the new History curriculum that emerged in the early 1990s, and a politically motivated attempt to discredit the reformist agenda of the Left by constructing "political correctness" as an attack on Australian culture (Clark, 2004). What is common in each of the criticisms documented above is the accusation that the new historiography is politically motivated and ideologically laden, while the critic's own version of history is "just the facts." It seems that the New Right from which such criticisms emerge yearns nostalgically for an unproblematic "white history" that has been "naturalized" to the point of its conflation with "reality" and the "real past." Such strategies are obviously ignorant of, and complicit with, the process by which "white privilege" and "white history" are rendered invisible and universal by presenting the "white story" as "common sense." However, the strategies of these neoconservatives indicate a desire to return to a "whitewashed history" that, in their color-blind ways, they see as "history as it was." By this they mean as it "really" was, and as it used to be taught. On the contemporary scene, the conservative position is committed to "the myth of realism" that conflates white history with history itself, as if "whiteness" meant translucent, without filters or "colored" lenses (Apple, 2004b; Kelen, 2005; Tonkin, 1990).

When Prime Minister Howard engaged in linking the narrative of the West with history, effectively selling our "white mythologies" as common sense, he did so for reasons both personal and political. Scholars have identified the values that underpin "white history" as a genre: a commitment to monotheism; liberal democracy; progress; industrialization; national unity; and law and order (Ferro, 1981; Preiswerk & Perrot, 1978). Such values are implicit in the histories of countries across Europe and the English-speaking world, and are what distinguishes "white history" from histories from other parts of the world. It is this set of "liberal" values—and not just a particular narrative—that Howard and his supporters saw as under threat by "black armband" histories. It is a position Howard appears to share, whether he admits it or not, with the one-time leader of the populist ultraconservative One Nation Party, Pauline Hanson. It is a position Howard continued to capitalize on throughout his political candidacy as he sought a power base among the white disenfranchised, who were perceived to have suffered at the hands of Keating's "depression we had to have" in the 1980s and were feeling nauseated by an apparently value-free diet of political correctness.

It is therefore possible to read the white backlash to the struggle for histories as a reaction to what Weis, Proweller, and Centrie (2004) describe as white working-class masculinity under siege. Although their analysis centers on the United States, it is equally applicable to the Australian context. The large losses of male-dominated jobs in labor-intensive industries during the economic restructuring of the 1980s; an increasing number of nonwhite immigrants moving into the suburbs, resulting in a sense of territorial encroachment; and challenges for dominance in the home as the result of gender role contestation all have resulted in men no longer having any definable material sphere in which they can openly assert patriarchal power. It is this sense of loss or disenfranchisement that has been capitalized on by New Right governments in both the United States and Australia, and it has resulted in the disturbing success of movements such as Hanson's One Nation Party in Australia. Feeling a sense of loss and disadvantage, however factual or illusory this may have been, white working-class males in the 1990s were eager to accept the political rhetoric of a conservative elite that implicated "political correctness" and "black armband" histories as responsible for the dethroning of patriarchy, and subsequently, the sense of cultural despair. The New Right's strategy gave them permission to recommit themselves to the "white mythology," a triumphant version of the national past that offered comfort to whites eager to reclaim their rightful status in Australian society. Howard's 2006 Australia Day speech on January 26 repeated his Blainey-inspired rhetoric of getting the balance of history right, and argued that a sense of national unity, to be provided by a History curriculum that focused on a coherent (all-embracing) narrative, was essential in the fight against "terror," his new Orwellian opponent.

Like conservatives in the United States, the United Kingdom, and Canada, Howard in his criticism of "black armband" history, and his call for a return to a triumphant national narrative, fails to understand that judgments made by serious historians are always cautious, tentative, and subject to ongoing investigation and careful evaluation. When criticizing the fact that particular perspectives on the past are taught in schools, Howard and his supporters would do well to remember that:

> [H]istorical knowledge is contingent; multiple perspectives on the past must be explored because people under study are seldom of one mind; historical objectivity should be pursued, but it can never be completely achieved; and . . . the historian's writings can never be detached from the persona of the writer. (Nash, et al., 1998, p. 40)

Dening is even more exacting about the dilemmas of history when he asserts that histories are "transformations of the past into expressions . . . they refer to a past in making a present . . . Histories are metaphors of the past . . . but histories are also metonymies of the present" (1996, p. 37). In other words, the meaning of "the past" is given to it from the present. Whatever meaning it once had as a living present is now more or less unrecoverable. That is not to say that the past provides nothing in this exchange; of course it does, as it operates as the ground of interpretation. What we have given up when we follow Dening's position is not meaning but certainty.

## Culture Wars and the Curriculum: Manufacturing the "Good Citizen"

Although the 1992 syllabus was a landmark document in the evolution of History curriculum in NSW, by the end of the 1990s the public backlash against "political correctness," the growing strength of the New Right at the national level, and a state Labor premier with a personal interest in history resulted in pressure placed upon education authorities to revise the curriculum once again. Installed as NSW premier in 1994, Bob Carr was keen to see History continued as a compulsory subject across Years 7-10 with emphasis on history as a definable body of knowledge, and coupled with a public examination for the school certificate at the end of Year 10, as a way of increasing academic rigor and teacher accountability (C. Harris, 2004). Carr's plans for history were paralleled by a directive from the federal Liberal government that required state education authorities to find ways of incorporating national "civics and citizenship" initiatives into the humanities curriculum. Following an inquiry conducted by the Civics Expert Group into the best way for civics and citizenship to be delivered, it was decided that in NSW civics and citizenship education should become part of the History curriculum. Interestingly, although historian Stuart Macintyre (1997) described the notion of using History curriculum to deliver civics and citizenship education as an innovation, its original appearance as a school subject in NSW around 1830 emphasized loyalty to the empire and civic duty. Far from being innovative, the idea to utilize History to produce the "good citizen" of the nation simply returned History to one of its original curricular purposes. In fact, there was discussion of the relationship between History and Civics education in Australia throughout the twentieth century. See, for example, Long's claim that the value of History as a school subject was "the bearing it has on the proper discharge of the duties of citizenship" (1909, p. 11); T. S. Hall's argument "that civics is not an independent school subject, but is necessarily dependent upon the teaching of history" (1914, p. 630) and his claim that "all history teaching should aim at creating an atmosphere of civic responsibility" (1914, p. 630); the discussion of History as self-evidently related to Civics education in Currey (1930); and "the incorporation of civics into comprehensive courses on Australian history or into Social Studies courses," depending on which state one was looking at, in the early 1950s (Collins, 1953, p. 92). Thus, the relationship between History and Civics education was well established by the time the call for a new History syllabus with a focus on civics and citizenship arose in NSW late in the 1990s.

The timing of the call for History curriculum to become the vehicle of civics and citizenship education and the release of a new syllabus after significant public debates over the teaching of the nation's past was hardly coincidental. Although the development of the 1998 syllabus followed a general trend in curriculum renewal, it was certainly ahead of schedule: previous revisions of the History curriculum had occurred approximately a decade apart. The production of the 1998 syllabus was accompanied by rhetoric about falling standards within History education, concerns over the politicization of curriculum content, and alarmist calls for a return to a more "traditional" History curriculum that would simply "tell the past as it was" (S. Macintyre, 1997; Nile, 2002). The importance of school History as a battlefield in the history wars of the 1990s should not be underestimated, given that curriculum performs an important role in the social reproduction of national identities by operating as a vehicle for national histories that connect the development of individuals to narratives and images of nationhood (Clark, 2004; Popkewitz, et al., 2001).

When the new syllabus was released by the NSW Board of Studies in 1998, some commentators suggested that the directive to incorporate civics and citizenship education into History curriculum was used as a lever to produce a totally reactionary document that signaled a return to the 1950s- and 1960s-style curriculum. According to Halse and Harris, the 1998 syllabus was significant in its return to "chronological history"; its movement away from an "issues-based" model due to "content overload"; its movement towards a preference for content over skills; and its incorporation of a focus on civics and citizenship that could "be seen as an effort to extol a particular vision of nationalism" (Halse & Harris, 2004, p. 20). As in the Canadian case I discuss below, the 1998 syllabus proved very unpopular with teachers, who were used to a syllabus that honored multiple perspectives, provided flexibility for teachers, and was not obsessed with nationalistic models of civics education. Consequently, the 1998 syllabus was superseded in 2003 by a syllabus that was more positively received, but it too will be annulled when the historic Australian K-10 History curriculum is released in 2012.

Looking back over the twentieth century, Schlesinger sees the conflation of history and civic nationalism as a "corruption of history . . . [that] continues to thrive because it taps into potent emotions of history and locality to give individual lives meaning in an increasingly baffling universe" (1992, p. 47). On both sides of politics, the central category for the analysis of history is the construct of "nation," which remains unproblematized in most debates and often is at the root of attempts to determine a shared public memory of the past. Typically, the type of nationalism that fuels these history wars is a racialized nationalism. The situation in Australia is little different. The political interest in school History comes out of the recognition that controlling what is taught as history is a way of influencing the course of the future. As I have noted repeatedly in this book, "the stories we tell ourselves about the past have serious consequences both for how we understand the present and for how we can imagine alternative futures" (Nugent, 2003, p. 33). Thus, given the politician's skill at manufacturing consent, the desire to produce a hegemonic narrative of the nation that speaks to and from one's own political position is probably irresistible (Curthoys, 2003).

In the United States in late 1994, Lynne Cheney, a conservative scholar, media personality, wife of the soon-to-be vice president Dick Cheney, and outgoing chair of the National Endowment for the Humanities, incited a culture war with an article in the *Wall Street Journal* criticizing the new National Standards for History education. Despite praise for the standards in public hearings and reviews, the endorsement of the National Council for History Standards, and affirmations of support from across the spectrum of participating organizations, Cheney's reservations about the National Standards triggered a media frenzy that was decidedly negative and prejudicial. Critics in the national press repeated the litany of culture war fighting phrases that have become common to the history wars across the English-speaking world, including the ideologically loaded terms *multiculturalists, revisionists, politically correct liberals*, and so on (Nash, et al., 1998, p. 197). Like the NSW case, the fight over the National Standards for History in the United States demonstrated a perception among the conservative intelligentsia that the nation's history was being hijacked for sectarian and minority political interests, while the triumphs of the mainstream majority were put in second place. Arguably, it was another example of white paranoia in which the curriculum came to represent the crucible of citizenship and cultural identity, and any attack on national mythologies was perceived to be an attack on national identity and thus the nation itself. In common with the controversy over the 1992 NSW History syllabus, the challenge to the National Standards in the United States demonstrated a concern that it was "historically false to view the entire panorama of . . . [national] history as one long conflict about race and gender, in which all ethnic groups except white males are portrayed as victims" (Phyllis Schlafly cited in Nash, et al., 1998, p. 219). Motivated by a perception that the collective memory of the nation was at risk, conservative commentators conflated history with public memory, and rather than supporting a

History curriculum in which students learn the skills of critical inquiry, source analysis, and considered judgment, they fought to install their own "version of the civic religion" (Kenneth Moynihan cited in Nash, et al., 1998, p. 277).

Politicians with ambitions to use the History curriculum as a vehicle for dispensing a diet of collective memory, national identity, and state mythology would do well to study G. H. Richardson's 2002 research on Canadian teachers working amidst the politicization of school History in Canada. According to Richardson, the articulation of national identity in the Canadian curriculum emerges from his research as a series of "frozen tropes" that have become irrelevant to both history teachers and their students: "Required to teach a curriculum whose assumptions and legitimacy they no longer uncritically assume, teachers find themselves trapped between the mythic structure of modernism and the postmodern realities the classroom presents to them" (G. H. Richardson, 2002, p. 135). This led Richardson to the conclusion that living with ambiguous conceptions of national identity is critically important for educators and their students living in postmodern pluralist societies. His research documents how working with this "ambiguity of identity" rather than a fixed national self allows teachers to seize the historical imagination and investigative passion of their students, for whom these issues have an immediate relevance. However, no discourse is ever innocent of a will to power, whether counter-revisionist (reactionary) or "black armband." So, it would be unfortunate if we avoided the teaching of national narratives altogether, because historical narratives provide templates that assist people to think intelligently about contemporary problems and issues, and "have the potential to provide personal moorings" (Nash, et al., 1998, p. 9).

One solution is to demonstrate the contingent nature of our social and cultural institutions that often are exhibited within traditional forms of history as unchanging, because presenting the world in this way creates the possibility of altering it (Nehamas, 1985). This is an activity that is frequently mentioned as a desired practice in the texts of critical pedagogues (whose work is discussed later in this chapter). What governments in our postindustrial, and/or postcolonial democracies need to realize is that

> lively debate over the meaning of the past and its relation to today's affairs does not signal national disunity and deterioration; rather it is a sign of a vibrant democracy. On the other hand, when these debates become rancorous and politicized, they threaten to impede the national mission to cure ourselves of historical amnesia. (Nash, et al., 1998, p. 272)

Certainly, we should be wary of any History that simply attempts to install a set of collective memories. The good historian produces a history that "organizes and exceeds memory, refusing to conflate the two" (A.-L. Shapiro,

1997, p. 130), and while history and memory both view the past from the perspective of the present, they both must be used to resist the desire to fix history, and they must be willing to make collective memories available for scrutiny, challenge, and revision (Popkewitz, et al., 2001). This critical engagement with history is unlikely to be achieved if stakeholders let governments dictate the national narrative taught in schools. As Peter Lee asserts, "History in schools is too important to be left to the politicians" (1991, p. 63).

## National History and the Challenge of Public Memory

One way of developing an understanding about what is at stake in the battle over the content of school History is to explore the historical narrative as a site of public or collective memory. The work in this area is useful for helping us to understand what happened to History curriculum after "the end of (metanarrative) history," particularly in terms of the development of Australia's 1992 syllabus and its replacement in 1998 by a more conservative document, because the territory that is contested in these curriculum documents might be read as the territory of collective or public memory.

In recent years, the complex and problematic relationship between history and memory has become one of the most important preoccupations in the historiographic field. There are many reasons why "memory" made its reappearance in academic circles after having been relegated to the religious domain and its practices of "remembrance" (Klein, 2000). One reason is linked to the perceived inability of the historical narrative to adequately capture the horror and experience of events such as the Shoah (LaCapra, 1998). Another is that talk of collective memory provides a new way to understand history after the collapse of history as a grand story, because the sense of "subjectivity" carried by the idea of memory readily invokes ideas of struggle over whose version of events gets sanctioned and "remembered" by the establishment. Thus, memory's "partial, fragmented, transient, and allusive nature become a kind of trope of memory that proposes itself . . . as a counter-historiographical force . . . [and a] discursive field available for analysis as part of the genealogy of the modem soul" (Spiegel, 2002, p. 150). The danger is that memory becomes positioned as somehow more "authentic" than history by laying claim to a vividness and psychic presence that is more accessible to public consciousness than the arcana of historical scholarship, despite warnings that the accuracy of a memory does not correspond to its vividness (Engel, 1999).

The idea that memory is not only a subjective experience, that it also operates as a collective phenomenon, is not a new concept; it can be traced back to scholars such as Hugo von Hofmannsthal and Maurice Halbwachs, who introduced the idea of "collective memory" in the early part of the twentieth century. Halbwachs (1950/1980) was careful to separate collective memory from history, arguing that the former lives in the consciousness of the group, keeping the memory alive and operating as a repository for tradition, whereas the latter operates as an impartial record of events. Although Halbwachs's conception of history now seems rather dated, his notion of collective memory raises an important point about the social, but discrete, ownership of public memory. Following Halbwachs's logic, history is made up of narratives that have been objectively verified and have universal applicability, whereas collective memory is an artifact of a particular social group's cultural repository. In this light, the history wars are the outcome of one group asserting its "cultural memory" over others. Such collective or cultural memory is, as Roth argues, "the key to personal and collective identity" (1995b, p. 8), and it ensures that memory itself is a battlefield upon which we engage in public struggles over different versions of the historical past. Thus, cultural identity is one of the potential causalities for those members of a group who lose the struggle to establish their group's collective memory as the public account of the past.

Historians have argued that history must critically test and remain suspicious of memory, that its mission is to suppress or destroy memory, by which they mean that the rigor of producing a history makes it an altogether different process than simply memorizing or remembering something that has occurred (LaCapra, 1998; Nora, 1995). From this viewpoint, history becomes a process of sorting, filtering, copying, rejecting, selecting, constructing, reworking, and ultimately sanctioning memories, whether they are our own or those of our broader communities and nations. Helping us to remember but also to forget, historical narratives "shape our social reality as much by what they exclude as what they include" (McLaren, 1995, p. 236). History, in this sense, becomes an important act of remembrance while it simultaneously works to erase conflicting alternative perceptions of "the past" from public memory. Thus, inclusion and exclusion are part of the same process of memorization, operating through the production of historical narratives, and in the construction of historical exhibits. Collingwood was thus correct when he asserted that history "does not depend upon memory" (1946/1994, p. 238); rather, memory depends on history.

The attempt to engage in "remembrance" of the past at a public level—to "escape from amnesia" (Urry, 1994)—is nowhere as obvious as it is in the museum. When a museum exhibit is constructed, artifacts are collected and arranged according to the concerns of the curator and, one might add, a range of cultural assumptions and a cultural perception of time and history (Karp & Lavine, 1991; D. D. Wilson, 2000). The illusion conjured by the nineteenth-century museum curator that objects could speak for themselves has given way to a new regime in which objects are "given meaning" by being arranged according to historically determined categories. The display of objects in "historical associations" in a modern exhibit is no less a product of a "regime of truth" than the display of artifacts in isolated display cases, organized according to the authority of "scientific" taxonomies, in the nineteenth-century museum. As studies of the changing form of museums over the past two centuries demonstrate, there is nothing "natural" about either of these arrangements. Those objects that make it into an exhibit (and those that are left out), as well as their placement in relation to one another, and in what sequence, constitute an attempt to tell a particular story, and thus to shape or "colonize" collective memory (Hooper-Greenhill, 1992). This also is true of "the archive" or library, which affects collective memory by tightly controlling "archival memory" through the documents it makes available in its collections (Sassoon, 2003).

Identifying the strategic processes at work in the formation of museum exhibits and library collections does not suggest that they can be avoided. The artifact once placed in a museum or added to the collection of a library becomes inevitably a rhetorical object (Bennett, 1995), and the goal of the "rhetoric object" is to mediate the viewer's relationship with "the past"; to legitimize through its cultural authority—and the force of the presence of its selected artifacts—a particular view of history. As much as the written historical narrative, and the archive from which documents are drawn, the museum is engaged in the production of a specific knowledge of the past that attempts to discipline and constitute the "public memory" of its interlocutors. The museum exhibit thus is not value-free; it is the product of a political agenda, intended or otherwise, that produces "public memory" rather than simply preserving it (S. Macdonald, 1996; Riegel, 1996).

This process of producing a collective consciousness of "the past" is often achieved at the expense of heterogeneity. It typically sanctions particular accounts while delegitimating others. It "invents" nations through its construction of a shared national narrative (Anderson, 1983; Gellner, 1994). The danger of this process of legitimation and delegitimation, of producing a single uniform historical narrative, has been demonstrated numerous times during the twentieth century when totalitarian governments acted to deliberately blot out certain memories from the national consciousness, effectively denying to specific people or particular groups a place in history (Todorov, 2001). In such cases, school History becomes a vehicle for sharing official stories of the nation. Often, the result is a pedagogy of indoctrination whose only antidote, according to Nash, Crabtree, and Dunn, is to encourage the "analysis and interpretation of the past based on rigorous weighing and judging of evidence from a variety of original sources" (1998, pp. 33-34). This is a useful strategy against universal history, assuming that a variety of sources are available to historians, and their alternative accounts are accessible to the wider society. In the totalitarian regimes of the twentieth century in which history was tightly controlled, however, this assumes a luxury that simply was not available.

## On the Pedagogy of Interjection: Counter-Memory as Critical History

Given the potentially political nature of the History curriculum, particularly when viewed as a venue for the production and circulation of public memory, radical educators frequently have advocated History and the Social Studies as a site for "critical" approaches to pedagogy. Interestingly, the curriculum shift in NSW represented by the 1992 syllabus, which involved what might be called a "pedagogy of interjection," coincided with an attempt among curriculum theorists in the United States (most significantly, Henry Giroux and Peter McLaren) and in Canada (most notably, Roger Simon) to develop a "critical pedagogy." Although I make no claim of a connection between these movements, the NSW History curriculum debates of the early 1990s paralleled the emergence of critical pedagogy in the United States, and it reflected wider social and intellectual trends that resulted in the simultaneous development in Australia of "critical literacy" and a "New English" (Green, 1995). Thus, a way of understanding the changes wrought by the 1992 syllabus is to conceptualize it as opening the space for a "critical" approach to History education.

Critical pedagogy often is described as a reaction against the technorational form of curriculum theorizing that aims at cultural transmission and reproduction. Although there is no single form of critical pedagogy, its multiple versions grow out of a common set of issues, problems, and conditions centered on the political nature of schooling and society. A fundamental assumption of critical pedagogy is that it is a broad educational venture that questions and negotiates the relationships between theory, practice, language, learning, power, and social change. It seeks to confront and transform the social norms and dominant values of our culture by challenging teachers and teacher educators to explore their own histories and to attempt to understand how our class, gender, and ethnic experiences have left their mark on how we think and act. Thus, critical pedagogy requires students to critically interrogate their personal histories, situating their lived experience in its "historicality-sociality" (Giroux, 2007; McLaren, 1998). Critical pedagogy recognizes "that all knowledge is created within a historical context," and that viewing knowledge as the product of a particular historical moment places emphasis on the "discontinuities, conflicts, differences, and tensions in history" (Darder, Baltodano, & Torres, 2003, p. 12). Thus, it should not surprise the reader to find Giroux advocating a "pedagogy of public memory" that "rejects the notion of knowledge as merely an inheritance with transmission as its only form of practice" (2000, p. 36).

The proposal to use History as a tool of "public" or "counter-memory" forms something of a recurring theme in critical pedagogy. "Skilled in the language of public memory" (Giroux, 2000, p. 36), the radical educator is admonished by Giroux "to develop a critical watch over the relationship between historical events and the ways in which those events are produced and recalled through the narratives in which they unfold" (2000, p. 36). He argues that:

> public memory suggests that history be read not merely as an act of recovery but as a dilemma of uncertainty, a form of address and remembering that links the narratives of the past with the circumstances of its unfolding and how such an unfolding or retelling is connected to "the present relations of power." (Giroux, 2000, pp. 36-37)

In other words, a critical History pedagogy works against the hijacking of collective memory by recognizing that historical knowledge is always the object of a political struggle. A pedagogy emerging from such a position sees History as the practice of "counter-memory," where "counter-memory represents a critical reading of how the past informs the present and the present reads the past" (Aronowitz & Giroux, 1991, p. 124).

The practice of counter-memory is often associated with Michel Foucault, who wanted "to write the history or trace the archaeology of what they [the medical, penal, psychiatric or pedagogical establishment] silenced, repressed, or excluded in constituting themselves and the institutions that house them" (LaCapra, 2000, p. 130). As a pedagogical practice in History classes, counter-memory is best aligned with "history from below"—"the rewriting of history through the power of [once silenced] student voice" (Giroux, 1995, p. 51). However, it has been suggested by Giroux that "remembrance as counter-memory opens up the past, not as nostalgia, but as *the invention of stories*" (1995, pp. 53-54, my emphasis); and the practice of counter-memory invites students "to *reclaim their identities* through the production of different historical narratives" (1995, p. 51, my emphasis). Rather than thinking about identity as static, and an already accomplished outcome, "we should think, instead, of identity as a 'production,' which is never complete, always in process, and always constituted within, not outside, representation. This view problematizes the very authority and authenticity to which the term, 'cultural identity,' lays claim" (S. Hall, 1997, p. 110). If we take seriously the idea that as "posthistorical subjects" we are all cyborgs, hybrids, or chimeras, then *reclamation of identity* would of necessity involve the recognition of ourselves as the site of intersection of a range of often conflicting, inscriptive forces, perhaps subject to multiple interpellations in the same moment. This provides us with the possibility of writing new scripts for ourselves that open the possibility of greater freedom, given appropriate tools to do so, rather than being limited by a nonnegotiable past.

Counter-memory as a practice would seem to be particularly useful in schools, because sociologists of school knowledge interested in curriculum reform often have argued that public schooling has a history of bureaucratic regulation and individual repression. However, it is naïve to believe that "minorities and the poor simply accept the efforts of the educational professions to mould them in the image dictated by the nation's political and social elite" (Popkewitz, et al., 2001, p. 11). Following a similar line, Simon (2000) argues that school is better conceptualized as a sphere of "transactive memory." It is Simon's view that

> memory is not just that which contributes to knowledge of the past and/or underwrites a claim to group or communal membership . . . memory may become transactional, enacting a claim on us, providing accounts of the past that may wound or haunt—that may interrupt one's self-sufficiency by claiming an attentiveness to an otherness that cannot be reduced to a version of our own stories. (Simon, 2000, p. 63)

In his detailed treatment of "transactional memory," Simon argues that:

> [I]f the limits of historical memory are fully constrained by notions of identity and identification, the possibilities for transactive public memory are clearly limited. For in such identity-based affiliations begins the refusal to take other people's memories seriously, as of no concern, as having nothing to do with you, as not your responsibility, unless, perhaps, one can forge an identification between one's own troubles and traumas and those of others. (Simon, 2000, p. 64)

In many ways, this is a description of the problems involved in the reaction to the 1992 History syllabus in NSW. There are few conservative politicians and historians who would support Simon's "pedagogy of transactive memory," which facilitates a situation in which one's memories of the past are placed alongside potentially opposing narratives, allowing for the possibility that one's own stories might be challenged and shifted as a result of the encounter with the stories of others.

Unconcerned by the inevitable resistance to his form of critical pedagogy, Simon asserts that "a transactive memory has the potential to expand that ensemble of people who count for us" (2000, p. 63). That is, we may come to empathize with the situation of others by hearing the recounting of public memories from their perspective. In this case, school becomes a transactional space, simultaneously connecting us with marginal narratives and problematizing the monomyths of our culture. Simon's pedagogy of transactive memory thus resists any tendency to reiterate valued stories that attempt to secure collective affiliations and shared identifications in a stable notion of the past. Instead, he argues that it must evoke an unrelenting sense "not of belonging but of being in relation to, of being claimed in relation to the experience of others" (2000, p. 63). In Simon's pedagogy of transactive memory there is the possibility of a critical History pedagogy that is the analogue of the changes made to the NSW History curriculum in the early 1990s that makes strange our collective memories by making us live the struggle for histories in our classrooms.

## On the Limitations of Counter-Memory as Critical History

Despite its good intentions, since the late 1980s critical pedagogy has sustained considerable criticism. Unlike the situation of the "new histories" of the 1992 syllabus, the most insistent critique has not come from a powerful New Right, but from fellow radicals working in the growing field of postmodern and poststructuralist feminist scholarship. Critical pedagogues such as Giroux and McLaren have been accused by a succession of poststructuralist feminists of using rhetoric that constructs the illusion of equality while leaving the power relations of the teacher/student relationship undisturbed. They have been criticized for overstating the power of rationality to free the subject from constraining metanarratives; for narrowly identifying power with forces of exploitation and repression; for not getting beyond the "missionary position" (Ellsworth, 1989; McWilliam, 1997; Yates, 1992). Further, critics have argued that failing to develop "a coherent and systematic engagement with theorisation of 'gender'" has led critical pedagogy to "an acritical reinstatement and revalorisation of history's 'great' patriarchal metanarratives" (Luke & Gore, 1992, p. 25). Added to this, Ellsworth argues that terms in the technical lexicon of critical pedagogy such as "'empowerment,' 'student voice,' 'dialogue,' and even the term 'critical'— are repressive myths that perpetuate relations of domination" (1989, p. 298), because "the intrinsically asymmetrical conditions of classrooms precluded the sort of dialogue envisioned by critical pedagogy" (Stanley, 1992, p. 142) that often unwittingly imposes its own set of particular communicative norms (Burbules, 2000). Gore (1992) has likewise questioned the notion of a pedagogy of "empowerment," as it appears to privilege those doing the empowering and thus fails to avoid the very relations of power it proposes to subvert. Further, it has been argued that radical pedagogy discourses have tended to hold zero-sum conceptions of power that over-simplify power relations and lead "to a kind of self righteousness that claims innocence, and risks the replacement of one orthodoxy with another," particularly through a tendency to generate grand narratives of its own (Gore, 1991, p. xx). While these critiques of critical pedagogy are undeniably important, there are other reasons for being cautious about a critical pedagogy of counter-memory as a way of teaching History.

The scholarship and climate of reform that influenced the production of the 1992 syllabus points to the impossibility of producing a standpoint-free history. At the level of curriculum documentation, this realization manifested in the 1992 syllabus as a call to teach History from multiple perspectives. However, my concern from the viewpoint of history theory is that such a strategy is only ever a partial solution to the problem of history, operating exclusively at the level of "content." As was the case in British Columbia, Canada, the interjection of counter-narratives into the curriculum "complicate[s] the nation-building story... [but] do[es] not necessarily upset it" (Seixas, 2000, p. 22). Based on an oppositional politics, the critical pedagogy of counter-memory often works to valorize narratives of the past emerging from the margins while challenging blind acceptance of "master narratives based on white, patriarchal, and class-specific versions of the world" (Aronowitz & Giroux, 1991, p. 120).

This kind of "pedagogy of polemics" involves pitting one version of the past against another in the hope of arriving at the kind of personal transformation sought by Simon through his pedagogy of transactive public memory. However, though it is likely that a pedagogy of counter-memory will support students in uncovering the vested interests behind various claims on the past, it is equally possible that it will achieve little more than creating conflict between those holding opposing views. In fact, according to Ashcroft in his analysis of cultural transformation in postcolonial societies, those deploying strategies of interjection typically accept (or at least appear to accept) "the basic premises of historical narrative," but supply "a contrary narrative, which claims to offer a more immediate or 'truer' picture... a record of those experiences omitted from imperial history" (2001, p. 101). The resultant game of truth between competing narratives, particularly where perspectives may differ but there is general agreement on "the facts," arguably places students in a situation in which celebration of "a democratic, multi-cultural, multi-perspectival, pluralism of historical approaches" leaves them able to adjudicate between alternative histories only on the basis of their own "political sympathies" (Fulbrook, 2002, p. 9). Indeed, it is likely that what this approach to History pedagogy does is to enshrine a cultural relativism that blunts critique rather than enhances it, making it politically incorrect to make value judgments about opposing historical narratives, a fear widely held within the historical establishment (see Evans, 1997). Furthermore, although the idea of a pedagogy of transactive public memory is appealing, it may be idealistic in its projected effects, for there is little in Simon's description of the pedagogy of transactive public memory that guarantees students will come to value the standpoints of others, or see this as a desirable aim. In both forms of critical pedagogy, there is perhaps an overconfidence in the rationality of the student (Yates, 1992). What these approaches to critical History elide is direct attention to historical representation (as social practice and cultural artifact).

It should be noted that the call for a critical pedagogy that attends to representational practices is not absent from the literature. Giroux has frequently called for a pedagogy that interrogates representation, arguing for pedagogy as a form of cultural politics in which "the act of representing can be addressed historically and semiotically" (1994, p. 39). Likewise, Kaufmann has argued that critical pedagogy may be advanced "through a strategic postmodern interpretation of discursive formations as shifting constructions" (2000, p. 444). Thus, the neglect of attention to historical representation (as practice and artifact) in attempts to manifest a critical History curriculum should not be understood as a failure of critical pedagogy itself. Rather, the problem appears to be in the uptake or translation of only certain aspects of critical pedagogy. Regardless, it would seem that additional pedagogic attention needs to be paid to the way in which histories are produced and reproduced through the mediating effects of particular disciplinary practices, narrative forms, and cultural tools if critical pedagogies are to be useful to students navigating the struggle for histories.

CHAPTER FIVE

# Returning the Historiographer's Gaze

The critical pedagogy of counter-memory and pedagogy of transactive public memory advocated by radical theorists in the United States and Canada, respectively, were analogues of the critical approach to history adopted in New South Wales with the 1992 syllabus. Documenting some of the limitations of counter-memory as critical history, I concluded chapter 4 by expressing a concern that a pedagogy of counter-memory is only ever a partial solution to the problem of history because it operates almost exclusively at the level of competing "content," leaving unchallenged the practice and forms of historical representation. In this chapter, I explore the nature and impact of school History's null curriculum, rethinking critical History education in relation to postmodern theory and its theorization of history as historiography. I begin by revisiting some important concepts I developed in the chapter on critical-reconceptualist curriculum theory, and draw upon both pedagogical and historiographic heuristics for understanding approaches to History teaching, insisting that the null curriculum may be what curriculum as a knowledge system must reject in order to maintain its claims to truth. I argue that the neglect of historiography in the NSW mandatory History curriculum not only limits the tools students have available in a critical engagement with history, but also creates the very conditions of possibility for History curriculum itself. Registering the contributions of a number of contemporary scholars to the debate over the narrative nature of history, I argue that historiography is vital for any critical approach to the study of histories, but lethal for a History curriculum that desires to maintain its claim to truth. Attempts to introduce historiography as a discrete course of study in the senior school, such as the NSW Senior History Extension Course (Board of Studies NSW, 2000), have the effect of quarantining historiography, effectively inoculating the mandatory History curriculum against "the problem of historical representation." Finally, drawing upon Nietzsche's anti-historicist historiography, together with Bill Ashcroft's analysis of the modes of action by which postcolonial subjects resist interpellation and inscription within dominant representations of the historic past, I examine the implications of reclaiming historiography as the "unsayable" in History education. Arguing that a critical approach to history demands the possibility of disengaging from historical discourse, I propose engagement in "a pedagogy of interpolation" as an appropriate critical curricular response to the end of history.

Earlier in this book I mapped the field of curriculum studies and located my own work within a critical-reconceptualist trend in curriculum inquiry. Whereas reconceptualist inquiry began by adopting phenomenological or hermeneutic orientations to the study of educational experience (making sense of curriculum as autobiographical text), critical or radical curriculum theory was marked by its concern with education's role in the reproduction of social inequality (challenging curriculum as political text). Thus, critical-reconceptualist curriculum inquiry may be understood as an approach to curriculum theorizing that attempts to both understand and transform the practice of education. A second wave of critical-reconceptualist theory, marked by a poststructural turn, shifted the emphasis in more recent years towards greater diversity in forms of curriculum inquiry (Malewski, 2010; W. M. Reynolds & Webber, 2004), including the study of curriculum as knowledge systems that constitute particular rationalities via their inclusions and exclusions (Cherryholmes, 1987; Popkewitz, 1997). I argued that in order to understand how curricula construct specific "rationalities," it is useful to draw on Eisner's much earlier tripartite model of curriculum. Eisner's (1979) model proposed that students learn an explicit curriculum (documented in state or district policy and syllabus documents), an implicit curriculum (embodied in the school's daily routines and practices), and a null curriculum (constituted by the knowledge and practices that are neglected or ignored). Cherryholmes adds, "the explicit, implicit, and null curricular, together, express what is valued and dis-valued and determine the course of study" (2002, p. 118). Poststructurally speaking, as Bill Green once shared with me, these three curricula may be interpreted as equivalents of the said (explicit curriculum), the unsaid (implicit curriculum), and the unsayable (null curriculum). One way of approaching postmodern critical-reconceptualist curriculum inquiry, therefore, is to study curriculum as a knowledge system that makes available, either explicitly or implicitly, particular forms of reasoning defined and constituted in part by the neglect or denial of alternate forms of reasoning. It is my argument that historiography—as the study of historical representation—functioned as a null curriculum within History education in NSW during the period under study; and that it has been likewise absent from discussion during the culture wars in the United Kingdom, Canada, and the United States.

A null curricula can arise for a variety of reasons, including "neglect because important questions of purpose and intent are not thought about and not asked . . . because of conservatism and a desire to maintain the status quo . . . [or] the decision to take one direction in a curriculum rather than another" (Stimpson, 1991, pp. 11-12). The least likely etiology of the 1992 NSW History syllabus' neglect of historiography was a desire to maintain the status quo, given its unique mandating of Australian history and its subversive valorization of counter-narratives of the nation. It is far more likely that as it had never been a part of the NSW History curriculum before, historiography was simply not considered a necessary part of the explicit curriculum. Although there is no real evidence for this, it may have been considered likely to arise in a general way during introductory discussion of history as method, mandated in the explicit curriculum, or in an ad hoc way, as part of the implicit curriculum, emerging through the teaching of rival national narratives. However, from a poststructuralist standpoint, there is a more significant reason why historiography has remained absent from school curricula.

According to poststructuralist theory, "rationalities" are the product of cultural-historical knowledge systems that define themselves as much by what they include as what they exclude. For example, according to Foucault (1965/1988), "reason" itself, as a construct of the European Enlightenment, was defined by its rejection of certain forms of behavior that now constitute what we know as "madness." For Foucault, "madness" does not describe some essential quality or condition of a human being. Rather, madness was historically constituted by "the caesura that establishes the distance between reason and non-reason, reason's subjugation of non-reason" (Foucault, 1965/1988, p. ix). Foucault asserts that his understanding of how systems of reasoning define themselves through the dynamic of what they include and exclude came as a result of his attempt "to see how these problems of constitution could be resolved within a historical framework, instead of referring them back to a constituent object (madness, criminality, or whatever)" (Foucault, 1972/1994, p. 118). We can take from this argument that concepts such as madness, criminality, sexuality, and even history do not refer to "essences," but remain floating signifiers whose meaning changes in different sociocultural and temporal contexts constituted by a system of justified, institutionalized, and operationalized differentiations that permit and enable one to act upon the actions of others. Thus, applying Foucault's insight to education, we could say that curriculum operates as a set of "justified, institutionalized, and operationalized differentiations" of particular forms of knowledge and reasoning, and that it is the exercise and embodiment of a "relation of power" that "puts into operation differences that are, at the same time, its conditions and its results" (Foucault, 1982/1994, p. 344).

These conditions and effects of curriculum as a "relation of power" should not be understood as simply repressive, but as actually productive of particular rationalities. As Foucault asserts, "the notion of repression is quite inadequate for capturing what is precisely the productive aspect of power" (1972/1994, p. 120). According to his analyses,

> what makes power hold good, what makes it accepted, is simply the fact that it doesn't only weigh on us as a force that says no; it also traverses and produces things, it induces pleasure, forms knowledge, produces discourse. It needs to be considered as a productive network that runs through the whole social body, much more than a negative instance whose function is repression. (Foucault, 1972/1994, p. 120)

Thus, the function of a curriculum that justifies its differentiations of knowledge on the basis of precedent or purpose, institutionalizes these differentiations via apparatuses such as policy and syllabus documents, and operationalizes these differentiations through particular forms of pedagogy or statewide examinations, is the production of particular "rationalities" rather than others. When curriculum is understood in this way, the null curriculum becomes that which cannot be said without challenging the "rationality" of the system.

As a result of differentiating history from historiography—an enduring legacy of the nineteenth century—History curriculum treats the representational practices and forms of history as objective, rational, natural, universal, unchanging, and unproblematic, because historiography as a metatheoretical discourse is that "system of reasoning" that extends the gaze of the historian to everything, even themselves, revealing the historical specificity of all forms of historical knowledge and practice. To maintain history's claim to truth, historiography (as metatheory) must remain "the unsayable," for if historiography as metatheory is made explicit, if it enters into historical discourse, then history is profoundly "interrupted." The result of this interruption is to render history's truths "relative" to time, place, culture, method, methodology, autobiography of the historian, and so on. Of course, this often scares historians who are reluctant to surrender realist epistemologies (see, for example, McCullagh, 2004). Without a metadisciplinary historiography, realism becomes a default logic that encourages focus on the success or otherwise of historical interpretations according to the methodological standards of the discipline. Any critique of a particular "history" thus remains "interior" to the disciplinary discourse. However, challenges have emerged from "exterior" discourses that open the possibility for a more profound form of criticism. It is my argument that the lack of historiography in the curriculum limits the possibilities for a critical

History. This can be demonstrated by examining Seixas's conceptualization of three possible approaches to History teaching.

According to Seixas's (2000) model, teachers may decide to present a single story as the best history we have available, perhaps because, as he notes elsewhere, this is the way they encounter history from historians (Seixas, 1999). He describes the approach of teaching "the best story" as enhancing collective memory. In the historiographic work of Jenkins and Munslow (2004), this approach to teaching history would seem to correspond with a "reconstructionist" epistemology held by those few historians who still claim to be able to *discover* through an "objective methodology" a "truthful interpretation" of the sources and to write up their "impartial thesis" in the form of an *unproblematic representation*. As I noted in chapter 4, many conservative politicians would have all schools adopt this approach to teaching history, given that it provides them with a sense of control over public memory. The 2006 Australia Day speech by conservative prime minister John Howard, in which he called for a return to teaching history as a "structured narrative" informed by "the central currents of our nation's development" (Howard, 2006, p. 4), is unreserved in its support for a reconstructionist pedagogy of collective memory. At its best, as Seixas suggests, this approach promises the possibility of group cohesion, shared identity, and common social purpose, echoed in the themes of Howard's Australia Day tome as "social cohesion" and "national unity" (Howard, 2006, p. 4). At its worst, it is likely to manifest in a doctrinaire, nostalgic, nation-centric "names and dates" pedagogy that has the potential to limit the development of more differentiated and sophisticated forms of historical consciousness.

An alternative approach identified by Seixas (2000), and one that parallels in some ways the advice of the 1992 syllabus, involves presenting conflicting interpretations of the past to students, with a view to reaching warranted conclusions about which interpretation best fits the available evidence that has been gleaned through studying a series of documents, including the assessments of other historians. In Jenkins and Munslow's (2004) heuristic, this approach seems to be underpinned by a "constructionist" epistemology held by historians who study the actions of people as members of groups, using a variety of forms and levels of social theory in order to develop more or less sophisticated forms of explanation. Constructionist historians use a range of concepts and theories such as race, class, gender, ethnicity, imperialism, colonialism, and nationalism to make sense of "the past." According to Jenkins and Munslow,

> unlike reconstructionists, constructionists accept that getting at *the* story is not simply assured by a detailed knowledge of the sources. However, for constructionists,

> knowing the truth of the past is still feasible in principle precisely because history is constructed through using the tools of sophisticated conceptualisation and social theory. (Jenkins & Munslow, 2004, pp. 11, emphasis in the original)

Given the constructionist's confidence in developing relatively reliable histories from the evidence, this approach is likely to engage students in learning "disciplinary criteria for what makes good history" (Seixas, 2000, p. 20), assuming that one is seeking to determine which interpretation among alternatives is the "best interpretation." Although the 1992 syllabus encouraged teachers to engage students in "historical inquiry" and to look at the past from "multiple perspectives" (underpinned by at least some understanding of social theory), the use of loaded words such as *invasion* in place of the traditional *settlement* to describe British colonization of Australia showed a commitment to a "constructionist pedagogy." Arguably, it also demonstrated the intrusion of a pedagogy of "collective memory," albeit one that operates as a pedagogy of "counter-memory" that has the potential to replace one master-narrative with another, even if that new master-narrative originated "from the margins." Of course, the 1992 syllabus does not preclude using different perspectives to push disciplined inquiry, but neither does it mandate or guarantee such an approach.

Importantly, engaging in disciplinary inquiry is not the equivalent of learning a metadisciplinary historiography, a point that Seixas acknowledges implicitly in his description of a third pedagogical strategy for teaching history that he depicts as a "postmodern" approach. According to Seixas, this third approach is identified by its resistance to any attempt to adjudicate between histories in terms of which story is the "best interpretation"; it aims instead to assist students to understand how different individuals and groups, as historical entities themselves, organize the traces of the past into histories, an approach that is distinctly historiographic in orientation. This approach seems to be based on what Jenkins and Munslow describe as a "deconstructionist" epistemology that engages historians in

> critique [of] correspondence and coherence theories of knowledge (referentiality); the notion of inference and the truthful statement (explanation to the best fit); the clear distinction between fact and fiction; the subject-object division (objectivity); representationalism (accurate representation), and the idea that the appropriate use of social theory (concept and argument) can generate truthful statements. (Jenkins & Munslow, 2004, p. 12)

Committed to an anti-representationalist position, deconstructionist historians often engage in the production of historical narratives that explore "the consequences of reversing the priority of content over form . . . experimenting with [various forms of] representation" (Jenkins & Munslow, 2004, p. 13).

Understanding history as a representational practice invites recognition that different groups, and indeed different historians, have organized their histories differently, underscoring Wineburg's assertion that historical thinking is an "unnatural act" (2001, p. 3). If we accept that history is in fact a thoroughly cultural-historical act, then systematic induction into the variety of methodologies, forms, and theories underpinning historical representation becomes even more pressing.

Without historiography, efforts to develop a critical History are inevitably limited to the questioning of particular interpretations, stopping short of questioning history as a disciplined form of knowing. A curriculum that neglects historiography can only be sustained by ignoring or rejecting the postmodern crisis of historical representation. It can be sustained only by allowing historical narrative to remain "outside" of history and historical discourse. Once a historical narrative is understood to be the artifact of a social/temporal situation, then the possibilities of resisting historical discourse become available. Thus, reclaiming historiography as the unsayable of historical discourse becomes a strategy for opening new curricular possibilities. In the section that follows, I explore important contributions to the postmodern debate over the nature of historical representation in order to begin the process of reclaiming historiography (as a metatheoretical discourse) for the development of a critical History curriculum.

## Theorizing History as Historiography

*Historiography*, like *history*, is a word with many meanings and associations. Sometimes it is used to refer to the study of the theories, methods and principles of historical research, the results of which are typically presented in the form of a historical narrative or typology that highlights changes and continuities in historical practice (see Iggers, 1997; and N. J. Wilson, 2005). It even may be used to define that category of texts that provide advice on research methods for aspiring historians. More importantly, it refers to literature that comments on methodological issues related to the practice of history as a discipline. It also has been used to refer to texts that explore or argue for a specific approach to historical research. *Historiography* also has been used to define studies that examine the writings of particular historians or philosophers of history as they relate to each other, a particular methodology, or a specific period, or writings that debate the reliability of the work of a particular group of historians. Likewise, the term may be used to refer to literature that attempts to describe or define the nature of historical research more generally. At other times, it has been used to refer to a discrete body of historical literature that focuses upon a particular topic—often using a common methodological approach—as in the use of a label such as "the new Aboriginal historiography" (see chapter 4). Further, it may be used to refer to existing findings and interpretations on a particular topic, answering the question about what we know at this point about a particular person, period, event, idea, culture, and so on. Finally, it may refer to the actual practice of writing histories, based on available methodologies. What these different meanings have in common is a focus on historiography as a metatheoretical discourse that explores the changing forms and methods of historical representation. Importantly, since the late 1960s a body of work has developed that collapses the distinction between history and historiography. In the discussion that follows, drawing upon the insights of postmodern theory and its critique of historical representation, I theorize history as historiography as a prelude to exploring possibilities for an appropriate "critical" curricular response to the end of history.

## Representation and the "Reality Effect"

I have argued at various points throughout this book that one of the central problems that postmodernism presents to history as both discipline and discourse is the problem of representation. Whether it is Rorty (1979) arguing that our representations can be said to constitute our "reality" rather than mirror it, Baudrillard (1995) arguing that reality and representation have imploded, Derrida (1976) arguing that there is nothing outside text, or R. J. C. Young (1990) arguing that what we think of as histories are actually "white mythologies," we are confronted with the problem of historical representation. Thompson has argued that "the concept of representation is at the heart of all postmodern thinking" (2004, p. 41), given that, from the perspective of postmodernism, our representations of the world constitute reality as we know it, and that, consequently, reality is never known outside of our systems of representation. As I noted in chapter 1, this does not mean that representations actually create the material world, but it does mean that our representations of reality predispose us to view and engage with the world in certain ways, leaving us in a Kantian state where "we can believe in reality but not know the true nature of things-in-themselves" (Munslow, 2003, p. 59). Thus, manifesting a "profound distrust of the idea that referential language works through mirroring or mapping reality" (Potter, 1996, p. 68), postmodern theory inverts our commonsense perspective that signs reflect things in the world and replaces it with the view that our understanding of things in the world is constituted by the semiotic systems we have inherited and appropriated.

In his essay "The Discourse of History," Barthes made his now famous pronouncement that "historical discourse is in its essence a form of ideological elaboration" (1967/1997, p. 121). Being a semiologist, and moving through both structuralist and poststructuralist phases of textual criticism, Barthes was, in a sense, arguing that "history" is historiography, a process of writing in which traces of the past are worked into a narrative form of representation. Barthes's skepticism about the truth-value of historical discourse did not come from the identification of biased content in a particular narrative, the weighing up of one historical account (or narrative) against another, or the testing of a narrative against the evidence. For Barthes, the recognition of the ideological nature of historical discourse emerged from an examination of the way in which historical narratives are structured. Any illusion of a direct link with the reality of the past is a result of the historian removing traces of their authorial presence from the text. The result is that the reader of a historical narrative is given the sense that what they are reading is fact rather than fiction (Kansteiner, 1993).

Barthes's claim was made amidst a series of debates in the French academy over the relationship between *histoire* and *discours* (the analogue, translation problems acknowledged, of English-speaking debates over the relationship between history and narrative). To some extent, his comments rested on arguments put forward by Morton White (1965) and Arthur Danto (1965), who asserted that narrative was the typical mode of explanation employed by historians. Barthes's argument prefigured much that was articulated later by scholars such as Hayden White at the level of rhetoric and Frank Ankersmit at the level of the statement. Barthes's contribution to theory—his argument that history was foremost a literary genre—paralleled other positions at the time. However, a number of those complementary constructions of history as story were derived, according to Ricoeur, "more from a psychology of reception than from a logic of configuration" (1983, p. 151), from research into reader expectation rather than from an analysis of textual form. The narrativist conception of history was also "advanced" in the work of Louis Mink, who argued that historical narrative was best understood as "an artifice, the product of individual imagination," that acted as a "cognitive instrument" whose function it was "not just to relate a succession of events but to body forth an ensemble of interrelationships of many different kinds as a single whole" (1978/2001, p. 218). Mink's vision of the events of the past being woven into a narrative whole was later seconded by Ricoeur, who described historical narrative as a "synthesis of heterogeneous elements" (2000, p. 297). Hans

Kellner's assertion that "the straightness of any story is a rhetoric invention" makes a similar point (1989, p. x). Together, these scholars developed a particular historiographic view of history in which the "real events" of the past are seen to be organized by the structuring effects of the narrative form, having no inherent structure in themselves. This view is sometimes referred to as "narrative impositionalism." The suggestion is that subject to the "gaze" and writing practices of the historian, the events of the past are transformed into, or reconceptualized as, a historical narrative. Alternatively, we could say that subject to the selective, ordering, recontextualizing strategies of the historian, the past becomes an object that we can "re-cognize" as history (Berkhoffer, 1995). Although many scholars have contributed to the narrative conception of history, and hence to this theorization of history as historiography, one theorist stands out in terms of the audacity of his claims and the impact of his ideas.

## Narrative, Rhetoric, and the Historical Imagination

The ideas of Hayden White have gotten a mixed reception from historians. Like Barthes, White has been accused of seeing historical narrative as "intrinsically no different than fictional narrative, except in its pretense to objectivity and referentiality" (Spiegel, 1987, p. 139). Sometimes White has been quite explicit about this, though he denies that he is saying that the past didn't really exist, or that certain events didn't really happen (H. White, 1978a). Sometimes characterized as an "unrepentant structuralist" (Ankersmit, 1998, p. 185), White argues that historical narratives are artifacts of an interpretive act constituted in part by a historian's aesthetic, epistemological, and ethical commitments, and in part by the underlying tropic forms of language itself. Exploring the literary structure of the historical text, White advanced a sophisticated "tropology," or poetic theory of historical discourse, which has proven important in the philosophy of history and has been championed as an important contribution to a postmodern approach to history (see Jenkins, 1995). According to Kellner, White's work "represents an aggressive move to turn historical thought from a logical to a rhetorical form, and a defensive entrenchment against any counter-movement from rhetoric to logic" (1980, p. 28), again suggesting the necessity of refiguring history as historiography in the process.

Synthesizing and extending Vico's eighteenth-century theory of master tropes, White (1973) has argued that when historians begin the process of writing a history, they are predisposed to organize their insights in one of four modes derived from and limited in choice by what he believes to be—in true structuralist or "formalist" fashion—the tropic "deep structure" of our language and historical or figural imagination. White put forward the theory that the four tropes of metaphor (representation), metonymy (reduction), synecdoche (integration), and irony (negation) prefigure the production of any historical narrative, and when combined with particular modes of argument (ideographic, organicist, mechanistic, contextualist), emplotment strategies (romance, comedy, tragedy, satire), and ideological commitments (anarchist, conservative, radical, liberal), constitute the historiographical "style" of a particular historian or philosopher of history. Further, he argued that most historical events can be emplotted in a range of different ways, providing alternative interpretations of those events and endowing them with different meanings (H. White, 1978b). It can be safely said that this is White's most controversial claim. His point is not that particular events didn't happen, as the revisionist narratives of anti-Semitic Holocaust-denying historians might argue. Rather, White is arguing that there is no inherent meaning in an event, and that it is meaningful to us only after we give the event significance through our narrativization of it, a position that R. J. Evans feels leaves "no objective criteria by which fascist or racist views of history can be falsified" (1997, p. 239). However, the work of Ankersmit refutes such a claim, a point I will return to later in this chapter.

White evidently holds "a distrust of narrativity itself which emerges from its potentiality as a repressive force, a potentiality which was increased when the emerging discipline of history rejected rhetoric and presented itself as a 'scientific discipline' in the nineteenth century" (Ashcroft, 2001, p. 89). Therefore, it should not be surprising to find that White makes no claims for the ontological reality to which historical narratives refer. The historic past comes to us, in White's view, always "mediated" by textual forms. Despite White's rejection of history as anything other than a literary artifact, there is an emancipatory agenda underlying his tropological scheme. White developed the scheme with the idea that it would provide historians with a way "beyond irony" (Roth, 1995a, p. 145) and beyond "narrative enclosure" (Jenkins, 1995, p. 144), giving them the opportunity to consciously elect to deploy a particular trope, emplotment strategy, etc., to render the past meaningful in a variety of ways. This "freedom" to select different ways of writing about the past surely involves the adoption of an ironic approach to history/historiography, which raises the question of whether one is really as free as White supposes. The very fact that he identifies irony as the mode in which he figures his own "metahistorical" work (H. White, 1973) is symptomatic of this problem. Given that White also assigns dominant tropes to periods of historical scholarship—

apparently after a particular interpretation of Foucault's notion of the episteme—, the scheme becomes quite complex. It is not without its critics.

Chartier has indicated an uneasiness about White's commitment to a semiological approach to the study of history texts that ignores questions about the text's "reliability as witness" to specific events (1997, p. 38), though he argues in defense of White that the event must be given some ontological status if it can be emplotted in a number of different ways. Despite this, Lorenz has challenged White on the basis that his theory of history does not allow historical narratives to appeal to "the evidence" in order to verify their truth claims, thus conflating history and fiction, projecting them "as two exemplars of the same species" (1998, p. 329). However, there is a clear difference between the processes of producing (and for that matter "reading") a historical account and a fictional novel, despite the universal presence of similar tropic structures, and adopting an aesthetic orientation towards history does not preclude such recognition. Indeed, according to Golob, "Collingwood showed with great precision how evidence limited the formation of historical narrative and how it disciplined imagination" (1980, p. 59). Thus, it should not be surprising to learn that later, White "allows that the data may resist representation in a given form and therefore require a different tropological structure" (Kansteiner, 1993, p. 279).

Other critics of White's "narrative impositionalist" theory have raised questions about whether the tropes are linguistic structures or are better understood as modes of consciousness, attitudes, moods, or directions of imagination (Nelson, 1980). Vann (1998) has expressed concern over the efficacy of the tropological theory, given that in his important work *Metahistory* (1973), White selected both historians and philosophers of history to test his thesis regarding the preconfigurational effects of the tropes. In view of the potential for cultural bias in schema such as White's, one also wonders whether it is necessary to go as far as White in defining the tropes as "deep structures" of "historical consciousness," given that his own investigations were limited to nineteenth-century European historians and philosophers of history. Surely, the usefulness of his scheme would not be disturbed by supposing the tropes as recurring strategies of a literary subculture, as Pomper (1980) has suggested. It may well be the case that White could have circumvented some of the criticism of his work had he avoided positing a general scheme based on concealed deep structures. Likewise, White's reductions of "history" to text, and neglect of history as a discipline, place him in "an extreme nominalist position" (Struever, 1980, p. 61) that focuses upon product at the expense of analyzing process. Despite these caveats, White's work remains important for the attention it draws to rhetorical, tropological, narratological, and ideological analyses of the content and form of history texts; for the liberation of history from its insensitivity to the modalities and figures of discourse; and for its central argument that history is intrinsically historiography, a literary artifact (Berkhoffer, 1995; Chartier, 1997; Ricoeur, 1983). However, though White, like Barthes, Mink, and others, argues that the past is radically heterogeneous, and only becomes "morally ordered" and "cognitively apprehended" as a history through its narrativization (Holton, 1994), not everyone agrees; there have been some interesting criticisms of this view, not the least of which have come from the phenomenologist David Carr.

## The Narrative Structure of Experience

Carr (1986) argues that our experience of reality is an experience of "being in time," complete with a past, present, and future, or beginning, middle, and end. He gives examples such as hitting a ball with a baseball bat to indicate that even an everyday action has a narrative-like structure consisting of a beginning (eyeing the ball released from the hand of the pitcher), middle (swinging for the ball), and end (connecting with the ball). Carr seems unconcerned about the completely arbitrary way in which such designations are assigned; he appears undisturbed that we might want to place the beginning at the commencement of the game, at the changing rooms where the team is getting dressed, at the start of the season, and so on. He mentions only the "follow through" of the swinging bat as slightly problematic for his threefold temporal sequence. Yet, this does not stop Carr from arguing that the experience of the temporal dimension of being is the ground from which narrative forms emerge. Carr believes that "narrative structure pervades our very experience of time and social existence," independent of "our contemplating the past as historians" (1986, p. 9). Thus, he argues that the past and history do not differ in form, only content.

Carr poses his argument against theorists such as Barthes and White who see narrative form as an imposition on an otherwise disordered past. If we take Carr seriously, then Carr's historian is relegated to the role of "stenographer" documenting events in a pre-existing sequence that is already determinate of the narrative that will emerge in the historian's writing (Norman, 2001). But we don't have to take up Carr's point this way. We could see narrative as a quest for self-knowledge, and recognize that "it is because we all live out narratives in our lives and because we understand our lives in terms of the narratives we live out, that the form of narrative is appropriate for understanding the actions of others" (A. MacIntyre, 1984, p. 214).

Nevertheless, this is not to say that our narratives are accurate representations of what really happened. It does not provide convincing evidence that events have a narratively organized existence of their own independent of their participant-narrator. The important point is that just because we live our lives as the unfolding of narratives that remain forever unfinished and subject to additions, deletions, rewrites, and revisions of all kinds, that does not mean that our narrative conception of the past is not an imposition upon the past. It is my position that narrative imposition is just as problematic at the level of memory and experience as it is at the level of the historical narrative. Explorations of episodic memory and its susceptibility to abuse (as in the case of repressed-memory syndrome) provide support for this position (Loftus & Ketcham, 1996).

It is useful to consider, at this point, the arguments of the environmental historian William Cronon, who asserts that historians use narratives "because narrative is the chief literary form that tries to find meaning in an overwhelmingly crowded and disordered chronological reality" (2001, p. 411). Thus, Cronon believes history is often constructed in narrative form not because events really unfold in a story-like fashion, but because narrative as a form does what historians need it to do. According to Cronon, "whenever we choose a plot to order our environmental histories, we give them a unity that neither nature nor the past possesses so clearly" (2001, p. 411). However, it is unlikely, in Cronon's view, that any experience can be explained in its entirety by a single story. Thus, we must concede that

> narrative succeeds to the extent that it hides the discontinuities, ellipses, and contradictory experiences that would undermine the intended meaning of its story. Whatever its overall purpose, it cannot avoid a covert exercise of power: it inevitably sanctions some voices while silencing others. (Cronon, 2001, p. 411)

Like Cronon, Friedman (1995) asserts that the narrative mode of knowing that is central to the production of histories involves the selection, organization, ordering, interpreting and allegorizing of traces of the past. It thus constructs as much as it reconstructs the past. This is an important rejoinder to Carr's thesis. Although we may accept that the experience of being has a temporal or narrative sense to it, this does not mean that a history built by documenting a person's experience of the past precludes it from critical analysis. On the contrary, such a history is just one story, and as Kurosawa's haunting masterpiece *Rashomon* (Jingo & Kurosawa, 1950) demonstrates with its exploration of four characters' conflicting versions of the murder of a man and the rape of his wife, people rarely experience any event in the same way. If we accept the "*Rashomon* effect," then there is a profound difference between the history text and the past, between what we tell ourselves about events and the events themselves—even though both our experience of the events and our retelling of the events as a history share a commitment to narrativization. The conclusion one must draw, then, is either that past events are effaced by "history" or, as Ankersmit (2005) argues, that historical representation arises as an inevitably partial attempt to overcome the profound rupture that exists between our present and our past. What we know as the past is not what actually happened in any trans-subjective sense, but our own narrative account of what happened. Making history is not just something a professional historian does, but something that engages us all. History is both the process of narrativizing the subjective experience of our lives and the production of the historical narratives that are written to document those experiences.

Failing to acknowledge the problematic nature of the truth claims that emerge from our own memories and stories is the flaw in the phenomenologist's argument. Experience should not be equated with truth. Just because our experience of being in time is a temporal, narratively organized experience does not mean that the history we write about it is a true depiction of "what happened," nor does it mean that it compromises the truth of the past. A narrative might be accurate to our experience, but it is a categorical mistake to believe that our perspective is universally shared, complete in itself, or an exact replica of the past, for "relics of the past come directly from the past but they are reconstituted in their meanings by all the cultural systems that give them meaning. They gain meaning out of every social moment they survive" (Dening, 1996, p. 43).

Carr's critique of "narrative impositionalism" may help explain why narrative is important in the production of histories, but it says nothing about the truth value of what is presented as a history (Crowell, 1998). If anything, it reinforces the importance of the narrative form for the historian, but does not commit us to viewing its products as any more or less credible. Whether we believe we are retelling a story that pre-exists our writing process, using the narrative form because it is the most "appropriate means" for telling the truth of the past, or believe we are the inevitable authors of the past we are attempting to represent, history is unavoidably "the texted past" (Dening, 1996, p. 42). It is precisely in understanding history as "the texted past" that History remains of value, even while its foundations have been shaken.

## The Limits of Historiographical Representation

One area of history that has presented a particular problem for the postmodern approach to history is Holocaust studies. Taking seriously the assertions of methodological postmodernism that there can never be "unmediated access" to the world (and therefore, by analogy, to the past), and that our mediating frameworks actually constitute what we come "to know" (about the world/past), can we answer with any conviction questions about the reality of the Holocaust? According to historian Deborah Lipstadt, postmodernists have placed themselves in a predicament that renders them silent on questions about the status of events such as the Holocaust. In her book on Holocaust denial Lipstadt aims her sights on "deconstructionism" as creating the conditions that have fostered Holocaust denial (1994, p. 18). In the United States, deconstruction—as it is more typically labeled—is associated with the Yale School of literary theory, founded by the alleged Nazi collaborator Paul de Man and further developed by Derrida, whose reading of de Man's work has been criticized as bordering on the apologist with reference to de Man's collaborationist past (LaCapra, 2000). Lipstadt argues that "deconstructionism," which stands in here as a symbol for all forms of methodological postmodernism, proposes

> that there was no bedrock thing such as experience. Experience was mediated through one's language. The scholars who supported this deconstructionist approach were neither deniers themselves nor sympathetic to the denier's attitudes; most had no trouble identifying Holocaust denial as disingenuous. But because deconstructionism argued that experience was relative and nothing was fixed, it created an atmosphere of permissiveness towards questioning the meaning of historical events and made it hard for its proponents to assert that there was anything "off limits" for this skeptical approach. The legacy of this thinking was evident when students had to confront the issue. Far too many of them found it impossible to recognize Holocaust denial as a movement with no scholarly, intellectual, or rational validity. (Lipstadt, 1994, p. 18)

Richard J. Evans agrees, arguing that:

> the increase in scope and intensity of the Holocaust deniers' activities since the mid-1970s has among other things reflected the postmodernist intellectual climate, above all in the USA, in which scholars have increasingly denied texts had any fixed meaning, and have argued instead that meaning is supplied by the reader. (Evans, 1997, pp. 240-241)

However, Guttenplan (2001) chides Evans for asserting that Holocaust denial is a direct effect of the spread of postmodern theory. Guttenplan argues for a more complex picture, noting that Irving and alleged Holocaust deniers like him are rarely if ever postmodernists, though they may have capitalized on postmodernism's skepticism towards truth claims and used it as a device to sanction their revisionism. But this is a form of misappropriation, not deconstruction or poststructural theory; misappropriation as a form of "selective attention" is the signature strategy of the deniers. More importantly, it might be possible to understand the rise of right-wing revisionism as, at least in part, a reaction to, rather than a creation of, the cultural pluralism espoused within postmodernism (see my comments on white disenfranchisement in chapter 4). Methodologically, it is important to note that revisionists tend to reject poststructuralist postmodernism's principle that texts are open to multiple interpretations, arguing instead that "every text has only one meaning or it has no meaning at all" (Faurisson cited in Guttenplan, 2001, p. 290). Hence, Holocaust denial, as a particular species of revisionism, works to put forward its own interpretation of "the sources" as an exclusive reading rather than simply one possible interpretation among many. This same practice is evident in the two published volumes of *The Fabrication of Aboriginal History* (Windschuttle, 2002, 2009). Windschuttle (1996) admits to being opposed to postmodern social theory in all its forms, but his work takes a much more "black and white" view of historical evidence than is typical among professional historians, raising legitimate questions about his own status as a "denier" of Indigenous Australian history (Taylor, 2008).

Traumatic events such as the Holocaust appear to demand and resist representation simultaneously. They work as "limit events" that "test our traditional conceptual and representational categories" (Friedlander, 1997, p. 389). LaCapra argues that "the traumatic event has its greatest and most clearly justifiable effect on the victim, but in different ways it also affects everyone who comes in contact with it: perpetrator, collaborator, bystander, resister, those born later" (LaCapra, 1998, pp. 8-9). There is, however, an ethical imperative to represent the Holocaust. Friedlander (1997) supports this view, arguing that the problem of representation is not solely aesthetic or intellectual, but also an issue of morality This must be tempered by Oliver's assertion that testimony of trauma is both a "necessity and impossibility" (2001, p. 53). It is a necessity because we must not be allowed to forget the tragedies that have occurred, particularly those like the Holocaust that have had a wide-ranging impact and raise ethical and political questions that demand answers. Yet, it is an impossibility, because no representation of the trauma can ever fully capture its totality; there will always be silences and blind spots. Along these lines, one scholar has compared Auschwitz to "an earthquake which destroys all seismographic devices and therefore cannot be measured and represented within the applicable sign systems . . . [leaving us with] a vague but powerful feeling of its enormity and unrepresentability" (Kansteiner, 1997, p. 416).

We should also add, though it seems self-evident, that part of the limit condition imposed on historiographic representation is that the depiction of an event is never the event itself—though as Baudrillard (1995) argues, sometimes it may be confused with it. Thus, we may learn about the traumatic past through its representation, and we may be affected by our encounter with that representation, but we can never claim to have experienced what happened. Our experience in this case is of the historiographic representation, not the event itself. No matter how much we are moved by the testimony, we remain at best onlookers whose understanding of the event is always limited by the horizon of our own sociohistorically constituted sense-making technologies, or what Kellner calls our "culturally available models" (1997, p. 398).

There is an additional point about the problem of representation that must be made. As Wyschogrod states:

> [T]he commonsense view of history presupposes that the historian aims to tell the truth about the past where truth is understood as a matching of event or pattern with what is said about it. Even if what is alleged about some specific detail happens to be false, the truth of a proposition is thought to depend upon its correspondence with an object or referent. (Wyschogrod, 1998, p. 2)

The problem for history and historians is that histories are never simply a series of propositions (statements of fact), each of which can be verified or falsified. According to White, history, as an account of the past, may be understood as "a list of facts [that] is transformed into a story" (1997, p. 393). Adhering to White's philosophy of history, Jenkins argues that "[if] 'facts' are to be significant [historically], they can only gain that significance through being narrativized. This narrativization in its emplotment and troping confers on the facts a significance that a different emplotment and troping could take away" (1997, p. 385).

Ankersmit (2001a) makes this problem clear in his example of the Renaissance. "The Renaissance" is a category that historians apply to a series of events that could have been ordered, described, selected, defined, periodized, or segregated in some other way. While "the facts of the matter" may include references to Leonardo da Vinci, Michelangelo, and a host of other "important" figures and their contributions to the intellectual and cultural life of their times, "the narrative" of the Renaissance, which furnishes these people and events with meaning, arises from particular interpretations of "the facts." Thus, a debate about what the Renaissance was or means is not a debate about the past as it happened, but about narrative interpretations of it. For Ankersmit, "interpretation is not translation. The past is not a text that has to be translated into narrative historiography; it has to be *interpreted*" (2001b, p. 237, emphasis in the original). Further, he asserts that "narrative interpretations *apply* to the past, but do not *correspond* or *refer* to it (as statements do)" (2001b, p. 239, emphasis in the original). As "proposals," narrative interpretations of the past "may be useful, fruitful, or not, but cannot be either true or false"

(2001b, p. 241). This is because in Ankersmit's view, only an individual statement can be verified as true or false.

Quite powerfully, Ankersmit also argues that "a historical narrative is a historical narrative only insofar as the (metaphorical) meaning of the historical narrative in its totality transcends the (literal) meaning of the sum of its individual statements" (2001b, p. 243). Where this is not the case, the set of statements is probably better described by the term *chronicle*. Ankersmit asserts that "the ultimate challenge for both historical writing and the historian is not factual or ethical, but aesthetic" (2001a, p. 176). Viewed in this way, historical research only becomes history as the traces of the past are given meaning within a narrative structure (a historiographic form). To quote Jenkins, "most historiography is the imposition of meaningful form onto a meaningless past" (1995, p. 137).

We might assert, once again, that some traumatic events, such as the genocide of the Jewish population of Western Europe by the Nazi regime, demand that we provide meaning for their existence whether we want to or not, whether impossible or not. We do this by transforming facts that we can derive from traces left behind into the narrative of "the Holocaust." Thus, "the Holocaust" operates at the level of narrative representation and not actually at the level of the statement, attempting to provide "meaning" to the acts of lethal violence committed against European Jewry during World War II through the particularities of its aesthetic construction.

For Ankersmit, like White, the problem of representation at the heart of Holocaust history is ultimately a question of the "appropriateness" or "respectfulness" of the aesthetic form, with regard to the trauma that occurred. From a postmodern perspective, at the level of the narrative, the meaning of a set of statements is always an (at least partly) open question (and "relative" to the reader or writer attempting understanding and interpretation). However, although this suggests that each historian will develop a narrative that makes the set of factual statements meaningful to themselves and their communities, interpretation has its socially (and linguistically) imposed limits. White (1997) has asserted that while a neo-Nazi revisionist might be able to represent the extermination of the Jews in some satirical form, this would never be acceptable for a serious historian, who is likely to depict the events as a tragedy. Importantly, Ankersmit contends that although interpretations may be challenged by alternative interpretations (narratives by competing narratives), only individual statements can be (and should be) challenged by "the facts." Thus, Holocaust denial is only such if it can be falsified at the level of the statement. This is precisely what Richard J. Evans put into play when he took the witness stand in the Irving libel case, annihilating Irving's suspect narratives by demolishing the statements upon which they stood, showing that the claims of reference that they intended were selective, false, or inaccurately rendered. If Evans had agreed that Irving had built his narrative interpretations upon an accurate set of the "available" factual statements (regarding the extermination of the Jews of Europe by the Nazi regime), he would have had to accept that Irving's interpretation could not be discounted as a possible rendering of the past. Evans could have provided a more plausible interpretation of "the facts" himself, but this would not, of itself, lead to a verdict that Irving was a Holocaust denier. What Evans showed, without necessarily accepting any of Ankersmit's premises, was that at the level of the statement, Irving's research was deficient. Likewise, Evans argued that there were better interpretations of "the facts" than the ones Irving provided, which for the most part was an argument accepted by the judge in the trial (Guttenplan, 2001).

Of course, there is a step between the determination of "statements of fact" and the production of an adequate or plausible narrative interpretation. That step is the determination of what will count as "evidence" for the specific history that is to be written. According to Jenkins, "nothing is ever *intrinsically* historical" (2003, p. 39, emphasis in the original); instead, objects of enquiry can be used as evidence within "any number of [historical] discourses without belonging to any of them" (2003, p. 39). Within the postmodernist approach to history, "evidence" does not simply equate with "facts." "Statements of fact" become "evidence" only when used to support a particular historical interpretation or explanation. The evidence needed to support a particular interpretation is typically only a partial collection of available "facts" determined by the questions that are guiding the research being conducted. For example, it may be a verifiable fact that almost six million Jews were murdered by the Nazi regime during World War II, but this fact becomes "evidence" for only particular types of historical inquiry. It may be useful if we are exploring questions related to the fate of European Jewry under the Nazi regime, or if we are exploring the National Socialist movement's attitudes and policies towards the Jews. However, it is unlikely to be mobilized as evidence if our question concerned the success of German military strategy during World War II. It might appear in the historical explanation as a statement of what was happening on the home front, but it is unlikely to be critical to an argument that seeks to understand or explain why German strategic decisions on the Russian front met with success or failure. Tweak the question only slightly and such a "fact" becomes "historically significant." Imagine if the historian had a question about whether or not German military strategy on the Russian front was motivated by a belief that large numbers of the Russian army were Jewish: In such a case, the extermination of European Jewry inside and outside of

German borders would become "historically significant." The point of this example is that research questions typically pre-exist the determination of what will constitute "data" or evidence (Popkewitz, 2001). Though facts might stimulate the generation of particular research questions, the evidence for a particular historical interpretation is always determined by the question or problem that the historian is attempting to solve or understand. Thus, postmodernists often talk about the evidence being constituted by the researcher's question. When this claim is made, it is the "historical significance" of "the facts," and not "the facts" themselves, that is at stake.

## Bringing Historiography Out of Quarantine

In the preceding discussion I explored a series of compelling arguments that history is an act of writing that transforms, rather than simply gathers, the traces of the past into a narrative text. Whether we are examining Barthes's notion of the way the impersonal style of the historical narrative encourages us to read it as fact; White's argument for the prefigurative power of an historian's aesthetic, epistemological, and ethical commitments operating in conjunction with the underlying tropic forms of language itself; Carr's case for the narrative structure of everyday experience; or Ankersmit's conception of the way the metaphorical meaning of a historical narrative transcends the literal meaning of the sum of its referential statements, the overall message surely must be that history is historiography.

Theorizing history as historiography comes at a price, and that price is the truth claim of the historical narrative. It is not, as Ankersmit (2001a) has argued, a complete dismissal of any claim history has to being a factual discourse. Rather, understanding history as the transformation of factual statements into a narrative form, or the imposition onto the evidence of a set of meanings that challenge the silences of the evidence, problematizes the truth claims of history as an explanatory or interpretive discourse. Importantly, if we accept this reconceptualization of history as historiography, then we are not simply trading history in for fiction. Historiography is as much process as it is product, a technology of representation as much as a narrative artifact. As Curthoys and Docker note, there is a particular quality of "doubleness" to history that prevents it from escaping either its sources or its representational forms (2006, p. 11). Historiography helps us to work "in the space between history as rigorous scrutiny of sources and history as part of the world of literary forms" (2006, p. 11). It leads us to the realization that "history is a method rather than a truth" (Ashcroft, 2001, p. 86). It also invites challenge to history's methods, given their own sociohistorical contingency, allowing for the possibility of "escaping" historical discourse, which, I will argue in the final section of this chapter, is vital for a critical History. However, I first want to examine what the theorization of history as historiography means for current curriculum prescriptions.

From the preceding discussion it is difficult to see how a curriculum that is critically oriented, and that takes seriously the postmodern critique of historical representation, can ignore historiography. However, it must also be clear that the solution to school History's null curriculum cannot be simply the insertion of a historiography course into the explicit curriculum. While I applaud the postmillennial development and inclusion of a historiography course as an option within the History strand of the Higher School Certificate (matriculation curriculum) in NSW, I am concerned about the way that placing a course such as this at an extension level in the postcompulsory years of schooling—which makes sound "developmental" sense, of course—effectively quarantines the effects of recent debates over history. Those who will be enrolled in this subject constitute a small number of the state's brightest history candidates, and those who teach it are but a very few committed teachers. Given its particular place in the hierarchy of history subjects, the History Extension course can only ever provide the critical tools of historiography to a small number of teachers and students, yet all teachers and students will encounter historical discourse daily throughout their lives, in a wide variety of forms (M. L. Davies, 2006; Groot, 2009). Such a course is likely, by virtue of its unique mandate to address historiography, to exclude most students from any sophisticated debates that seek to question the truth claims made for historical representation. Thus, it reduces the likelihood of students thinking critically about their own histories and the histories they encounter in the wider world. Students will, no doubt, continue to have the chance to develop historical explanations and interpretations by critically evaluating alternative or rival sources, encountering the cornerstone methodology of the discipline. However, divorced from historiography, this encounter with the disciplinary practices of history is likely to hide the controversy that is central to historical inquiry and representation, in much the same way that Apple's (1975) early work demonstrated how controversies at the center of the scientific enterprise are hidden from students in Science curriculum because of its neglect of the history and philosophy of science. Regardless, it seems unlikely that the claim of history to be able to represent the past will ever get anything like the scrutiny it would get if historiography were considered integral, rather than supplemental, to the study of history.

If simply incorporating historiography into the curriculum as a discrete unit is unsatisfactory within a postmodern frame of reference, then it is necessary to explore what a more effective curricular response to the problem of historical representation might be. One possible curricular response is to do away with History (as the study of the past) altogether and replace it with Historiography (as the study of historical representations). This would radically reclaim History curriculum as a site of "critical" history, but it also would transform the school subject into little more than a branch of literary interpretation. Certainly those dedicated to curriculum as a vehicle of cultural reproduction might reject such a radical form of critical history in schools, and those who advocate for school History to develop a student's historical (methodological) skills might find such an approach limiting. Further, those committed to a developmental continuum would be likely to perceive a critical History curriculum based on historiography as beyond the capability of junior high school students. However, looking at the growing body of North American scholarship into the development of historical reasoning among youth (Wineburg, 2005), I would argue that, given appropriate instruction, students are capable of far more complex forms of historical reasoning than politicians and many educators realize. Therefore, I reject the views expressed in media-led debates by conservative journalists such as Luke Slattery (2005a, 2005b) and Sarah Golsby-Smith (2005) that challenge the appropriateness of the teaching of "postmodern theory" and "critical literacy" in Australian schools, but I accept that a nuanced approach to their incorporation into an area such as History education is needed.

Typically, the journalists and educationalists involved in polemics against postmodernism in schools present attempts to incorporate critical approaches to knowledge and postmodern theory into the curriculum as "irresponsible" and "doctrinaire" (L. Slattery, 2005a, p. 10) and "a cause for unease" (Donnelly, 2004, p. 60). Their usual strategy is to construct postmodern theory as confusing and ideologically loaded and their own content-driven curricula as supported by "common sense." Their arguments against postmodern theory typically consist of tired misconceptions and inaccuracies such as the notion that postmodernism's assumptions include "truth is a matter of opinion . . . [and] there is no real world outside of language and hence no facts independent of our descriptions of them" (L. Slattery, 2005a, p. 10). Given the highly significant yet subtle difference between these claims and the actual assumptions of postmodern theory, it is unlikely that the public—particularly in Australia, where they are known for their ambivalence towards academe—will be persuaded by a defense that seems to be intellectual nitpicking. However, this renewed conservative assault against the deployment of postmodern theory in schools need not stop the project of rethinking history as historiography that I am fleshing out here. To avoid a doomed battle with the conservative critics of postmodernism whose voices currently dominate the media, and likewise, to avoid simply replacing one set of beliefs about history with another, other ways of bringing historiography out of quarantine must be sought. Certainly, if historiography is incorporated into History curriculum as an integral part of History education, then its implications are far-reaching.

## Historiography and/as Effective History

To use historiography to understand (after Foucault, 1969/1972) the conditions of existence and possibility for a given historical representation is to extend the gaze of a historian from the traces of the past to his or her narrativization of the enduring "evidence." In their attempt at writing a historical narrative that explains or interprets the past, historians exceed the evidence. The resultant historical narratives form discourses that can be compelling and seductive. From a structuralist perspective, historical discourse can be said to "hail" us in a variety of ways, providing the conditions of self-formation (Althusser, 1971). In the Althusserian sense, we are "born into" ideology; the subject positions offered by the discourse of history provide "a sense of identity and social meaning" that is reinforced "by ideological state apparatuses" that include institutions such as the church, the police, and education (Ashcroft, 2001, p. 36). Foucault's poststructuralism, which owes a debt to Althusser's structuralist Marxism, describes this situation as having "a body totally imprinted by history" (Foucault, 1971/1994, p. 376). That is, contra Rousseau (and his position on "society"), Foucault sees discourse not as a power that corrupts the "natural human self," but as a force that is productive of particular subject positions rather than others. As Grosz argues, discourses through which subjectivities are constituted "make the body into a particular kind of body—pagan, primitive, medieval capitalist, Italian, American, Australian" (1995, p. 172). It is the productive differentiation of subject positions within discourse that has an enabling effect on our capacity to act in particular ways, and that simultaneously acts upon us to limit our capabilities, our desires, and what we feel is possible, a point I have argued elsewhere, using the martial arts as an example (Parkes, 2010). Importantly, Foucault (1984/1996) argues that it is not simply the institutions of the state that exercise these coercive relations, but also what individuals do to themselves, through what he describes as "technologies of the self": discourses and social practices that are appropriated and applied to oneself as part of the process of self-formation.

As beings "totally imprinted by history," we are in many ways bound within historical discourse. According to Ashcroft's examination of transformation in postcolonial societies,

> this capacity [of cultural institutions and technologies] to interpellate imperial subjects, to inculcate a particular view of the world, a particular morality, a range of aesthetic, ethical, political and social values in the colonized, is a very good demonstration of hegemony. (Ashcroft, 2001, p. 37)

However, this focus on the way discourse shapes available subject positions should not suggest, as some have argued, that poststructuralism cannot account "for the subject's ability to act as an agent, to contravene the subject-forming power" (Ashcroft, 2001, p. 36). Foucault's argument that history becomes critical or "effective" "to the degree that it introduces discontinuity into our very being" (1971/1994, p. 380) suggests the possibility of resistance. Further, if subjectivity is a by-product or artifact of historical discourse, then freedom is a problem of (personal and social) history. Foucault (1984/1996) defines freedom throughout his later work as resisting who we are, because if human subjectivity is constituted through a historical process, then who we are is the subject of historical contingencies, and to be free would mean being other than how we have been constituted to be within historical and other cultural discourses. By definition, then, critical history must provide the opportunity for developing a capacity to interrupt or disengage from historical representation. For without the capacity to disengage from historical discourse, we are unlikely to be able to resist interpellation. One of the earliest attempts to conceptualize a critical history that aimed at building just such a capacity to interrupt or disengage from historical discourse can be found in Nietzsche's "On the Uses and Disadvantages of History for Life" (1874/1983).

In his "untimely meditation" Nietzsche posited the idea of an unhistorical sense that would protect the individual against the excesses of a variety of forms of historicization. For Nietzsche, an absent or deficient historical sense might make us beasts, but an "excess" of history, by constraining us within the borders of a moribund past, renders life inert (Bambach, 1990). Nietzsche's essay on history emerged from his concern with "the chauvinistic nationalism" of Germany under Bismarck (Davison, 2000, pp. 10-11). Contemplating the uses and disadvantages of history as deployed by conservatives, liberals, and radicals, Nietzsche proposed his threefold anti-historicist historiography. According to Nietzsche, history typically manifested in the form of: (1) the monumental (in which past events and deeds were valorized and venerated); (2) the antiquarian (in which attempts were made to preserve the past as cultural heritage and source of identity); and (3) the critical (in which aspects of the past were challenged from the standpoint of present "truths"). According to Nietzsche's scheme, each of these uses of history was subject to abuse (by being used exclusively, or to excess), in which case it would lead to human subjugation rather than freedom. His answer was to pit the various forms of history against each other in a complex balancing act. Although Nietzsche's conceptualization of critical history is intriguing, it seems overly complex for any sort of translation into a critical History curriculum. However, it does raise the interesting problem of how students might be taught to disengage from historical discourse while still "doing history."

There are a number of ways to resist historical discourse that can be revealed through an analysis of the strategies used by postcolonial subjects to challenge their interpellation and inscription within dominant representations of the historic past. In his book *Post-Colonial Transformation* (2001), Ashcroft addresses "some of the fundamental issues which arise in post-colonial responses to imperial discourse" (p. 13). Particularly interested in the problem of resistance, he argues that across many postcolonial societies (and he counts Australia among them), one sees four reactions to the discourse of history. First, there is acceptance of historical discourse, and one's location within it. The history that was taught prior to the 1992 syllabus in NSW was underpinned by an acceptance of the grand narrative of Australia's great achievements in the context of a larger history of the British Empire, and thus reflected precisely this acquiescence in regard to historical discourse. Secondly, Ashcroft identifies a reaction characterized as rejection, in which the very concept of history is challenged as a cultural or imperial construct. Ashcroft warns that because rejection involves "a powerful statement of a different cultural consciousness . . . [it] may function as a group insularity, neglecting the transformative way in which cultures may develop by using appropriated influences" (Ashcroft, 2001, pp. 100-101). Struggles over an "authentic" Aboriginality or a single Aboriginal history are one of the ways this particular response to historical discourse has played out in the Australian context (Russell, 2001). The result is that even a radical curriculum document such as the 1992 History syllabus proposes a singular "Indigenous perspective" as an antidote to the dominance of "white mythologies."

Alongside rejection, Ashcroft argues that it will be possible to identify resistance to the discourse of history emerging as the interjection of counter-narratives into the popular arena. He argues that, as a response to historical discourse, interjection demonstrates an acceptance of "the basic premises of historical narrative . . . [but presents] a contrary narrative, which claims to offer a more immediate or 'truer' picture of post-colonial life, a record of those experiences omitted from imperial history" (2001, p. 101). He sees "this insertion of contesting narratives, a 're-writing' of history . . . [as] an important strategy in the process of discursive resistance" (2001, p. 102). The strategy of interjection was the signature of the 1992 History syllabus, with its incorporation of the counter-histories of women and Indigenous peoples. Importantly, this form of resistance seeks to operate "*within* the spaces opened up by history, and in this way [to] redirect it" (2001, p. 102, emphasis in the original). The limitations of this strategy, as noted at the end of chapter 4, include its failure to engage with the problem of historical representation itself. This brings us to the final strategy that Ashcroft has identified in his analysis of postcolonial resistance to historical discourse.

In the strategy of *interpolation*, the dominant discourse is interrupted not by outright dismissal or by challenging narrative closure through the construction and circulation of one's own counter-stories, but by destabilizing the very forms through which the dominant discourse is produced, consumed, and exchanged. This final strategy involves a meta-awareness of the genres and disciplines through which the dominant discourse operates, and it disturbs and disrupts by reconfiguring forms, crossing boundaries, and challenging disciplinarities via their strategic reconstitution. Ashcroft's conceptualization of interpolation is worth quoting at length:

> [R]esponding to this ubiquitous master narrative, the aims of post-colonial writing seem curiously contradictory: the aim is on one hand to insert post-colonial experience into the programme of history, on the other to reject history because of its imperial narrativization of the past. But the problem here is that in history, as in other discursive formations, the post-colonial exists outside representation itself. The remedy is not "re-insertion" but "re-vision"; not the re-insertion of the marginalized into representation but the appropriation of a method, the re-vision of the temporality of events. This is interpolation in its fullest sense, and is crucial to the political interpretation of post-colonial experience because it is an attempt to assume control of the processes of representation . . . to re-inscribe the "heteroglossia," the hybrid profusion of life, into the linear and teleological movement of imperial history and, by so doing, to change our view of what history is. (Ashcroft, 2001, p. 98)

According to Ashcroft, "the key function of the post-colonial interpolation of history is to subvert the unquestioned status of the 'scientific record' by re-inscribing the 'rhetoric' of events" (2001, p. 92). Ashcroft thus provides a good description of the required characteristic of a critical or transformative History curriculum. It must interrupt historical discourse by drawing attention to its representational practices. Of course, the ways it does this may vary widely. Critically, interpolation as pedagogy must involve returning the gaze of the historiographer. Historiography renders visible the genealogy of a given historical representation by refurnishing it with a set of temporal moorings, opening the possibility for students, teachers, and historians to resist the interpellating effects of the well-told narrative. Recognizing the historicity and rhetorical construction of a history compels us to see that all stories of the past have contingent foundations. Invoking the contingency of historical representation invites us to apprehend it as open to change, never the final word. Thus, a pedagogy of interpolation, by drawing attention to the historicity and rhetorical forms of all histories taught, would seem to be an appropriate curricular response to postmodernism's challenge to historical representation.

CHAPTER SIX

# Ghosts and Visions in the Curriculum

I began this volume by suggesting that history is haunted by predictions of its imminent end; I conclude by exploring history, given its posthumous status, as a series of ghosts and visions that haunt the curriculum. First, I acknowledge a debt to *Curriculum Visions* (2002), edited by William Doll and Noel Gough. Its idea of thinking about curriculum as haunted by ghosts and invoking new visions provoked me to think through the implications of interpolation as pedagogy, in which history, after its "end," is haunted by historiography. I complement this exploration by engaging with history as political "vision" in the sense that can be found in the work of Wendy Brown (2001). In considering history as ghost and vision, I hope to provide a meaningful conclusion that addresses the (im)possibilities of History curriculum after "the end of history."

In taking seriously postmodernism's rejection of naïve realism, essentialism, and foundationalism, my argument is at odds with those of Willie Thompson and others who see postmodernism as "a quasi-theological form of discourse, repellent to all but the initiated and which will certainly come to figure as no more than a bizarre curiosity of intellectual history" (Thompson, 2004, p. 128). I can say little in response to such wonderfully crafted hyperbole except to confess that over the last decade I have been one of those "possessed" by postmodernism. Unlike Thompson, I am not prepared to speculate how long this possession will last, but I think it will take some powerful incantations to exorcise it from me, for I find postmodernism compelling, at least in what I have called its poststructural/methodological form. Reviewing the chapters of this volume, I remain confident that writing histories involves the transformation of traces of the past into a narratively organized explanatory or interpretive text, exceeding, rather than simply gathering, what counts as "evidence" for the questions asked or problem posed (see, in particular, my discussion of Ankersmit, 2001a, in chapter 5). This is not to deny that beyond tropological choices, important discipline-informed cognitive processes are at work in this act of transformation (Evans, 1997; McCullagh, 2004), a point often overlooked or downplayed by some "postmodern" history theorists. Certainly, there are many objections to the "narrative impositionalist" view revisited above, and perhaps I could be criticized for in not engaging with them more comprehensively, but my goal was not to weigh up the worth of postmodernism, but to re-examine historical and methodological postmodernism's apparent "threat" to history and the subsequent implications of this threat for History as curriculum.

It is not always clear to the critics of methodological postmodernism—particularly those who, like Windschuttle (1996), lump together poststructuralists, critical theorists, hermeneuticists, semioticians, multiculturalists, social constructionists, and literary theorists—that often there are highly significant epistemological differences between these disciplinary fields and practices, despite some overt similarities and complementarities. One important difference between critical theory and poststructuralism, for example, has implications for how we understand the idea of the "critical." The many forms of critical theory are supported by a common epistemology that posits language as an ideological medium that often distorts our vision of reality, preventing interlocutors from communicating without static or distortion. The practice of critique in critical theory becomes the means by which "to unmask the lies of the established disorder that appears as transparently normal" (Haraway cited in Gough, 2002, p. 4).

In alignment with critical theory, poststructuralism agrees that language is opaque, but sees our visions of reality as both productive and repressive simultaneously. Poststructuralists typically reject the idea that our representations ever unproblematically correspond with reality, and thus resign themselves to a position that reality is never known outside our systems of representation. Thus, you will hear poststructuralists saying that our systems of representation constitute reality as we know it. Unlike the notion of "critical" that is often mobilized in the Marxist-inspired literature of radical pedagogy, which implies a capacity to challenge representations in order to uncover an obscured truth, poststructuralism's notion of "critical" amounts to a concern that even our best attempts at revealing reality are suspected of producing new hallucinations. When Neo knocks down the sentinel robots in the closing moments of *The Matrix Reloaded* (2003), the critical theorist applauds his escape from ideology and acknowledges that he is the Messiah (or messiah-like). At the same moment, the poststructuralist sits back and takes a breath, resigned to the view that Neo has simply moved out of one matrix into another. Critique, in a poststructuralist sense, thus involves an attempt to expose normalized and naturalized discourses and systems of logic as cultural-historical enterprises. In the act of critique, however, is the construction of a new discourse, or new system of representation. There is no final liberation from discourse or systems of representation after the exercise of poststructural critique. Yet, recognizing the historicity of a discourse or knowledge system means acknowledging that it is always in transit, always open to the possibility of "transformation" (LaCapra, 2004). Thus, the poststructuralist notion of "critical" is about opening what Foucault (1988/1994) describes as spaces of freedom, spaces to think and act differently, rather than emancipation through the unveiling of an ultimate or final truth. This has been both the method and argument of this book.

I have argued in this book that if History curriculum is to be a critical/transformative enterprise, then it must attend to the problem of historical representation. In my analysis of History curriculum in NSW during the 1990s, it became apparent that while there was institutionalized resistance to the idea of a single "grand story" of the nation, operationalized in the form of a "radical" syllabus, historiography failed to register as part of the curriculum. This neglect of historiography was common to the parallel curricular reforms that took place in the United States, United Kingdom, and Canada, and it meant that while metanarratives might be challenged through a "pedagogy of counter-memory," historical discourse itself remains beyond the horizon of critique. It is my conclusion that after postmodernism, History curriculum remains possible, but in a reconceptualized form in which historiography haunts the curriculum as a disruptive force.

As a "disruptive force" in the study of histories, historiography functions like "the stranger" of Wang's 2002 text whose presence promises to "shatter taken-for-granted perceptions and assumptions, to challenge conventional truth, and to bring the promise of new life" (p. 294). Wang's warning that "to encounter the stranger can be threatening" (2002, p. 296) and "to invite the stranger into our horizon is to risk questioning our own views and ways of being" (p. 294) is instructive here. Historiography as the "stranger" for History curriculum comes as "someone alien to us" (Wang, 2002, p. 294). We might even go so far as to call it the "unsayable" that helps constitute history by its absence. Historiography, as a metahistorical discourse, is history's "stranger" because its presence challenges history's claims to stand "outside" of time. By rendering the gaze of the historian panoptical, historiography forces history into a painful reflexivity that paradoxically provides the possibility for the historian (or history student) to disengage from historical discourse as a result of historicizing historical representation. As LaCapra argues, "history in the sense of historiography cannot escape *transit* unless it negates itself by denying its own historicity and becomes identified with transcendence or fixation"

(2004, pp. 1-2, my emphasis). Acknowledging history's historicity through an encounter with historiography is tantamount to killing history, because it leaves us with only the practices and forms of historiographic representation. After historiography, history can function only as a ghost, an apparition that stands in for an unrecoverable original. According to Doll, "ghosts have an ethereal presence; they can be seen, often felt, but have no material substance" (2002, p. 24). History as specter plays in such a space, constructing visions that haunt both the present and the future.

To place the problems of historical representation at the center of a critical History curriculum is to teach History *under erasure*, to conjure a pedagogical situation in which histories are both presented and deconstructed in the same lesson. A History curriculum that places historical representation at its center must also of necessity develop a historical hermeneutics. Such a hermeneutics must find ways of illuminating the epistemologies that haunt representations of the past, summoning them to the fore. Mobilizing Jenkins and Munslow's (2004) *reconstructionist, constructionist,* and *deconstructionist* heuristic as a frame through which to "read" histories in the classroom could be one manifestation of this historical hermeneutics, channeling historiography's disruptive force in the same way that history as genealogy, after Foucault, interrupts the logic of the disciplines by re-establishing their historicity. This movement towards the development of a pedagogical hermeneutics is a project for the future (in both the senses that this phrase conjures). It need not deny the importance of "disciplined inquiry" in the sense described by Seixas (2000), but it does add an extra dimension to critical historical study that is frequently ignored.

If we accept that all histories are colored by their sociohistorical circumstances, even highly "empirical" histories (since they too are determined by what historical questions are or are not asked, and what evidence is collected or ignored), then systematic induction into ways of "reading" history, perhaps drawn from literary theory such as those advocated by LaCapra (2000), become even more pressing. As the Australian historians Ann Curthoys and John Docker note, there is a particular quality of "doubleness" to history that prevents it from escaping either its sources or its representational forms, and in the form of historiography it assists us to work "in the space between history as rigorous scrutiny of sources and history as part of the world of literary forms" (Curthoys & Docker, 2006, p. 11). It leads us to the realization that "history is a method rather than a truth" (Ashcroft, 2001, p. 86). Embracing this insight into the way history functions means paying attention to how we read our sources and how we read the historical narratives we encounter. It means understanding "historical method" as a thoroughly hermeneutic or interpretive act. When history is understood as "historical representation," engaging with histories historiographically becomes a tool to navigate through and between multiple and conflicting historical narratives. This historiographic move allows us to understand and appreciate rival historical narratives, and it also provides at least some criteria to adjudicate between them. However, I must add a note of caution here. There is another important criteria that is absent if we stop at simply understanding history as the product of historiographic processes and ignore the ethics and political value of the vision of the future that a particular historiographic construction of the past produces. As Brown (2001) contends:

> the play between present and past in a particular political moment... transforms past and present into the "then" and "now" as a form of mutual illumination. Heavily dependent on memory, this play is also fueled by anxiety about certain losses in the past and about losing position in the present, and hence by anxiety about the capacity to make a future. (p. 168)

We can see this in the way the various history wars have transformed school History into a battlefield. Curriculum operates as a site of struggle between these same polarities of past and present, seeking to create ideal futures. Historical representation, as both a form of and a challenge to collective remembering, can never escape its pedagogic tendencies. Historiography provides a means by which to engage these pedagogic tendencies directly, interrupting history and revealing the apparatus at work in its modes and forms of representation.

In practice, teaching history as historiography presents a number of challenges for history educators. In order to enact a historiographic approach to teaching history, it is necessary to have knowledge beyond the recall of facts, dates, and interesting anecdotes (aligned with the "reconstructionist" or "collective memory" approach described above). It is also necessary to have knowledge beyond "historical method" (central to the "constructionist" or "disciplinary" approach described earlier). What teachers need in order to enact the historiographic approach advocated here is knowledge of historiographic traditions themselves, including an understanding and awareness of historiographic debates that inform the "topics" they are teaching. As Avner Segall argues, "a critical perspective poses the following: according to what conventional and methodological practices, whose discourse, whose standards, whose past?" (Segall, 2006, p. 138). These questions invite an engagement with historiography and its competing traditions, each with their own conventions, methodologies, discourses, standards, and representations of the past. Faced with competing accounts of a single event, students learning within a historiographic approach to teaching history can be tasked to explore not only alternative perspectives, but develop an understanding of how each of these perspectives has its own history, and is derived from the application of different principles, standards, and methodological approaches. Again, as Segall clearly states, "Questions of this sort help make visible and problematic the presuppositions of discourses, values, and methodologies that legitimate and enforce particular versions and visions as to what the past is and what knowing and acting upon it entail" (Segall, 2006, p. 139). This means that it is necessary for History educators, and certainly History teacher educators, to address historiography in the education and development of History teachers. Knowledge of historiography and its impact on methodology and forms of representation become central to the endeavor of representing history in classrooms. Applied to the example of the colonization of Australia, the case explored in detail in this book, it becomes evident how historiographic study can provide adjudicating frames of reference through which to read alternative historical accounts by exposing the value-laden methodological practices operating as the conditions of possibility for rival histories.

Through the lens of what might be called the "traditional" view of Australia's contact or colonization history, Australia was a "vacant land" by European standards, and it was settled peacefully from 1788 by three waves of transported convicts, and from the late 1820s by assisted and unassisted "free" immigrants looking for a new life. This view depicts Aboriginal resistance to occupation as marginal and of little significance to the march of progress as civilization gained a foothold in the Great Southern Land. It constructs Australia's Indigenous peoples as a "dying race," inferior in every imaginable way to the Europeans who were displacing them. This view was taught in schools up to the 1970s as the received account of Australia's past (Reynolds, 1989). When we examine this account from a historiographic perspective, it is easily identified as a Whig interpretation of history that presents progress towards European social structures and Enlightenment values as natural (read "inevitable") development. Within the Whig interpretation, the forced removal of "half-caste" children from their Aboriginal mothers is enacted and read as a paternalist gesture designed to "save" the children by civilizing them. In some ways, the reactionary account of the colonial period put forward by Keith Windshuttle (2002) is a return to elements of Whig historiography, but it is tempered by a strong injection of positivist empiricism that treats oral history with suspicion and thus not only rejects much of the "evidence" that underpins the revision of the late 1980s and early 1990s, but also almost systematically excludes Indigenous testimony as a reliable historical source.

The rival "revisionist" view that emerged in earnest in public consciousness at the time of the bicentennial of the nation (1988) presents a significantly different vision of the interaction between Australia's Indigenous peoples and its European colonizers. This revisionist account argues that Aboriginal resistance had been significant, organized, and far more widespread and frequent than the national mythology had allowed. In fact, historians who presented this revisionist interpretation of the colonization of Australia made the case that nothing less than a frontier war had ensued (Reynolds, 1982); and that far from being an inferior "dying race" with a primitive nature and uncivilized culture, the Aboriginal peoples of Australia were the custodians of a successful and enduring ancient culture, and the victims of an act of genocide, deliberate or otherwise, that actively sought their displacement and eradication. This "social history" account, in which the removal of children from Aboriginal families is represented by the idea of a "stolen generation," asks us to understand Australia's contact history as traumatic and shameful (Curthoys & Docker, 2001; Markus, 2001; Read, 2002). As with many forms of standpoint history, this representation of the past tells its story from the perspective of the marginalized. As a result, it weights witness testimony more highly than other accounts, and constructs remembrance of trauma as an ethical and pedagogical imperative (Simon, 2000). Though often presented by its adherents as a more accurate representation of the past, this perspective has a tendency to encourage in the national consciousness the elision of differences between different groups of European settlers, and to construct its own value-laden categories (such as "frontier" and "genocide") that impact on how the past is constructed, interpreted, and understood.

In taking on a historiographic approach to teaching History, two things become important. Firstly, we need to understand that historical representation emerges from within particular historiographic traditions (such as feminism, Marxism, social history, intellectual history, cultural history, etc.), and hence is marked "historically" by the biases of those methodological traditions. Understanding the historiographic frame within which a historical narrative has been constructed becomes the first step in understanding the historian's value-laden assumptions, disposition towards particular forms of interpretation, and concern with different forms of evidence. The second thing that becomes important is that we come to understand how our own acts of reading and interpretation are prejudiced by the methodological biases of the historiographic traditions we have been initiated into, and for that matter, our personal sociohistorically situated experiences. In teaching history as historiography we become receptive to what Foucault (1969/1972) has called "the conditions of possibility" for any historical narrative we encounter. At least potentially, we come to know what was possible for this history to tell, and perhaps what was impossible for it to tell. Further, like Falzon (1998), we come to realize that interpretation is not only historically shaped, but also inevitable and unavoidable. We cannot avoid passing judgment on the interpretations of the past we encounter, and we do this within the limits of our methodological prejudices. Where history pedagogy is able to emphasize the historiographic and hermeneutic dimensions of "history" in this way, we are not left at the mercy of an uncritical relativism. Rather, there is potential for us to take a "critical pluralist" stance towards history in which we accept narrative diversity in the curriculum (recognizing the inevitable and almost endless proliferation of historical interpretations) but have the capacity to make value judgments about the historical narratives we encounter and to advocate for those stories of the past that are generated from defensible historical methodologies and provide hopeful visions for the future. In this struggle for critical and effective histories, a historiographic hermeneutics becomes an important feature of history pedagogy rather than something reserved for after you have "learned the facts." When we believe that "truth" can be separated from "method," and we subsequently try to do History without some form of historiographic hermeneutics, there can be no easy disengagement from historical discourse, and thus we will remain haunted by our histories.

# References

Allport, C. (1987). A rationale for teaching women's history. *Teaching History*, 20(4), 3-7.

Althusser, L. (1971). Ideology and ideological state apparatuses (Notes towards an investigation) (B. Brewster, Trans.). In L. Althusser (Ed.), *Lenin and philosophy and other essays* (pp. 127-186). New York: Monthly Review Press.

Anderson, B. (1983). *Imagined communities*. London: Verso.

Anijar, K. (2004). The world connected on a tenuous string: Looking at the movie threads. *Journal of Curriculum and Pedagogy*, 1(2), 125-149.

Ankersmit, F. R. (1998). Hayden White's appeal to the historians. *History and Theory*, 37(2), 182-193.

Ankersmit, F. R. (2001a). *Historical representation*. Stanford, CA: Stanford University Press.

Ankersmit, F. R. (2001b). Six theses on narrativist philosophy of history. In G. Roberts (Ed.), *The history and narrative reader* (pp. 237-245). London: Routledge.

Ankersmit, F. R. (2005). *Sublime historical experience*. Stanford, CA: Stanford University Press.

Aoki, T. T. (2005). *Curriculum in a new key: The collected works of Ted T. Aoki* (W. F. Pinar & R. L. Irwin, Trans.). Mahwah, NJ: Lawrence Erlbaum Associates.

Apple, M. W. (1975). The hidden curriculum and the nature of conflict. In W. Pinar (Ed.), *Curriculum theorizing: The reconceptualists* (pp. 95-119). Berkeley, CA: McCutchan.

Apple, M. W. (2004a). *Ideology and curriculum* (3rd ed.). New York: Routledge.

Apple, M. W. (2004b). Making white right: Race and the politics of educational reform. In M. Fine, L. Weis, L. Powell Pruitt, & A. Burns (Eds.), *Off white: Readings on power, privilege, and resistance* (pp. 74-85). New York: Routledge.

Aronowitz, S., & Giroux, H. A. (1991). *Postmodern education: Politics, culture, and social criticism*. Minneapolis: University of Minnesota Press.

Ashcroft, B. (2001). *Post-colonial transformation*. London: Routledge.

Attwood, B. (Ed.). (1996). *In the age of Mabo: History, Aborigines and Australia*. Sydney: Allen & Unwin.

Attwood, B. (2005). *Telling the truth about Aboriginal history*. Crows Nest, Australia: Allen & Unwin.

Baker, B. (2009). Borders, belonging, beyond: New curriculum history. In B. Baker (Ed.), *New curriculum history* (pp. ix-xxxv). Rotterdam, Netherlands: Sense Publications.

Baker, B., & Heyning, K. E. (2004). Introduction: Dangerous coagulations? Research, education, and a traveling Foucault. In B. Baker & K. E. Heyning (Eds.), *Dangerous coagulations? The uses of Foucault in the study of education* (pp. 1-79). New York: Peter Lang.

Ball, S. J. (1993). What is policy? Texts, trajectories and tool boxes. *Discourse*, 13(2), 10-17.

Bambach, C. R. (1990). History and ontology: A reading of Nietzsche's second "Untimely Meditation." *Philosophy Today*, 34(3), 259-272.

Barthes, R. (1967/1997). The discourse of history. In K. Jenkins (Ed.), *The postmodern history reader* (pp. 120-123). London: Routledge.

Barthes, R. (1968/1977). The death of the author (S. Heath, Trans.). In R. Barthes (Ed.), *Image-music-text* (pp. 142–148). London: Fontana.

Baudrillard, J. (1983). *Simulations*. New York: Semio-text(e).

Baudrillard, J. (1988). The system of objects (J. Mourrain, Trans.). In M. Poster (Ed.), *Jean Baudrillard: Selected writings* (pp. 10–29). Stanford, CA: Stanford University Press.

Baudrillard, J. (1992). *The illusion of the end* (C. Turner, Trans.). Cambridge, UK: Polity Press.

Baudrillard, J. (1995). *The Gulf War did not take place* (P. Patton, Trans.). Bloomington & Indianapolis: Indiana University Press.

Baudrillard, J. (1998). The end of the millenium or the countdown. *Theory, Culture and Society*, 15(1), 1–10.

Bayard, C., & Knight, G. (1995). Vivisecting the 90s: An interview with Jean Baudrillard. Retrieved January 15, 2004 from http://www.ctheory.net/text_file.asp?pick=66

Bell, D., & Kennedy, B. (Eds.). (2000). *The cybercultures reader*. New York: Routledge.

Bennett, T. (1995). *The birth of the museum: History, theory, politics*. London: Routledge.

Berkhofer, R. F. (1995). *Beyond the great story: History as text and discourse*. Cambridge, MA: The Belknap Press of Harvard University Press.

Bernstein, B. (1990). *The structuring of pedagogic discourse: Vol. 4. Class, codes, and control*. London: Routledge.

Bertram, C. (1994). The end of history: One more push! In C. Bertram & A. Chitty (Eds.), *Has history ended? Fukuyama, Marx, modernity* (pp. 167–180). Aldershot, UK: Avebury.

Best, S., & Kellner, D. (1991). *Postmodern theory: Critical interrogations*. Hampshire, UK: Macmillan.

Best, S., & Kellner, D. (1997). *The postmodern turn*. New York: The Guildford Press.

Best, S., & Kellner, D. (2001). *The postmodern adventure: Science, technology, and cultural studies at the third millennium*. New York: The Guildford Press.

Bhabha, H. (1983/1997). The other question. In P. Mongia (Ed.), *Contemporary postcolonial theory: A reader* (pp. 37–54). London: Arnold.

Bhabha, H. (1996). Culture's in-between. In S. Hall & P. du Gay (Eds.), *Questions of cultural identity* (pp. 53–60). London: Sage Publications.

Biskup, P. (1982). Aboriginal history. In G. Osborne & W. F. Mandle (Eds.), *New history: Studying Australia today* (pp. 11–31). Sydney: Allen & Unwin.

Blainey, G. (1993a). Drawing up a balance sheet of our history. *Quadrant*, 37(7–8), 10–15.

Blainey, G. (1993b). There is a rival view, which I call the "black armband" view: The John Latham memorial lecture. In S. Warhaft (Ed.), *Well may we say... The speeches that made Australia* (pp. 267–278). Melbourne: Schwartz Publishing.

Board of Studies NSW (1992). *History years 7–10 syllabus*. Sydney: Author.

Board of Studies NSW (2000). *HSC history extension syllabus*. Sydney: Author.

Boje, D. M. (2001). *Narrative methods for organizational and communication research*. London: Sage Publications.

Breisach, E. (2003). *On the future of history: The postmodernist challenge and its aftermath*. Chicago: University of Chicago Press.

Brickley, P. (1994). Teaching post-modern history: A rationale proposition for the classroom? *Teaching History*, 74, 17–21.

# References

Brown, C. G. (2005). *Postmodernism for historians*. Harlow, UK: Pearson Longman.
Brown, W. (2001). *Politics out of history*. Princeton, NJ: Princeton University Press.
Brown, W. (2005). *Edgework: Critical essays on knowledge and politics*. Princeton, NJ: Princeton University Press.
Bullock, A. (1970). The historian's purpose: History and metahistory. In L. M. Marsak (Ed.), *The nature of historical inquiry* (pp. 25-28). New York: Holt, Rinehart and Winston.
Burbules, N. (2000). The limits of dialogue as critical pedagogy. In P. P. Trifonas (Ed.), *Revolutionary pedagogies: Cultural politics, instituting education, and the discourse of theory* (pp. 251-273). New York: Routledge Falmer.
Cahoone, L. (1996). Introduction. In L. Cahoone (Ed.), *From modernism to postmodernism: An anthology* (pp. 1-23). Cambridge, MA: Blackwell.
Callinicos, A. (1989). *Against postmodernism*. Cambridge, UK: Polity Press.
Caputo, J. D. (1987). *Radical hermeneutics: Repetition, deconstruction, and the hermeneutic project*. Bloomington: Indiana University Press.
Carr, B. (2003). *What Australia means to me*. Camberwell, Australia: Penguin Books.
Carr, D. (1986). *Time, narrative, and history*. Bloomington: Indiana University Press.
Carr, E. H. (1990). *What is history?* (2nd ed.). London: Penguin Books.
Chabot, C. B. (1988). The problem of the postmodern. *New Literary History*, 20(1), 1-20.
Chakrabarty, D. (1997). Postcoloniality and the artifice of history: Who speaks for "Indian" pasts? In P. Mongia (Ed.), *Contemporary postcolonial theory: A reader* (pp. 223-247). London: Arnold.
Chartier, R. (1997). *On the edge of the cliff: History, language, and practices*. Baltimore: Johns Hopkins University Press.
Cherryholmes, C. H. (1987). A social project for curriculum: Post-structural perspectives. *Journal of Curriculum Studies*, 19(4), 295-316.
Cherryholmes, C. H. (2002). Curriculum ghosts and visions—and what to do? In W. E. Doll & N. Gough (Eds.), *Curriculum Visions* (pp. 116-126). New York: Peter Lang.
Clark, A. (2002, December). "Getting back to the facts": When politics meets pedagogy in history education. *The History Teacher*, 20-25.
Clark, A. (2003). What do they teach our children? In S. Macintyre & A. Clark (Eds.), *The history wars* (pp. 171-190). Melbourne, Australia: Melbourne University Press.
Clark, A. (2004). Teaching the nation: Politics and pedagogy in Australian history. Ph.D. diss., University of Melbourne.
Clement, C. (2003). The Humpty Dumpty factor in Aboriginal history. *The History Teacher*, 37(4), 26-32.
Cole, M. (1985). The zone of proximal development: Where culture and cognition create each other. In J. V. Wertsch (Ed.), *Culture, communication, and cognition: Vygotskian perspectives* (pp. 187-214). New York: Cambridge University Press.
Collingwood, R. G. (1946/1994). *The idea of history* (rev. ed.). Oxford, UK: Oxford University Press.
Collins, N. R. (1953). The teaching of history in Australian secondary schools. In J. D. Legge (Ed.), *University studies in history and economics* (pp. 79-98). Perth: University of Western Australia.

Comaroff, J., & Comaroff, J. L. (2000). Millennial capitalism: First thoughts on a second coming. *Public Culture*, 12(2), 291-343.

Connor, S. (1997). *Postmodernist culture: An introduction to theories of the contemporary* (2nd ed.). Oxford, UK: Blackwell Publishers.

Cormack, P., & Green, B. (2009). Re-reading the historical record: Curriculum history and the linguistic turn. In B. Baker (Ed.), *New curriculum history* (pp. 223-236). Rotterdam, Netherlands: Sense Publishers.

Cronon, W. (2001). A place for stories: Nature, history, and narrative. In G. Roberts (Ed.), *The history and narrative reader* (pp. 409-434). London: Routledge.

Crowell, S. G. (1998). Mixed messages: The heterogeneity of historical discourse. *History and Theory*, 37(2), 220-244.

Currey, C. H. (1930). *The study and teaching of history and civics*. Sydney: Whitcombe & Tombs and Teachers' College, University of Sydney.

Curthoys, A. (2003). Cultural history and the nation. In H.-M. Tiq & R. White (Eds.), *Cultural history in Australia* (pp. 22-37). Sydney: University of New South Wales Press.

Curthoys, A., & Docker, J. (2001). Genocide: definitions, questions, settler-colonies. *Aboriginal History*, 25, 1-15.

Curthoys, A., & Docker, J. (2006). *Is history fiction?* Sydney: University of New South Wales Press.

Cutler, R. L. (2001). Warning: Sheborgs/cyberfems rupture image-stream! In B. Grenville (Ed.), *The uncanny: Experiments in cyborg culture* (pp. 187-200). Vancouver: Vancouver Art Gallery and Arsenal Pulp Press.

Danto, A. C. (1965). *Analytical philosophy of history*. New York: Cambridge University Press.

Danto, A. C. (1997). *After the end of art: Contemporary art and the pale of history*. Princeton, NJ: Princeton University Press.

Darder, A., Baltodano, M., & Torres, R. D. (2003). Critical pedagogy: An introduction. In A. Darder, M. Baltodano & R. D. Torres (Eds.), *The critical pedagogy reader* (pp. 1-23). New York: Routledge Falmer.

Davies, B. (1993). *Poststructuralist theory and classroom practice*. Melbourne, Australia: Deakin University Press.

Davies, M. L. (2006). *Historics: Why history dominates contemporary society*. Abingdon, UK: Routledge.

Davis, N. Z. (1987). *Fiction in the archives: Pardon tales and their tellers in sixteenth-century France*. Stanford, CA: Stanford University Press.

Davison, G. (2000). *The use and abuse of Australian history*. Sydney: Allen & Unwin.

Dawson, J. (2004). *Washout: On the academic response to the fabrication of Aboriginal history*. Sydney: Macleay Press.

de Alba, A., Gonzalez-Gaudiano, E., Lankshear, C., & Peters, M. (2000). *Curriculum in the postmodern condition*. New York: Peter Lang.

De Bont, J., & Foster, L. (Producers) & Wimmer, K. (Director). (2002). *Equilibrium* [Motion picture]. United States: Dimension Films.

Dening, G. (1996). *Performances*. Melbourne, Australia: Melbourne University Press.

Denzin, N. K. (1994). Postmodernism and deconstructionism. In D. R. Dickens & F. Andrea (Eds.), *Postmodernism and social inquiry* (pp. 182-202). New York: The Guildford Press.

# REFERENCES

Derrida, J. (1976). *Of grammatology*. Baltimore: Johns Hopkins University Press.

Derrida, J. (1984). Deconstruction and the other. In R. Kearney (Ed.), *Dialogues with contemporary continental thinkers: The phenomenonlogical heritage* (pp. 107-126). Manchester, UK: Manchester University Press.

Derrida, J. (1989). *Of spirit: Heidegger and the question* (G. Bennington & R. Bowlby, Trans.). Chicago: University of Chicago Press.

Derrida, J. (1990). Some statements and truisms about neo-logisms, newisms, postisms, parasitisms, and other small seisisms (A. Tomiche, Trans.). In D. Carroll (Ed.), *The states of "theory": History, art and critical discourse* (pp. 63-95). New York: Columbia University Press.

Derrida, J. (1994). *Specters of Marx: The state of the debt, the work of mourning, and the new international* (P. Kamuf, Trans.). New York: Routledge.

DeVito, D., Shamberg, M., & Sher, S., (Producers) & Niccol, A. (Director). (1997). *Gattaca* [Motion picture]. United States: Columbia Pictures.

Doll, W. E. (2002). Ghosts and the curriculum. In W. E. Doll & N. Gough (Eds.), *Curriculum visions* (pp. 23-70). New York: Peter Lang.

Doll, W. E., & Gough, N. (Eds.). (2002). *Curriculum visions*. New York: Peter Lang.

Donnelly, K. (1997). The black armband view of history. *Agora*, 32(2), 15.

Donnelly, K. (2004). *Why schools are failing: What parents need to know about Australian education*. Sydney: Duffy & Snellgrove.

Dreyfus, H. L., & Rabinow, P. (1982). *Michel Foucault: Beyond structuralism and hermeneutics*. Brighton, UK: Harvester Press.

Duncan, G. (1992). History, historians in an age of anxiety. *Teaching History*, 26(1), 41-46.

Eagleton, T. (1983). *Literary theory: An introduction*. Oxford, UK: Basil Blackwell.

Ebert, T. (1996). *Ludic feminism and after: Post-modernism, desire, and labor in late capitalism*. Ann Arbor: University of Michigan Press.

Eisner, E. W. (1979). *The educational imagination: On the design and evaluation of school programs*. New York: Macmillan.

Eisner, E. W., & Vallance, E. (Eds.). (1974). *Conflicting conceptions of curriculum*. Berkeley, CA: McCutchan.

Elam, D. (1997). Feminism and deconstruction. In K. Jenkins (Ed.), *The postmodern history reader* (pp. 66-74). London: Routledge.

Ellsworth, E. (1989). Why doesn't this feel empowering? Working through the repressive myths of critical pedagogy. *Harvard Educational Review*, 59(3), 297-324.

Engel, S. (1999). *Context is everything: The nature of memory*. New York: W. H. Freeman.

Engestrom, Y. (1999). Activity theory and individual and social transformation. In Y. Engestrom, R. Miettinen & R.-L. Punamaki (Eds.), *Perspectives on activity theory* (pp. 19-38). Cambridge, UK: Cambridge University Press.

Ermarth, E. D. (1992). *Sequel to history: Postmodernism and the crisis of representational time*. Princeton, NJ: Princeton University Press.

Evans, R. J. (1997). *In defence of history*. London: Granta Books.

Evans, R. J. (2002). *Telling lies about Hitler: The Holocaust, history and the David Irving trial*. London: Verso.

Fairclough, N. (1995). *Critical discourse analysis: The critical study of language*. London: Longman.

Falzon, C. (1998). *Foucault and social dialogue: Beyond fragmentation.* London: Routledge.

Farrell, F. (1980). Aboriginal history. *Teaching History,* 14(3), 4-24.

Feldstein, R. (2001). Multimedia pedagogy and Sunday morning millenial fever. In H. A. Giroux & K. Myrsiades (Eds.), *Beyond the corporate university: Culture and pedagogy in the new millennium* (pp. 309-330). Lanham, MD: Rowman & Littlefield Publishers.

Ferro, M. (1981). *The use and abuse of history, or how the past is taught.* London: Routledge & Kegan Paul.

Fosket, J. R., & Fishman, J. (1999). Constructing the millennium bug: Trust, risk, and technological uncertainty. *CTHEORY, Event-Scene 83,* 13 October.

Foucault, M. (1965/1988). *Madness and civilization: A history of insanity in the age of reason* (R. Howard, Trans.). New York: Vintage Books.

Foucault, M. (1966/1994). *The order of things: An archaeology of the human sciences.* New York: Vintage Books.

Foucault, M. (1969/1972). *The archaeology of knowledge.* London: Routledge.

Foucault, M. (1969/1994). What is an author? (J. V. Harari, Trans.). In J. D. Faubion (Ed.), *Essential works of Foucault, 1954-1984: Vol. 2. Aesthetics* (pp. 205-222). London: Penguin Books.

Foucault, M. (1971/1994). Nietzsche, genealogy, history (D. F. Brouchard & S. Simon, Trans.). In J. D. Faubion (Ed.), *Essential works of Foucault, 1954-1984: Vol. 2. Aesthetics* (pp. 369-391). London: Penguin Books.

Foucault, M. (1972/1994). Truth and power (C. Gordon, Trans.). In J. D. Faubion (Ed.), *Essential works of Foucault, 1954-1984: Vol. 3. Power* (pp. 111-133). London: Penguin Books.

Foucault, M. (1978/1994). Questions of method (G. Burchell, C. Gordon, & P. Miller, Trans.). In J. D. Faubion (Ed.), *Essential works of Foucault, 1954-1984: Vol. 3. Power* (pp. 223-238). London: Penguin Books.

Foucault, M. (1980). *The history of sexuality: Vol. 1. An introduction* (R. Hurley, Trans.). New York: Vintage.

Foucault, M. (1982/1994). The subject and power (P. Rabinow & H. Dreyfus, Trans.). In J. D. Faubion (Ed.), *Essential works of Foucault, 1954-1984: Vol. 3. Power* (pp. 326-348). London: Penguin Books.

Foucault, M. (1983/1994). Structuralism and post-structuralism (J. Harding, Trans.). In J. D. Faubion (Ed.), *Essential works of Foucault, 1954-1984: Vol. 2. Aesthetics* (pp. 433-458). London: Penguin Books.

Foucault, M. (1984/1996). The ethics of the concern for the self as a practice of freedom (P. Aranov & D. McGrawth, Trans.). In S. Lotringer (Ed.), *Foucault live: Interviews, 1961-1984* (pp. 432-449). New York: Semiotext(e).

Foucault, M. (1988/1994). The political technology of individuals. In J. D. Faubion (Ed.), *Essential works of Foucault, 1954-1984: Vol. 3. Power* (pp. 403-417). London: Penguin Books.

Foucault, M. (1991). Politics and the study of discourse. In G. Burchell, C. Gordon & P. Miller (Eds.), *The Foucault effect: Studies in governmentality* (pp. 53-72). Chicago: University of Chicago Press.

Friedlander, S. (1997). Probing the limits of representation. In K. Jenkins (Ed.), *The postmodern history reader* (pp. 387-391). London: Routledge.

Friedman, S. S. (1995). Making history: Feminism, narrative and desire. In D. Elam & R. Wiegman (Eds.), *Feminism beside itself*. New York: Routledge.

Fuery, P., & Mansfield, N. (2000). *Cultural studies and critical theory* (2nd ed.). Melbourne, Australia: Oxford University Press.

Fukuyama, F. (1989). The end of history? *The National Interest*, 16, 3-18.

Fukuyama, F. (1990). Are we at the end of history? *Fortune*, 121(2), 75-78.

Fukuyama, F. (1992). *The end of history and the last man*. New York: Avon Books.

Fukuyama, F. (1995). Reflections on *The end of history*, five years later. *History and Theory*, 34, 27-43.

Fukuyama, F. (1999). *The great disruption*. New York: The Free Press.

Fukuyama, F. (2002a). Has history restarted since September 11? The Nineteenth Annual John Bonython Lecture, Melbourne, Australia, August 8.

Fukuyama, F. (2002b). *Our posthuman future: Consequences of the biotechnology revolution*. New York: Farrar, Straus & Giroux.

Fulbrook, M. (2002). *Historical theory*. New York: Routledge.

Furedi, F. (1994). The enthronement of low expectations: Fukuyama's ideological compromise for our times. In C. Bertram & A. Chitty (Eds.), *Has history ended? Fukuyama, Marx, modernity* (pp. 31-46). Aldershot, UK: Avebury.

Gallagher, S. (1993). *Hermeneutics and education*. Albany: State University of New York Press.

Gane, M. (2000). *Jean Baudrillard: In radical uncertainty*. London: Pluto Press.

Gee, J. P. (1990). *Social linguistics and literacies: Ideology in discourses*. London: Falmer Press.

Gee, J. P. (1992). *The social mind: Language, ideology, and social practice*. New York: Bergin and Garvey.

Gellner, E. (1994). *Encounters with nationalism*. Cambridge, MA: Blackwell.

Gergen, K. J. (2009). *An invitation to social construction* (2nd ed.). London: Sage Publications.

Giroux, H. A. (1994). Living dangerously: Identity politics and the new cultural racism. In H. A. Giroux & P. McLaren (Eds.), *Between borders: Pedagogy and the politics of cultural studies* (pp. 29-55). New York: Routledge.

Giroux, H. A. (1995). Border pedagogy and the politics of postmodernism. In P. McLaren (Ed.), *Postmodernism, postcolonialism, and pedagogy* (pp. 37-64). Sydney: James Nicholas Publishers.

Giroux, H. A. (2000). *Impure acts: The practical politics of cultural studies*. New York: Routledge.

Giroux, H. A. (2001). Mis/Education and zero tolerance: Disposable youth and the politics of domestic militarization. *Boundary*, 2(28), 61-94.

Giroux, H. A. (2007). Introduction: Democracy, education, and the politics of critical pedagogy. In P. McLaren & J. L. Kincheloe (Eds.), *Critical pedagogy: Where are we now?* (pp. 9-42). New York: Peter Lang.

Golob, E. O. (1980). The irony of nihilism. *History and Theory*, 19(4), 55-65.

Golsby-Smith, S. (2005, November 14). Theory throttles classroom discourse. *The Australian*, 8.

Goodson, I. F. (1992). Studying school subjects. *Curriculum Perspectives*, 12(1), 23-26.

Goodson, I. F., & Marsh, C. J. (1996). *Studying school subjects*. London: Falmer Press.

Gore, J. M. (1991). Neglected practices: A Foucauldian critique of traditional and radical approaches to pedagogy. Paper presented at the the Liberating Curriculum Conference,

University of Adelaide, July 11-14.

Gore, J. M. (1992). What we can do for you! What can "we" do for "you"? Struggling over empowerment in critical and feminist pedagogy. In C. Luke & J. Gore (Eds.), *Feminisms and critical pedagogy* (pp. 54-73). New York: Routledge.

Gough, N. (1994). Narration, reflection, diffraction: Aspects of fiction in educational inquiry. *Australian Educational Researcher*, 21(3), 47-76.

Gough, N. (1998). Reflections and diffractions: Functions of fiction in curriculum inquiry. In W. F. Pinar (Ed.), *Curriculum: Toward new identities* (pp. 94-127). New York: Garland.

Gough, N. (2002). Voicing curriculum visions. In W. E. Doll & N. Gough (Eds.), *Curriculum visions* (pp. 1-22). New York: Peter Lang.

Gough, N. (2003). Intertextual turns in curriculum inquiry: Fictions, diffractions and deconstructions. Ph.D. diss., Deakin University, Geelong, Australia.

Gould, S. J. (1997). *Questioning the millennium*. New York: Harmony Books.

Gray, C. H. (2001). *Cyborg citizen: Politics in the posthuman age*. New York: Routledge.

Green, B. (1993). Literacy studies and curriculum theorizing; or, the insistence of the letter. In B. Green (Ed.), *The insistence of the letter: Literacy studies and curriculum theorizing* (pp. 195-225). London: Falmer Press.

Green, B. (1995). Post-curriculum possibilities: English teaching, cultural politics, and the postmodern turn. *Journal of Curriculum Studies*, 27(4), 391-409.

Green, B. (2003). Curriculum inquiry in Australia: Toward a local genealogy of the curriculum field. In W. F. Pinar (Ed.), *Handbook of international curriculum research* (pp. 123-141). Mahwah, NJ: Lawrence Erlbaum Associates.

Groot, D. (Ed.). (2009). *Consuming history: Historians and heritage in contemporary popular culture*. Abingdon, UK: Routledge.

Grosz, E. (1995). *Space, time, and perversion*. New York: Routledge.

Guttenplan, D. D. (2001). *The Holocaust on trial: History, justice and the David Irving libel case*. London: Granta Books.

Halbwachs, M. (1950/1980). *The collective memory* (F. J. Ditter Jr & V. Y. Ditter, Trans.). New York: Harper Collins Books.

Hall, J. R. (1999). *Cultures of inquiry: From epistemology to discourse in sociohistorical research*. Cambridge, UK: Cambridge University Press.

Hall, S. (1997). Cultural identity and diaspora. In P. Mongia (Ed.), *Contemporary postcolonial theory: A reader* (pp. 110-121). London: Arnold.

Hall, T. S. (1914). Report of the fourteenth meeting of the Australasian Association for the Advancement of Science, University of Melbourne, 1913.

Halliday, M. A. K. (1985). *An introduction to functional grammar*. London: Edward Arnold.

Halse, C., & Harris, C. (2004). National identity and social cohesion: The social use of history curriculum in the United Kingdom, the US and Australia. Paper presented at the Annual Conference of the Australian Association for Research in Education, University of Melbourne, November 28-December 2.

Halse, C., Khamis, M., Dinham, S., Harris, B., Buchanan, J., & Soeters, C. (1997). *The state of history in New South Wales*. Leichardt, Australia: History Teachers' Association of New South Wales.

Haraway, D. (1985). A manifesto for cyborgs: Science, technology, and socialist feminism in the

1980s. *Socialist Review*, 80, 65-108.

Haraway, D. (1997). *Modest_Witness@Second_Millennium.FemaleMan(c)_Meets_OncoMouse(TM): Feminism and technoscience*. New York: Routledge.

Harris, C. (1996). The impact of outcomes and the National Profile for Studies of Society and Environment on the development of the 1992 years 7-10 history syllabus. Unpublished thesis, University of Sydney.

Harris, C. (2004). History curriculum development in New South Wales: Issues of control and its impact on teachers. Paper presented at the Annual Conference of the Australian Association for Research in Education, Melbourne, November 28-December 2.

Harris, J. (2003). Hiding the bodies: The myth of the humane colonisation of Aboriginal Australia. *Aboriginal History*, 27, 79-101.

Healy, C. (1997). *From the ruins of colonialism: History as social memory*. Cambridge, UK: Cambridge University Press.

Henriques, J., Holloway, W., Urwin, C., Venn, C., & Walkerdine, V. (Eds.). (1984). *Changing the subject: Psychology, social regulation, and subjectivity*. London: Methuen.

Herbert, F. (1965/1981). *Dune*. London: New England Library.

Herbert, F. (1966/1976). *The eyes of Heisenberg*. London: New English Library.

Hlebowitsh, P. S. (1993). *Radical curriculum theory reconsidered: A historical approach*. New York: Teachers College Press.

Holton, R. (1994). *Jarring witnesses: Modern fiction and the representation of history*. Hemel Hempstead, UK: Harvester Wheatsheaf.

Hooper-Greenhill, E. (1992). *Museums and the shaping of knowledge*. London: Routledge.

Hopenhayn, M. (1993). Postmodernism and neoliberalism in Latin America. *Boundary*, 20(3), 93-109.

Horgan, J. (1996). *The end of science*. New York: Addison Wesley.

Horrocks, C. (1999). *Baudrillard and the millennium*. Cambridge, UK: Icon Books.

Howard, J. (2006, January 26). Unity vital in battle against terrorism. *Sydney Morning Herald*, p. 11.

Huebner, D. E. (1966/1999). Curricular language and classroom meanings. In V. Hillis (Ed.), *The lure of the transcendent: Collected essays by Dwayne E. Huebner* (pp. 101-117). Mahwah, NJ: Lawrence Erlbaum Associates.

Huebner, D. E. (1975). The tasks of the curricular theorist. In W. F. Pinar (Ed.), *Curriculum theorizing: The reconceptualists* (pp. 250-270). Berkeley, CA: McCutchan.

Hutcheon, L. (1989). *The politics of postmodernism*. London: Routledge.

Huxley, A. (1931/1989). *Brave new world*. New York: HarperPerennial.

Iggers, G. G. (1997). *Historiography in the twentieth century: From scientific objectivity to the postmodern challenge* (with a new epilogue). Middletown, CT: Wesleyan University Press.

Jameson, F. (1991). *Postmodernism, or, the cultural logic of late capitalism*. Durham, NC: Duke University Press.

Jameson, F. (1998). *The cultural turn: Selected writings on the postmodern, 1983-1998*. London: Verso.

Jenkins, K. (1991). *Re-thinking history*. London: Routledge.

Jenkins, K. (1995). *On "What is history?": From Carr and Elton to Rorty and White*. London:

Routledge.
Jenkins, K. (Ed.). (1997). *The postmodern history reader*. London: Routledge.
Jenkins, K. (1999). *Why history?: Ethics and postmodernity*. London: Routledge.
Jenkins, K. (2003). *Refiguring history: New thoughts on an old discipline*. London: Routledge.
Jenkins, K., & Munslow, A. (2004). Introduction. In K. Jenkins & A. Munslow (Eds.), *The nature of history reader* (pp. 1-18). London: Routledge.
Jingo, Minoru (Producer), & Kurosawa, A. (Director). (1950). *Rashomon* [Motion picture]. Japan: Daiei Motion Picture Company.
Johnston, G. (1982). An historical perspective of the 1980 syllabus in history for years 7-10. *Teaching History*, 15(4), 65-81.
Kansteiner, W. (1993). Hayden White's critique of the writing of history. *History and Theory*, 32(3), 273-295.
Kansteiner, W. (1997). From exception to exemplum. In K. Jenkins (Ed.), *The postmodern history reader* (pp. 413-417). London: Routledge.
Karp, I., & Lavine, S. D. (Eds.). (1991). *Exhibiting cultures: The poetics and politics of museum display*. Washington, DC: Smithsonian Institution Press.
Kaufmann, J. (2000). Reading counter-hegemonic practices through a postmodern lens. *International Journal of Lifelong Education*, 19(5), 430-447.
Kelen, C. (2005). Hymns for and from white Australia. In A. J. Lopez (Ed.), *Postcolonial whiteness: A critical reader on race and empire* (pp. 201-229). Albany: State University of New York.
Kellner, D. (1989). *Jean Baudrillard: From Marxism to postmodernism and beyond*. Cambridge, UK: Polity Press.
Kellner, H. (1980). A bedrock of order: Hayden White's linguistic humanism. *History and Theory*, 19(4), 1-29.
Kellner, H. (1989). *Language and historical representation*. Madison: University of Wisconsin Press.
Kellner, H. (1997). "Never again" is now. In K. Jenkins (Ed.), *The postmodern history reader* (pp. 397-412). London: Routledge.
Kemmis, S. (1993). Curriculum as text. In B. Green (Ed.), *Curriculum, technology, and textual practice*. Geelong, Australia: Deakin University.
Kemmis, S., & Fitzclarence, L. (1986). *Curriculum theorizing: Beyond reproduction theory*. Geelong, Australia: Deakin University.
Kincheloe, J. L. (2004). *Critical pedagogy primer*. New York: Peter Lang Publishing.
Kincheloe, J. L., & McLaren, P. (2003). Rethinking critical theory and qualitative research. In N. K. Denzin & Y. S. Lincoln (Eds.), *The landscape of qualitative research: Theories and issues* (2nd ed., pp. 433-488). Thousand Oaks, CA: Sage Publications.
Klein, K. L. (2000). On the emergence of memory in historical discourse. *Representations*, 69(Winter), 127-150.
Kliebard, H. M. (1987). *The struggle for the American curriculum, 1893-1958*. New York: Routledge.
Koch, T. (1994, February 8). Furore over "invasion" text: Govt refuses to intervene. *Courier-Mail*.
Kojeve, A. (1969). *Introduction to the reading of Hegel*. New York: Basic Books.
Kroker, M., & Weinstein, M. A. (2001). *Data crash: The theory of the virtual class*. Montreal: New

World Perspectives and Ctheory Books.

Kuhn, T. (1970). *The structure of scientific revolutions* (2nd ed.). Chicago: University of Chicago Press.

Kumar, K. (1995). *From post-industrial to post-modern society: New theories of the contemporary world.* Oxford, UK: Blackwell.

Kurzweil, R. (1999). *The age of spiritual machines: When computers exceed human intelligence.* Cambridge, MA: MIT Press.

LaCapra, D. (1998). *History and memory after Auschwitz.* Ithaca, NY: Cornell University Press.

LaCapra, D. (2000). *History and reading: Tocqueville, Foucault, French studies.* Carlton South, Australia: Melbourne University Press.

LaCapra, D. (2004). *History in transit: Experience, identity, critical theory.* Ithaca, NY: Cornell University Press.

Lainsbury, G. P. (1996). Generation X and the end of history. *Essays on Canadian Writing, 58,* 229-241.

Le Goff, J. (1992). *History and memory.* New York: Columbia University Press.

Lee, A. (2000). Discourse analysis and cultural re(writing). In A. Lee & C. Poynton (Eds.), *Culture and text: Discourse and methodology in social research and cultural studies* (pp. 188-202). St. Leonards, Australia: Allen & Unwin.

Lee, P. (1991). Historical knowledge and the national curriculum. In R. Aldrich (Ed.), *History in the national curriculum* (pp. 39-65). London: Institute of Education, University of London.

Lemke, J. L. (1995). *Textual politics: Discourse and social dynamics.* London: Taylor & Francis.

Lipstadt, D. E. (1994). *Denying the Holocaust: The growing assault on memory and truth.* New York: Plume.

Loftus, E., & Ketcham, K. (1996). *The myth of repressed memory : False memories and allegations of sexual abuse.* New York: St. Martin's Press.

Long, C. R. (1909). *The aim and method in history and civics: Based on a lecture delivered before the teachers of the Daykesford district, Victoria, September, 1908.* Melbourne, Australia: Macmillan.

Lorenz, C. (1998). Can histories be true? Narrativism, postivism, and the "metaphorical turn." *History and Theory, 37*(3), 309-329.

Lucas, G. (Producer & Director). (2002). *Star Wars II: Attack of the clones* [Motion picture]. United States: Lucasfilm.

Luke, C., & Gore, J. M. (1992). Introduction. In C. Luke & J. Gore (Eds.), *Feminisms and critical pedagogy* (pp. 1-14). London: Routledge.

Lundgren, U. P. (1991). *Between education and schooling: Outlines of a diachronic curriculum theory.* Geelong, Australia: Deakin University.

Lyon, D. (1999). *Postmodernity* (2nd ed.). Buckingham, UK: Open University Press.

Lyotard, J. F. (1979). *The postmodern condition: A report on knowledge* (G. Bennington & B. Massumi, Trans.). Minneapolis: University of Minnesota.

Lyotard, J. F. (1989). Universal history and cultural differences (D. Macey, Trans.). In A. Benjamin (Ed.), *The Lyotard reader* (pp. 314-323). Oxford, UK: Blackwell.

Lyotard, J. F. (1991). *The inhuman: Reflections on time.* Cambridge, UK: Polity Press.

Macdonald, J. B. (1975). Curriculum theory. In W. Pinar (Ed.), *Curriculum theorizing: The reconceptualists* (pp. 5-13). Berkley, CA: McCutchan.

Macdonald, S. (1996). Introduction. In S. Macdonald & G. Fyfe (Eds.), *Theorizing museums* (pp. 1-19). Oxford, UK: Blackwell Publishers.

MacIntyre, A. (1984). *After virtue*. South Bend, IN: University of Notre Dame Press.

Macintyre, S. (1997). The genie and the bottle: Putting history back into the school curriculum. *Australian Journal of Education*, 41(2), 189-215.

Macintyre, S., & Clark, A. (2003). *The history wars*. Melbourne, Australia: Melbourne University Press.

MacLure, M. (2003). *Discourse in educational and social research*. Buckingham, UK: Open University Press.

Malewski, E. (Ed.). (2010). *Curriculum studies handbook: The next moment*. New York: Routledge.

Mann, J. S. (1975). Curriculum criticism. In W. Pinar (Ed.), *Curriculum theorizing: The reconceptualists* (pp. 133-148). Berkeley, CA: McCutchan.

Markus, A. (2001). Genocide in Australia. *Aboriginal History*, 25, 57-69.

Marsh, C. J., & Willis, G. (2003). *Curriculum: Alternative approaches, ongoing issues* (3rd ed.). Upper Saddle River, NJ: Merrill/Prentice Hall.

McCarney, J. (1994). Shaping ends: Reflections on Fukuyama. In C. Bertram & A. Chitty (Eds.), *Has history ended? Fukuyama, Marx, modernity* (pp. 13-30). Aldershot, UK: Avebury.

McCullagh, C. B. (2004). *The logic of history: Putting postmodernism in perspective*. London: Routledge.

MCEETYA (Ministerial Council for Education, Early Childhood Development and Youth Affairs). (1989). Hobart declaration on schooling. Available from http://www.mceecdya.edu.au/mceecdya/hobart_declaration,11577.html.

MCEETYA (Ministerial Council for Education, Early Childhood Development and Youth Affairs). (1999). Adelaide declaration on national goals for schooling in the twenty-first century. From http://www.mceecdya.edu.au/mceecdya/adelaide_declaration,11576.html.

MCEETYA (Ministerial Council for Education, Early Childhood Development and Youth Affairs). (2008). Melbourne declaration of educational goals for young Australians. From http://www.mceecdya.edu.au/mceecdya/melbourne_declaration,25979.html.

McGuinness, P. (1994, June 15). History of invasion ignores more balanced school of thought. *The Australian*, p. 15.

McLaren, P. (1995). Post-colonial pedagogy: Post-colonial desire and decolonized community. In P. McLaren (Ed.), *Postmodernism, postcolonialism, and pedagogy* (pp. 227-268). Albert Park, Australia: James Nicholas Publishers.

McLaren, P. (1998). Revolutionary pedagogy in post-revolutionary times: Rethinking the political economy of critical education. *Educational Theory*, 48(4), 431-462.

McLaren, P., & Leonardo, Z. (1998). Jean Baudrillard: From Marxism to terrorist pedagogy. In M. Peters (Ed.), *Naming the multiple: Poststructuralism and education* (pp. 215-243). New York: Bergin & Garvey.

McWilliam, E. (1997). Beyond the missionary position: Teacher desire and radical pedagogy. In S. Todd (Ed.), *Learning desire: Perspectives on pedagogy, culture, and the unsaid* (pp. 217-235). New York: Routledge.

Melleuish, G. (2006). The teaching of Australian history in Australian schools: A normative approach. Paper presented at the the Australian History Summit, Canberra, August 17.

Memmi, A. (1967). *The colonizer and the colonized*. Boston: Beacon Press.

Miedema, S., & Wardekker, W. L. (1999). Emergent identity versus consistent identity: Possibilities for a postmodern repoliticization of critical pedagogy. In T. S. Popkewitz (Ed.), *Critical theories in education: Changing terrains of knowledge and politics* (pp. 67-83). New York: Routledge.

Mills, S. (1997). *Discourse*. New York: Routledge.

Mink, L. O. (1978/2001). Narrative form as a cognitive instrument. In G. Roberts (Ed.), *The history and narrative reader* (pp. 211-220). London: Routledge.

Morrison, K. R. B. (2004). The poverty of curriculum theory: A critique of Wraga and Hlebowitsh. *Journal of Curriculum Studies, 36*(4), 487-494.

Munslow, A. (2003). *The new history*. Essex, UK: Pearson Longman.

Nash, G. B., Crabtree, C., & Dunn, R. E. (1998). *History on trial: Culture wars and the teaching of the past*. New York: Alfred A. Knopf.

Nehamas, A. (1985). *Nietzsche: Life as literature*. Cambridge, UK: Cambridge University Press.

Nelson, J. S. (1980). Tropal history and the social sciences: Reflections on Struever's remarks. *History and Theory, 19*, 80-101.

Niethammer, L. (1992). *Posthistoire: Has history come to an end?* (P. Camiller, Trans.). London: Verso.

Nietzsche, F. (1874/1983). On the uses and disadvantages of history for life (R. J. Hollingdale, Trans.). *Untimely meditations* (pp. 57-123). Cambridge, UK: Cambridge University Press.

Nile, R. (2002). Australian studies: Australian history, Australian studies, and the new economy. *Journal of Australian Studies, 74*, 201-216.

Nora, P. (1995). Between memory and history: Les lieux de mémoire. In J. Revel & L. Hunt (Eds.), *Histories: French constructions of the past* (pp. 632-636). New York: New Press.

Norman, A. P. (2001). Telling it like it is: Historical narratives on their own terms. In G. Roberts (Ed.), *The history and narrative reader* (pp. 181-196). London: Routledge.

Norris, C. (1990). *What's wrong with postmodernism?* Hemel Hempstead, UK: Harvester-Wheatsheaf.

Nugent, M. (2003). Botany Bay: Voyages, Aborigines, and history. *Journal of Australian Studies*, 76.

Oliver, K. (2001). Witnessing otherness in history. In H. Marchitello (Ed.), *What happens to history: The renewal of ethics in contemporary thought* (pp. 41-66). London: Routledge.

Olsen, B. (1990). Barthes: From sign to text. In C. Tilley (Ed.), *Reading material culture* (pp. 163-205). Oxford, UK: Basil Blackwell.

Osborne, G., & Mandle, W. F. (Eds.). (1982). *New history: Studying Australia today*. Sydney: Allen & Unwin.

Ozga, J. (2000). *Policy research in educational settings: Contested terrain*. Buckingham, UK: Open University Press.

Palermo, J. (2002). *Poststructuralist readings of the pedagogical encounter*. New York: Peter Lang.

Parkes, R. J. (2007). Reading history curriculum as postcolonial text: Towards a curricular response to the history wars in Australia and beyond. *Curriculum Inquiry, 37*(4), 383-400.

Parkes, R. J. (2010). Discipline and the dojo. In Z. Millei, T. G. Griffiths, & R. J. Parkes (Eds.), *Re-theorising discipline in education: Problems, politics, and possibilities* (pp. 76-90). New York: Peter Lang.

Parkes, R. J., Gore, J. M., & Elsworth, W. A. (2010). After poststructuralism: Rethinking the discourse of social justice pedagogy. In T. Chapman & N. Hobbel (Eds.), *Social justice pedagogy across the curriculum: The practice of freedom* (pp. 164-183). New York: Routledge.

Partington, G. (1987). History education in bicentennial Australia. *Forum*, December.

Patton, P. (1995). Introduction. In J. Baudrillard (Ed.), *The gulf war did not take place* (pp. 1-21). Bloomington: Indiana University Press.

Paul, G. S., & Cox, E. D. (1996). *Beyond humanism: Cyberevolution and future minds*. Rockland, MA: Charles River Media.

Peters, M. (1998). *The "post-historical" university*. Paper presented at the Winter Lecture Series (The University in the 21st Century), University of Auckland, August 25.

Petrina, S. (2004). The politics of curriculum and instructional design/theory/form: Critical problems, projects, units, and modules. *Interchange*, 35(1), 81-126.

Phelan, A. (2010). "Bound by recognition": Some thoughts on professional designation for teachers. *Asia-Pacific Journal of Teacher Education*, 28(4), 317-329.

Phillips, R. (1998). Contesting the past, constructing the future: History, identity and politics in schools. *British Journal of Educational Studies*, 46(1), 40-53.

Pinar, W. F. (Ed.). (1975). *Curriculum theorizing: The reconceptualists*. Berkeley, CA: McCutchan.

Pinar, W. F. (1979). The reconceptualization of curriculum studies. In P. H. Taylor (Ed.), *New directions in curriculum studies* (pp. 13-22). Sussex, UK: Falmer Press.

Pinar, W. F. (2004). *What is curriculum theory?* Mahwah, NJ: Lawrence Erlbaum Associates.

Pinar, W. F., & Grumet, M. R. (1981). Theory and practice and the reconceptualisation of curriculum studies. In M. Lawn & L. Barton (Eds.), *Rethinking curriculum studies: A radical approach* (pp. 20-42). London: Croom Helm.

Pinar, W. F., & Reynolds, W. M. (Eds.). (1992). *Understanding curriculum as phenomenological and deconstructed text*. New York: Peter Lang.

Pinar, W. F., Reynolds, W. M., Slattery, P., & Taubman, P. M. (1995). *Understanding curriculum*. New York: Peter Lang.

Pirenne, H. (1970). What are historians trying to do? In L. M. Marsak (Ed.), *The nature of historical inquiry* (pp. 29-34). New York: Holt, Rinehart and Winston.

Poad, D. (2003). Keith Windschuttle's *The fabrication of Aboriginal history*—A critique. *The History Teacher*, 37(4), 19-32.

Pomper, P. (1980). Typologies and cycles in intellectual history. *History and Theory*, 19(4), 30-38.

Popkewitz, T. S. (1997). The production of reason and power: Curriculum history and intellectual traditions. *Journal of Curriculum Studies*, 29(2), 131-164.

Popkewitz, T. S. (2001). The production of reason and power: Curriculum history and intellectual traditions. In T. S. Popkewitz, B. M. Franklin, & M. A. Pereyra (Eds.), *Cultural history and education: Critical essays on knowledge and schooling* (pp. 151-183). New York: Routledge Falmer.

Popkewitz, T. S., Franklin, B. M., & Pereyra, M. A. (2001). History, the problem of knowledge, and the new cultural history of schooling. In T. S. Popkewitz, B. M. Franklin, & M. A. Pereyra (Eds.), *Cultural history and education: Critical essays on knowledge and schooling* (pp. 3-44). New York: Routledge Falmer.

Popper, K. (1957/1986). *The poverty of historicism*. London: Ark Paperbacks.

Poster, M. (1984). *Foucault, Marxism, and history: Mode of production versus mode of information*. Cambridge, UK: Polity Press.

Potter, J. (1996). *Representing reality: Discourse, rhetoric, and social construction.* London: Sage Publications.

Prakash, G. (1994). Subaltern studies as postcolonial criticism. *American Historical Review,* 99(5), 1475-1490.

Preiswerk, R., & Perrot, D. (1978). *Ethnocentrism and history: Africa, Asia, and Indian America in western textbooks.* New York: NOK Publishers.

Prentis, M. D. (1993). Aboriginal history, heritage, and religion: Some thoughts on the junior syllabus. *Teaching History,* 27(4), 3-11.

Rayment-Pickard, H. (2000). Posthistory. In R. M. Burns & H. Rayment-Pickard (Eds.), *Philosophies of history: From enlightenment to postmodernity* (pp. 301-309). Oxford, UK: Blackwell Publishers.

Read, P. (2002). Clio or Janus? Historians and the stolen generations. *Australian Historical Studies,* 118, 54-60.

Reynolds, H. (1982). *The other side of the frontier: Aboriginal resistance to the European invasion of Australia.* Ringwood, Australia: Penguin.

Reynolds, W. M. (1989). *Reading curriculum theory: The development of a new hermeneutic.* New York: Peter Lang.

Reynolds, W. M., & Webber, J. A. (Eds.). (2004). *Expanding curriculum theory: Dis/positions and lines of flight.* Mahwah, NJ: Lawrence Erlbaum Associates.

Richardson, G. H. (2002). *The death of the good Canadian: Teachers, national identities, and the social studies curriculum.* New York: Peter Lang.

Richardson, L. (2001). Getting personal: Writing-stories. *International Journal of Qualitative Studies in Education,* 14(1), 33-38.

Ricoeur, P. (1983). *Time and narrative* (Vol. 1, K. McLaughlin & D. Pellauer, Trans.). Chicago: University of Chicago Press.

Ricoeur, P. (1991). *From text to action: Essays in hermeneutics, II* (K. Blamey & J. B. Thompson, Trans.). London: Athlone Press.

Ricoeur, P. (2000). Life in quest of narrative. In R. M. Burns & H. Rayment-Pickard (Eds.), *Philosophies of history: From Enlightenment to postmodernity* (pp. 297-300). Oxford, UK: Blackwell Publishers.

Riegel, H. (1996). Into the heart of irony: Ethongraphic exhibitions and the politics of difference. In S. Macdonald (Ed.), *Theorizing museums* (pp. 83-104). Oxford, UK: Blackwell Publishers.

Ritter, D., & Flanagan, F. N. A. (2003). Stunted growth: The historiography of native title litigation in the decade since Mabo. *Public History Review,* 10, 21-39.

Roberts, D. D. (1995). *Nothing but history.* Berkeley, CA: Regents of the California Press.

Rorty, R. (1979). *Philosophy and the mirror of nature.* Princeton, NJ: Princeton University Press.

Rosenau, P. (1992). *Post-modernism and the social sciences: Insights, inroads, and intrusions.* Princeton, NJ: Princeton University Press.

Roth, M. S. (1995a). Cultural criticism and political theory: Hayden White's rhetorics of history. In M. S. Roth (Ed.), *The ironist's cage: Memory, trauma, and the construction of history* (pp. 137-147). New York: Columbia University Press.

Roth, M. S. (1995b). Introduction. In M. S. Roth (Ed.), *The ironist's cage: Memory, trauma, and the construction of history* (pp. 1-20). New York: Columbia University Press.

Royle, N. (2000). What is deconstruction? In N. Royle (Ed.), *Deconstructions: A user's guide* (pp. 1-13). Houndmills, UK: Palgrave.

Rusen, J. (2005). Rethinking utopia: A plea for a culture of inspiration. In J. Rusen, M. Fehr, & T. W. Rieger (Eds.), *Thinking utopia: Steps into other worlds* (pp. 276-281). New York: Berghahn Books.

Russell, L. (2001). *Savage imaginings: Historical and contemporary constructions of Australian Aboriginalities*. Melbourne: Australian Scholarly Publishing.

Said, E. W. (1978). *Orientalism*. London: Routledge.

Sassoon, J. (2003). Phantoms of remembrance: Libraries and archives as "the collective memory." *Public History Review*, 10, 40-60.

Sawyer, R. K. (2002). A discourse on discourse: An archaeological history of an intellectual concept. *Cultural Studies*, 16(3), 433-456.

Schlesinger, A. M. J. (1992). *The disuniting of America: Reflections on a multicultural society*. New York: W.W. Norton & Company.

Seddon, T. (1983). The hidden curriculum: An overview. *Curriculum Perspectives*, 3(1), 1-6.

Segall, A. (2006). What's the purpose of teaching a discipline, anyway? In A. Segall, E. E. Heilman & C. H. Cherryholmes (Eds.), *Social studies - the next generation: Re-searching in the postmodern* (pp. 125-139). New York: Peter Lang.

Segall, A., Heilman, E. E., & Cherryholmes, C. H. (Eds.). (2006). *Social studies—the next generation: Re-searching in the postmodern*. New York: Peter Lang.

Seixas, P. (1993). Parallel crises: History and social studies curriculum in the USA. *Journal of Curriculum Studies*, 25(3), 235-250.

Seixas, P. (1994). A discipline adrift in an "integrated" curriculum: History in British Columbia schools. *Canadian Journal of Education*, 19(1), 99-107.

Seixas, P. (1999). Beyond "content" and "pedagogy": In search of a way to talk about history education. *Journal of Curriculum Studies*, 31(3), 317-337.

Seixas, P. (2000). Schweigen! die Kinder! or does postmodern history have a place in the schools? In P. N. Stearns, P. Seixas, & S. Wineburg (Eds.), *Knowing, teaching, and learning history: National and international perspectives* (pp. 19-37). New York: New York University Press.

Shapiro, A.-L. (1997). Fixing history: Narratives of World War I in France. *History and Theory: Studies in the Philosophy of History*, 36(4), 111-130.

Shapiro, S. (1995). The end of radical hope? Postmodernism and the challenge to critical pedagogy. In P. McLaren (Ed.), *Postmodernism, postcolonialism, and pedagogy* (pp. 187-204). Sydney: James Nicholas Publishers.

Shelley, M. (1818/1993). *Frankenstein*. Sydney: Modern Publishing Group.

Short, E. C. (1991). Inquiry methods in curriculum studies: An overview. *Curriculum Perspectives*, 11(2), 15-26.

Silver, J. (Producer) & Wachowski, A., & Wachowski, L. (Directors). (1999). *The Matrix* [Motion picture]. United States: Village Roadshow Pictures.

Silver, J. (Producer) & Wachowski, A., & Wachowski, L. (Directors). (2003). *The Matrix Reloaded* [Motion picture]. United States: Village Roadshow Pictures.

Silverman, E. K. (1990). Clifford Geertz: Towards a more "thick" understanding? In C. Tilley (Ed.), *Reading material culture: Structuralism, hermeneutics, and post-structuralism* (pp. 121-159).

Oxford, UK: Basil Blackwell.

Sim, S. (1999). *Derrida and the end of history*. Cambridge, UK: Icon Books.

Simon, R. I. (2000). The touch of the past: The pedagogical significance of a transactional sphere of public memory. In P. P. Trifonas (Ed.), *Revolutionary pedagogies: Cultural politics, instituting education, and the discourse of theory* (pp. 61-80). New York: Routledge Falmer.

Simpson, I. (2000). The nature and purpose of history education in schools. Paper presented at the Annual Conference of the Australian Association for Research in Education, University of Sydney, December 2-6.

Slattery, L. (2005a, July 23-24). Fading theory has no place in schools. *Weekend Australian*, p. 10.

Slattery, L. (2005b, July 23-24). This little pig goes postmodernist. *Weekend Australian*, pp. 1, 10.

Slattery, P. (1997). Postmodern curriculum research and alternative forms of data presentation. Paper presented at the Curriculum and Pedagogy Institute, University of Alberta, September 29.

Smith, D., & Lovat, T. (1995). *Curriculum: action on reflection* (3rd ed.). Sydney: Social Science Press.

Sochen, J. (1982). *Herstory: A record of the American woman's past*. Palo Alto, CA: Mayfield.

Southgate, B. (2003). *Postmodernism in history: Fear or freedom?* London: Routledge.

Spiegel, G. M. (1987). Social change and literary language: The textualization of the past in thirteenth-century old French history. *Journal of Medieval and Renaissance Studies*, 17(2), 129-148.

Spiegel, G. M. (2002). Memory and history: Liturgical time and historical time. *History and Theory*, 41(2), 149-162.

Spielberg, S., Curtis, B., & Kennedy, K. (Producers) & Spielberg, S. (Director). (2003). *A. I. Artificial Intelligence* [Motion picture]. United States: Warner Bros Pictures.

Spivak, G. C. (1997). Poststructuralism, marginality, postcoloniality and value. In P. Mongia (Ed.), *Contemporary postcolonial theory: A reader* (pp. 198-222). London: Arnold.

St.Pierre, E. A., & Pillow, W. S. (2000). Introduction: Inquiry among the ruins. In E. A. St.Pierre & W. S. Pillow (Eds.), *Working the ruins: Feminist poststructural theory and methods in education* (pp. 1-26). New York: Routledge.

Stanford, M. (1994). *A companion to the study of history*. Oxford, UK: Blackwell.

Stanley, W. B. (1992). *Curriculum for utopia: Social reconstructionism and critical pedagogy in the postmodern era*. Albany: State University of New York Press.

Stearns, P. N. (1982). Social history and the teaching of history. In M. T. Downey (Ed.), *Teaching American history: New directions* (pp. 51-63). Washington, DC: National Council for the Social Studies.

Stelarc (1997). From psycho to cyber strategies: Prosthetics, robotics and remote existence. *Cultural Values*, 1(2), 241-249.

Stimpson, P. (1991). The null curriculum: Beliefs about education and geography in Hong Kong. *Curriculum Perspectives*, 11(4), 11-17.

Straub, J. (Ed.). (2005). *Narration, identity, and historical consciousness*. New York: Berghahn Books.

Struever, N. S. (1980). Topics in history. *History and Theory*, 19(4), 66-79.

Taylor, T. (2000). *The future of the past: Final report of the national inquiry into school history*.

Churchill, Australia: Faculty of Education, Monash University.

Taylor, T. (2008). *Denial: History betrayed.* Carlton, Australia: Melbourne University Press.

Thompson, W. (2004). *Postmodernism and history.* London: Palgrave Macmillan.

Tilley, C. (1990). Michel Foucault: Towards an archaeology of archaeology. In C. Tilley (Ed.), *Reading material culture: Structuralism, hermeneutics, and post-structuralism* (pp. 281-347). Oxford, UK: Basil Blackwell.

Todorov, T. (2001). The uses and abuses of memory. In H. Marchitello (Ed.), *What happens to history: The renewal of ethics in contemporary thought* (pp. 11-22). London: Routledge.

Tonkin, E. (1990). History and the myth of realism. In R. Sameul & P. Thompson (Eds.), *The myths we live by* (pp. 25-35). London: Routledge.

Urry, J. (1994). Time, leisure and social identity. *Time and Society*, 3, 131-150.

Vann, R. T. (1998). The reception of Hayden White. *History and Theory*, 37(2), 143-161.

Vattimo, G. (1988). *The end of modernity: Nihilism and hermeneutics in post-modern culture* (J. R. Snyder, Trans.). Cambridge, UK: Polity Press.

Vattimo, G. (1991). The end of (hi)story. In I. Hoesterev (Ed.), *Zeitgeist in Babel: The post-modern controversy* (pp. 132-141). Bloomington: Indiana University Press.

Veracini, L. (2003a). The evolution of historical redescription in Israel and Australia: The question of the "founding violence." *Australian Historical Studies*, 34(122), 326-345.

Veracini, L. (2003b). Of a "contested ground" and an "indelible stain": A difficult reconciliation between Australia and its Aboriginal history during the 1990s and 2000s. *Aboriginal History*, 27, 224-239.

Virilio, P. (1989). *Looking back on the end of the world.* New York: Semiotexte.

Wang, H. (2002). The call of the stranger: Dwayne Huebner's vision of curriculum as a spiritual journey. In W. E. Doll & N. Gough (Eds.), *Curriculum visions* (pp. 287-299). New York: Peter Lang.

Warhaft, S. (1993). *Well may we say... The speeches that made Australia.* Melbourne, Australia: Schwartz Publishing.

Wark, M. (1997). *The virtual republic: Australia's culture wars of the 1990s.* St. Leonards, Australia: Allen & Unwin.

Weis, L., Proweller, A., & Centrie, C. (2004). Excavating a "moment in history": Privilege and loss inside white working-class masculinity. In M. Fine, L. Weis, L. Powell Pruitt, & A. Burns (Eds.), *Off white: Readings on power, privilege, and resistance* (pp. 128-144). New York: Routledge.

Wells, H. G. (1896/1996). *The time machine; [and] The island of Dr. Moreau.* New York: Oxford University Press.

Wertsch, J. V., & Penuel, W. R. (1998). Historical representation as mediated action: Official history as a tool. In J. F. Voss & M. Carretero (Eds.), *International review of history education: Vol. 2. Learning and reasoning in history* (pp. 23-38). London: Woburn Press.

White, H. (1973). *Metahistory.* Baltimore: Johns Hopkins University Press.

White, H. (1978a). The fictions of factual representation. In H. White (Ed.), *Topics of discourse* (pp. 121-134). London: Johns Hopkins University Press.

White, H. (1978b). The historical text as literary artifact. In H. White (Ed.), *Topics of discourse* (pp. 81-100). London: Johns Hopkins University Press.

White, H. (1997). Historical emplotment and the problem of truth. In K. Jenkins (Ed.), *The *postmodern history reader* (pp. 392-396). London: Routledge.

White, M. (1965). *Foundations of historical knowledge.* Westport, CT: Greenwood Press.

Wilkins, M. (1994, June 19). Nationals condemn Chadwick "invasion." *Sunday Telegraph.*

Williams, H., Sullivan, D., & Mathews, E. G. (1997). *Francis Fukuyama and the end of history.* Cardiff: University of Wales Press.

Wilson, D. D. (2000). Realizing memory, transforming history: Euro / American / Indians. In S. A. Crane (Ed.), *Museums and memory* (pp. 115-136). Stanford, CA: Stanford University Press.

Wilson, N. J. (2005). *History in crisis? Recent directions in historiography.* Upper Saddle River, NJ: Pearson Prentice Hall.

Windschuttle, K. (1996). *The killing of history: How literary critics and social theorists are murdering our past.* New York: The Free Press.

Windschuttle, K. (2002). *The fabrication of Aboriginal history: Vol. 1. Van Diemen's land, 1803-1847.* Sydney: Macleay Press.

Windschuttle, K. (2009). *The fabrication of Aboriginal history: Vol. 3. The stolen generations. 1881-2008.* Sydney: Macleay Press.

Wineburg, S. (2001). Historical thinking and other unnatural acts. Paper presented at the Canadian Historical Consciousness in an International Context Conference, University of British Columbia, Vancouver, August 26-28.

Wineburg, S. (2005). The psychological study of historical consciousness. In J. Straub (Ed.), *Narration, identity, and historical consciousness* (pp. 187-210). New York: Berghahn Books.

Wraga, W. G. (1999). Extracting sun-beams out of cucumbers: The retreat from practice in reconceptualized curriculum studies. *Educational Researcher*, 28(1), 4-13.

Wright, H. K. (2000). Nailing jell-o to the wall: Pinpointing aspects of state-of-the-art curriculum theorizing. *Educational Researcher*, 29(5), 4-13.

Wyschogrod, E. (1998). *An ethics of remembering: History, heterology, and the nameless others.* Chicago. University of Chicago Press.

Yates, L. (1992). Postmodernism, feminism, and cultural politics: Or if master narratives have been discredited, what does Giroux think he is doing? *Discourse*, 13(1), 124-141.

Young, C. (1987). Aboriginal education and the teaching of history. *Teaching History*, 21(4), 9-14.

Young, C. (1993). Rethinking history—Innovation and change. *Teaching History*, 27(2), 3-8.

Young, R. J. C. (Ed.). (1981). *Untying the text: A post-structuralist reader.* Boston: Routledge & Kegan Paul.

Young, R. J. C. (1990). *White mythologies: Writing history and the west.* London: Routledge.

Young, R. J. C. (2001). *Postcolonialism: An historical introduction.* Oxford, UK: Blackwell Publishers.

Zagorin, P. (1999). History, the referent, and narrative: Reflections on postmodernism now. *History and Theory*, 38(1), 1-24.

Zakaria, F. (2001, September 24). The end of the end of history: The great political fights were over. Or so we thought. Government matters again. *Newsweek*, p. 70.

## Studies in the Postmodern Theory of Education

*General Editor*
*Shirley R. Steinberg*

Counterpoints publishes the most compelling and imaginative books being written in education today. Grounded on the theoretical advances in criticalism, feminism, and postmodernism in the last two decades of the twentieth century, Counterpoints engages the meaning of these innovations in various forms of educational expression. Committed to the proposition that theoretical literature should be accessible to a variety of audiences, the series insists that its authors avoid esoteric and jargonistic languages that transform educational scholarship into an elite discourse for the initiated. Scholarly work matters only to the degree it affects consciousness and practice at multiple sites. Counterpoints' editorial policy is based on these principles and the ability of scholars to break new ground, to open new conversations, to go where educators have never gone before.

For additional information about this series or for the submission of manuscripts, please contact:

>Shirley R. Steinberg
>c/o Peter Lang Publishing, Inc.
>29 Broadway, 18th floor
>New York, New York 10006

To order other books in this series, please contact our Customer Service Department:
>(800) 770-LANG (within the U.S.)
>(212) 647-7706 (outside the U.S.)
>(212) 647-7707 FAX

Or browse online by series:
>www.peterlang.com

www.ingramcontent.com/pod-product-compliance
Ingram Content Group UK Ltd.
Pitfield, Milton Keynes, MK11 3LW, UK
UKHW021838210426
5322IPUK00021B/356